FINNO-UGRIAN LANGUAGES
AND PEOPLES

THE LANGUAGE LIBRARY

EDITED BY ERIC PARTRIDGE AND SIMEON POTTER

Peter Hajdu

FINNO-UGRIAN LANGUAGES AND PEOPLES

TRANSLATED AND ADAPTED BY
G. F. Cushing

ANDRE DEUTSCH

First published 1975 by
André Deutsch Limited
105 Great Russell Street London WC1

Printed in Great Britain by
William Clowes & Sons Limited
London, Beccles and Colchester

ISBN 0 233 96552 1

Contents

᠗᠗᠗᠗᠗᠗

Contents

List of Maps and Figures

🔟🔟🔟🔟🔟🔟

MAPS

FIGURES

Note on Transcription

𝕤𝕤𝕤𝕤𝕤𝕤

Hungarian and Finnish words are written in the established orthography of these languages. The main variations from English are shown below, together with the appropriate International Phonetic Association (IPA) symbols.

Hungarian		*IPA symbol*
a	cf. y*a*cht	ɑ
á	long, open a	aː
c	*ts* in i*ts*	ts
cs	*ch* in *ch*urch	tʃ
e	more open than English *e*	ɛ
gy	palatalized *d*, cf. French a*di*eu	dj
h	silent in the final position	
í	long, cf. p*ee*l	iː
j *ly* }	*y* as in *y*es	j
ny	palatalized *n*	nj
ó	long *o*	oː
ö	*eu* as in French p*eu*	ø
ő	long form of *ö*	øː
s	*sh* as in a*sh*	ʃ
sz	*s* as in *s*ee	s
ty	palatalized *t*	tj
ü	*u* as in French t*u*	y
ű	long from of *ü*	yː
zs	*s* as in plea*s*ure	ʒ

Long consonants are written double, e.g. re*gg*el 'morning'; in the case of digraphs, only the first element is duplicated; e.g. a*ss*zony 'woman'.

9

Finnish		*IPA symbol*
ä	short and open, as in h*a*t	æ
j	*y* as in *y*es	j
ö	*eu* as in French p*eu*	ø
y	*u* as in French t*u*	y

Long vowels and consonants are written double, e.g. *ottaa* 'he takes'.

In the other Finno-Ugrian languages the following symbols are used. It should be noted that the IPA alphabet is not normally found in Finno-Ugrian linguistic works. The usual system of transcription is based on E. N. Setälä's article 'Über Transskription der finnisch-ugrischen Sprachen' in *Finnisch-Ugrische Forschungen*, Vol. I, Helsinki, 1901, but has often been modified by later scholars.

Vowels

å	(Lapp), the so-called 'dark' *a*	ɔ
ä	as in Finnish	æ
ε	the vowel in 'b*i*rd'	ɜ
õ	(Estonian),	ɤ,ɨ
ü	as in Hungarian	y
y	the Russian ы	ɨ

Consonants

Palatalization is shown by ' either above (*ć*) or alongside (*l'*) the appropriate consonant.

č	*ch* as in *ch*urch	tʃ
đ	*th* as in *th*is	ð
θ	*th* as in *th*in	θ
χ	*ch* as in lo*ch*	x
γ	voiced equivalent of x	γ
ŋ	*n* before *g* as in lo*ng*	ŋ
q	velar occlusive	q
š	*sh* in a*sh*	ʃ
ž	*s* in plea*s*ure	ʒ
ʔ	glottal stop	ʔ

Abbreviations

Cher.	Cheremis
Chuv.	Chuvash
Est.	Estonian
Finn.	Finnish
FU	Finno-Ugrian
Hu.	Hungarian
Mord.	Mordvin
Osty.	Ostyak
Voty.	Votyak
Zyr.	Zyryan

Preface

🔯🔯🔯🔯🔯🔯

THIS book is based on Péter Hajdu's *Finnugor népek és nyelvek* (Gondolat kiadó, Budapest, 1963). The aim of the author was to describe the Finno-Ugrian peoples and languages to an interested, but non-specialist, reading public. The present work is designed for the same kind of reader, but in the English-speaking world. This has necessarily meant changes, particularly in the first part of the book; certain explanatory passages have been added to meet the needs of readers unfamiliar with the Finno-Ugrian world. The book is still Hungarian orientated, since this is the largest and most widely known of the languages concerned.

In the second part of the book, more space has been devoted to the lesser known Finno-Ugrian peoples than to the Hungarians and Finns, concerning whom ample information is readily available. The bibliography is highly selective and is intended to guide those who wish for more detailed information to the appropriate sources.

In conclusion, those readers who may object to the use of the term 'Finno-Ugrian' instead of 'Uralic' in the title of this book are referred to p. 32.

G. F. Cushing

Introduction

᭥᭥᭥᭥᭥᭥

THE Finno-Ugrian group of languages consists of the following members: Hungarian (Magyar), Vogul (Mansi), Ostyak (Chanti), Zyryan (Komi), Votyak (Udmurt), Cheremis (Mari), Mordvin, the Finnic languages (Finnish, Carelian, Ingrian, Vepsian, Vodian, Estonian, Livonian) and Lapp. To these the Samoyed languages (Nenets or Yurak-Samoyed, Enets or Yenisei-Samoyed, Nganasan or Tavgi-Samoyed, Selkup and the extinct Sayan-Samoyed) are added to form the Uralic family of languages, but the term 'Finno-Ugrian' is frequently used to include all the languages mentioned here.

The relationship between them was first postulated a thousand years ago. Ottar of Heligoland, a Norwegian vassal of Alfred the Great, sailed along the northern coast of the Scandinavian peninsula towards the end of the ninth century and anchored on the White Sea coast near the present town of Archangel. In his report on the journey, he observed that the language of the Lapps of northern Norway resembled that of the 'Bjarmas' he found on the White Sea coast. This name was probably that of a group of Finnic speakers then populating that area.

The similarity between Hungarian, Vogul and Ostyak was first noted by a monk of Verona; his observations were recorded by Aeneas Silvius Piccolomini (1405–64), who later became Pope Pius II. Later references to this relationship were made by Mathias de Miechow, physician to the Polish court at the beginning of the sixteenth century, and by Siegmund Herberstein, author of *Rerum Moscovitarum Commentarii* (1549). During the first half of this century, Herberstein made two diplomatic journeys to Russia, where he heard news of the Ob-Ugrians from witnesses who had met them during the campaigns then launched in order to conquer Siberia.

These feelers in the dark continued in the following century, when the Hungarian János Tröstler included a few Finnish-Hungarian etymologies in his work *Das elte und neue Dacia* (1666). Of much more importance in the history of linguistic scholarship is a work by the Hamburg scholar Martin Fogel, which survives in manuscript only (1669). Naturally this had no influence upon the development of Finno-Hungarian linguistics, but it postulated a number of Finnish-Hungarian etymologies which are recognized as valid today; moreover it also contained certain structural similarities.

Quite independently of Fogel and Tröstler, a Swedish scholar and poet, Georg Stiernhielm, discovered the affinity between Hungarian and Finnish (1671).

More detailed scholarly comparison between the languages begins in the eighteenth century. The linguists of this period were greatly influenced by Gottfried Wilhelm von Leibniz (1646–1716), the precursor of the German idealists, who made outstanding contributions to both mathematics and linguistic studies. He advanced the proposition that comparison of languages and their relationships might shed light on the origins of nations, and under his influence linguistic material was collected from widely differing languages; the collections of words made in Russia during the eighteenth century are of particular interest and use to research in the Finno-Ugrian field.

As the horizon widened, so the number of important works increased. Philip Johann Strahlenberg (1730), Johann Eberhard Fischer (1756, 1768), August Ludwig Schlözer (1770, 1771) are the authors of such studies.

Strahlenberg, a Swedish captain made prisoner at the Battle of Poltava (1709), spent thirteen years in exile in Siberia, where he collected valuable material about the people living there. After his return home, he published *Das Nord- und Ostliche Theil von Europa und Asia* in 1730, in which he lists the first large group of 'Boreo-Oriental' (i.e. North-East) languages, Mordvin, Cheremis, Permian, Votyak, Vogul and Ostyak, which he regards as related to Hungarian, Finnish, Lappish and Estonian.

Fischer was a member of the Imperial Russian Academy, and several of his works touched on Finno-Ugrian problems. *De origine Ungrorum*, a manuscript thesis of 1756, discusses the Finno-Ugrian origin of the Hungarians. In his *Siberische Geschichte* (1768), he gives a comprehensive survey of what was then known about the Finno-Ugrian peoples and languages in Russia, and includes some valuable observations on them. His unpublished Siberian dictionary (*Vocabularium continens trecenta vocabula triginta quatuor gentium* . . .) contains exceptionally valuable material for comparative etymological studies in Finno-Ugrian.

Schlözer's *Questiones Petropolitanae* (1770) and *Allgemeine Nordische Geschichte* (1771) include useful studies of the Finno-Ugrian peoples for scholars in this field.

In Hungary, organized comparative linguistic studies began with the publication in 1770 of János Sajnovics's *Demonstratio idioma Ungarorum et Lapponum idem esse*; this was followed in 1799 by Sámuel Gyarmathi's *Affinitas linguae Hungaricae cum linguis fennicae originis*. Sajnovics restricted himself to proving the relationship between Lappish and Hungarian. It is greatly to his credit that he examined not merely etymologies, but also morphological and syntactical congruences: his method makes him a precursor of modern comparative linguistics. His work was continued by Gyarmathi, who was primarily interested in grammatical forms, although he included certain etymological observations. Gyarmathi spread his net more widely, examining all the Finno-Ugrian languages and Samoyed.

These first steps in the discovery of the linguistic relationships of Hungarian could not be expected to receive general acceptance while knowledge of the more remote Finno-Ugrian languages was obtainable only at second or third hand. New, reliable material was needed, and means provided to examine this methodically on comparative historical lines. This work began in the 1840–50 period. The pioneer work carried out by the Hungarians Reguly, Hunfalvy and Budenz, the Finns Sjögren, Castrén, Ahlqvist, Donner, Setälä and their associates led to the acceptance of the Finno-Ugrian group of languages as a proven fact and to the classification of the relationships within the group. The main lines of development of these languages were established, and the broad outline of the original primeval common language successfully reconstructed.[1]

1 For the relationship between Finno-Ugrian and Samoyed see Fig. 1, p. 41.

METHODS OF DETERMINING LINGUISTIC
RELATIONSHIP

The methods used by the Finno-Ugrian scholars were similar to those pursued in the Indo-European field. Similar words existed in some of the languages, e.g.

Hu. *jég* 'ice' ~ Finn. *jää* ~ Mord. *jej* ~ Vogul *jänk*[1]
Hu. *vaj* 'butter' ~ Finn. *voi* ~ Mord. *vaj* ~ Vogul/Ostyak *woj*.

It is possible to construct whole sentences containing words of similar form, e.g.

Finnish *Kala uiskelee elävänä vesien alla.*
Hungarian *Hal úszkál elevenen a víz alatt.*
(A fish swims about alive under water.)

or

Vogul: *χūs nē luwä ēläl' mini*
Hu.:　　*Húsz nő lova előre megy (mén)*
(Twenty women's horses go on ahead.)

Even the more distant Nenets is not entirely strange to the Hungarian speaker:

Nen.: *χāl'ē wit ylna jil'ē*
Hu.:　　*A hal víz alatt él*
(The fish lives under water.)

It would be possible to construct similar examples involving various other languages, but these artificially contrived sentences owe their existence chiefly to whimsical linguists and have little real purpose, except to emphasize one particular aspect of linguistic affinity. Moreover they sometimes involve deception, as in the Nenets sentence already quoted: the four words are taken from three different dialects merely to demonstrate more vividly the similarity between Nenets and Hungarian. The truth emerges from the table below, which demonstrates that the forms nearest to Hungarian have been deliberately selected:

1 See Note on transcription, p. iv.

	Hu.	Kanin dial.	Tundra dial.	Forest dial.
fish	hal	χāl'ē	χāl'ē	karreä
water	víz	jiʔ	jiʔ	wit
under	alatt	ylna	ŋylna	ŋyrnaɛ
lives	él	iīl'ē	jīl'ē	jirrī

It must not, however, be assumed that such sentences are totally misleading; they are realistically based on the known characteristics of the languages concerned, even though they do not represent everyday usage.

In practice the linguistic affinity is not so obvious. In Hungarian the usual greeting is *jó napot* (Good day!), which corresponds to Finn. *Hyvää päivää*, Voty. *d'ʒeč bur*, Cher. *poro keče*, Lapp *puörri peäivi* and Vogul *pāśä*. This example clearly shows the wide divergences, which are not confined to distant relatives like Hungarian and Finnish, but include Ostyak and Vogul, which are closely related to each other.

Where a fairly close relationship exists it may be possible for native speakers of one language to comprehend another, though with some difficulty. Such affinities exist between Finnish and Estonian or Carelian, Carelian and Vepsian, Estonian and Vodian. But even these provide plenty of sources for misunderstanding, e.g. Finn. *piimä* = buttermilk, sour milk, while Est. *piim* = milk. Compare also

Estonian: *haige* = sick		Finnish: *haikea* = bitter, sad	
kask = birch-tree		*kaski* = clearing	
linn = town		*linna* = castle	

Sometimes the same word has acquired two opposing meanings, as in Finn. *siunata* = bless, Est. *siunama* = curse. Both Finnish *hiili* and Vod. *ili* = coal, whereas in Estonian the cognate means 'brightness, light' and at the same time refers to the signal fires made on the beach to guide homecoming fishermen; the cognate Livon. *il'* is used by fishermen merely to denote 'fire'.

In general there are wide differences between the Finno-Ugrian languages, which have developed separately, in most cases, for several thousand years. During this period there have been radical changes in vocabulary, phonology, grammar and syntax, all of which have affected their common inheritance. Indeed, it requires

extensive linguistic research to discover what this common inheritance was. Certain regular features may be discerned in the
development of these languages. For example, the phonetic
changes in the words and grammatical elements inherited from
the basic languages have generally been subject to different but
recognizable sound-laws and not whimsical and self-induced
changes. The establishment of such sound-laws has a very important role in the recognition of related phenomena to show
linguistic affinity.

A casual observer would not, for example, associate the Hu.
ín (=tendon, sinew) with Finn. *suoni*, Mord. *san*, Voty. *sεn*, Vogul
tān, Osty. *ton* and Nenets *tεn*, yet all are derived from the same
root. The same is true of Hu. *eszik* (=eat), Vogul *tāj-*, Osty.
tew- and Finn. *syö-*, and of Hu. *epe* (=spleen) Finn. *sappi*, Lapp
sappe, Zyr. and Voty. *sep*, and Vogul *tēp*. All three of these groups
can be traced back to a common origin, and the differences that
have developed between them, as we shall see, are regular. But
first a brief interpolation.

Great importance is attached to etymology to prove linguistic
affinity, but etymology must be based on a sound knowledge of
the phonological development of each related language. Without
a knowledge of historical phonology it is impossible to obtain
correct etymological observations. Historical phonology is concerned with the changes which have taken place in the course of
time in the sounds of the various languages. These can be deduced
from variations in dialectal data, changes in loanwords and from
the study of old documents. In Hungarian, for example, early
documents play a very important rôle. An examination of the oldest of them shows among other things that those words which
today are monosyllabic and terminate in consonants were disyllabic and ended in vowels in the eleventh century. In the Foundation Deed of Tihany Abbey (1055 AD) we find the words *hodu, utu*
and *uuaru*, which are still known and used today in the forms *had*
(=army), *út* (=way), *vár* (=castle). From such examples one may
deduce that certain final open vowels of the Old Hungarian
period have been lost. From later documents it can be seen that
this process was completed during the thirteenth century. With
this knowledge, the relationship between Finn. *kala* (=fish), *käsi*
(=hand), *lintui* (=bird), *suoni* (=sinew) and Hungarian *hal, kéz,*

lúd and *ín* becomes clearer. The original final vowel, preserved in Finnish, has been lost in Hungarian.

Comparative historical phonology traces the course of sound-changes in the various languages (on the basis of the sound-laws that have been discovered in them) back to periods which have left no written records for posterity. The methods used may be illustrated by the following examples:

(i) Finno-Ugrian initial **p-* generally appears in Hungarian as initial *f-*, e.g.

Hu. *fej* 'head', *fő* 'chief' ~ Finn. *pää*, Vogul *päŋk*, Votyak *pun*, Mordvin *pe*.

Hu. *fészek* 'nest' (the final *-k* is an old diminutive form) ~ Finn. *pesä*, Ostyak *pit*, Zyryan *poz*.

Hu. *fon-* 'weave' ~ Finn. *puno-*, Votyak *pun-*, Vogul *pun-*.

Hu. *fa* 'wood' ~ Finn. *puu*, Zyryan/Votyak/Cheremis *pu*, Vogul *po*.

From these examples it is clear that in Hungarian *f-* is a secondary development; all the other Finno-Ugrian languages show *p-*, from which it is to be deduced that the original common language also had *p-* in these cases. Therefore FU **p-* > Hu. *f-*.

(ii) Finno-Ugrian initial **k-* > Hu. *h-* shows a similar development:

Hu. *hab* 'foam' ~ South Vogul *kup*, Ostyak *komp*, Mordvin *kumboldo-* 'undulate', Finn. *kummuta* 'well forth'.

Hu. *hal* 'fish' ~ Vogul/Ostyak *kul*, Cheremis *kol*, Finn. *kala*.

Hu. *hat* 'six' ~ Ostyak *kut*, Zyryan *kvat'*, Cheremis *kut*, Mordvin *koto*, Finn. *kuusi* (*kuute-*) etc.

Here, however, it must be noted that certain words in Hungarian retain an initial *k-*:

Hu. *kéz* 'hand' Vogul *kāt*, Cheremis *kit*, Finn. *käsi* (*käte-*).

Hu. *kő* 'stone' Vogul *kü*, Votyak *kö*, Cheremis *kü*, Mordvin *kev*, Finn. *kivi*.

Hu. *két* 'two' Vogul *kat*, Ostyak *kät*, Finn *kaksi* (*kahte-*).

FU **k-* thus gives rise to two variants in Hungarian. The observant reader will already have noted that the following vowel is the deciding factor: initial *k-* + a front vowel (*e, é, ö, i*) remains unchanged in Hungarian, while initial *k-* + a back vowel (*a, á, o, ó, u, ú*) becomes *h-*.

If we now examine -*z* in the following Hungarian words, and compare them with cognates in other Finno-Ugrian languages, we shall see that Finno-Ugrian **-t* is the origin:

Hu. *kéz* (see previous list).

Hu. *fazék* (=pot; the -*k* here is a diminutive suffix) ~ Vogul *pōt*, Osty. *put*, Cher. *pat*, Finn. *pata*.

Hu. *víz* (=water) ~ Vogul *wit*, Cher. *wüt*, Finn. *vesi* (*vete-*).

Hu. *száz* (=100) ~ Vogul *sāt*, Osty. *sat*, Finn. *sata*.

Hu. *méz* (=honey) ~ Finn. *mesi* (*mete-*).

This, then, constitutes another law, that Finno-Ugrian medial and final *t* > Hu. -*z*. We may also observe that a somewhat similar sound-change has occurred in Finnish: where *t* is followed by *i*, it becomes *s*. Old Finnish *käti*, *veti*, *meti* > Modern Finnish *käsi*, *vesi*, *mesi*. But the root form retains the original *t*: *käte-*, *vete-*, *mete-*. This change is naturally as peculiar to Finnish as *t* > *z* is to Hungarian; they are independent of each other.

The examples we have seen are among the most easily recognizable phenomena of Finno-Ugrian phonology. Exceptions to regular sound-changes frequently complicate the situation. Suffice it to say that most of the exceptions have a more or less satisfactory explanation. Regular development may have been prevented, for example, by the operation of some other sound-law or by analogy.

It must not be assumed from the above examples that only Hungarian shows a wide divergence from the Finno-Ugrian common language in its phonological structure. On page 20 above some of the equivalents of Hu. *in*, *eszik* and *epe* were shown. It will be noted that Finnish, Lapp, Mordvin and Permian examples have an initial *s-*, while Vogul and Ostyak show *t-*, and Hungarian has an initial vowel in each case. Once again the difference between these forms is the result of regular development. In common Finno-Ugrian, all of them showed an initial *s-*, which remained unaltered only in the western FU languages. In the Ugrian and incidentally the Samoyed branches also there were extensive changes: common Ugrian shows *s* > θ (as in *thin*), which in Vogul and Ostyak became *t-*[1]; in Old Hungarian, however, it disappeared altogether, probably via *h-*.

1 This *t-* now appears only in southern dialects of Ostyak, FU *s-* > *l-* in northern dialects and *j-* in certain eastern dialects: Hu. *in* ~ S. Osty. *ton*, N. Osty. *lan*, E. Osty. *jan*.

FU initial *š* shows a similar development in the Ugrian languages. It is preserved only in Zyryan, Votyak and Mordvin, while in Finnish it has become *h-*:

Hu. *egér* (=mouse) ~ Vogul *täŋker*, Zyr./Voty. *šyr*, Mordvin *šejɛr*, Finn. *hiiri*. In Vodian and Livonian the Finn. *š-* > *h-* went one step further and disappeared, as in Hungarian: Vod. *iri*, Liv. *ir*.

From the examples given it is clear that the etymologist must be fully aware of the sound-laws operating throughout the realm of comparative FU phonology. Since vocalic harmony is one of the features of most modern languages in the family, for many years vowels were rightly treated with considerable caution by scholars in this field. Now, however, they are frequently used to test the correctness of certain etymologies.

During the last century, with increasing knowledge of comparative phonology, it has become possible to reconstruct forms in common FU. The forms of the words already mentioned are as follows (only the Hungarian and Finnish equivalents are shown):

Hu.		Finn.		FU	
egér	=	*hiiri*	=	*šiŋere*	
epe	=	*sappi*	=	*säppä*	
e-szik	=	*syö-*	=	*seɣe*	
fa	=	*puu*	=	*pū*	
fazé-k	=	*pata*	=	*pata*	
fej, fő	=	*pää*	=	*päŋe*	
fésze-k	=	*pesä*	=	*pesä*	
fon	=	*puno-*	=	*puna*	
hab	=	*kumpua-*	=	*kumpa*	
hal	=	*kala*	=	*kala*	
hat	=	*kuusi, kuute-*	=	*kuttɛ*	
in	=	*suoni*	=	*sɛnɛ*	
jég	=	*jää*	=	*jäŋe*	
két	=	*kaksi, kahte-*	=	*kakte*	
kéz	=	*käsi, käte-*	=	*käte*	
kő	=	*kivi*	=	*kiwe*	
lúd	=	*lintu*	=	*lunta*	
méz	=	*mesi, mete-*	=	*mete* or *medе*	
száz	=	*sata*	=	*šata*	
vaj	=	*voi*	=	*wojɛ*	
víz	=	*vesi, vete-*	=	*wete*	

Use of the comparative method in historical phonology has brought to light the common vocabulary of the Finno-Ugrian languages. The results – and there are certain lesser-known Finno-Ugrian and Samoyed languages where research is still in its infancy – will undoubtedly entail revision of this vocabulary in the future, but the etymologies so far known are quite numerous and amply sufficient to demonstrate the relationship between these languages. Further reference will be made to this common vocabulary. Suffice it to note here that the following types of word may be distinguished:

1 *Pronouns*: I, thou, he/she, who?, what?
2 *Family relationships*: ancestor, boy, husband, wife, girl, bridegroom, bride, mother-in-law, father-in-law
3 *Certain numerals*
4 *Plants and animals*: hare, mouse, marten, hedgehog, dog, partridge, goose, bee, fish, burbot, tench, wood, bark, black cherry, elm, beech, privet
5 *Natural phenomena*: night, sky, dawn, spring, autumn, winter, rain, foam, current, water, lake, etc.
6 *Parts of the body*: finger, hand, mouth, tooth, head, tongue, spleen, liver, fang, etc.
7 *Verbs*, mainly denoting elementary functions: exist, become, live, die, eat, drink, bear, sleep, stand, go, hear, etc.

The number of Finno-Ugrian basic roots in Hungarian may be estimated at 1,000, possibly less. This does not appear to be a very large figure, taken in isolation. But when we consider that Géza Bárczi's *Magyar szófejtő szótár* (Hungarian Etymological Dictionary, Budapest, 1941) contains a total of some 5,000 words, of which 25 per cent are deemed to be of Finno-Ugrian origin, about 1,000 have developed during the independent life of Hungarian, and some 900 are of uncertain origin, it will be seen that they form an important item in the basic vocabulary of Hungarian. Only 35 per cent of the words in this dictionary prove to be loanwords. We may compare this with Albanian, where only 8 per cent of the vocabulary is original, and Armenian, where the figure is 23 per cent.

In everyday language, the number of Finno-Ugrian words used is even more striking. Vilmos Tolnai once calculated, using a variety of literary and colloquial texts, that of 100,000 words used in them, 88,400 were of Hungarian (i.e. FU and internally derived) origin. In poetic language the proportion tends to be even higher, though in Hungarian the frequent occurrence of the definite article, FU in origin, distorts the figures. In Finnish, which has no definite article, the figure of 90 per cent is reduced to 82–3 per cent. Géza Bárczi analysed the first stanza of the Hungarian National Anthem (*Himnusz*), written in 1823; it contains 21 words of FU or Ugrian origin, 4 Turkic, 1 Latin, 1 possible Iranian and 6 unknown roots. In Ady's *Magyar jakobinus dala* (Song of a Hungarian Jacobin, 1908), there are 86 words of FU or Ugrian origin, 35 of unknown or internally derived origin, 6 Turkic, 6 Slavonic and 7 loanwords from various other languages. Other statistical evidence also proves the indispensable nature of the FU elements in the Hungarian vocabulary.

Etymology alone is insufficient to prove the common origin of the Finno-Ugrian languages. A very important rôle is played by common structural elements. We shall return to this subject in greater detail; suffice it for the present to note that the primary noun-suffixes[1] show a very large measure of agreement in all Finno-Ugrian languages. The possessive suffixes can be traced to a common origin. Evidence can also be found in a few conjugational elements and noun and verb formatives.

Once again comparative historical phonology comes to the aid of the scholar investigating grammatical elements. If two such elements appear at first sight to agree, it is natural to assume that they are related; but if this supposition is not supported by phonological evidence, it must be abandoned. For example, Hu. plural -*k* (*hal* 'fish' plural *halak*) was for a long time assumed to be identical in origin with Lapp plural -*k* (*akšo-k*: 'axe-s'). It was discovered, however, that the Lapp plural -*k* had evolved from an earlier -*t*, as is also the case with the verbal 2nd person singular suffix (cf. Finn. *kuulet* = Lapp *gulâk*, 'you hear'). Thus the Lapp plural cannot be related to Hungarian, where no such change occurs, but is connected with the -*t* plural found in Finnish, Mordvin, Vogul and Ostyak.

1 Primary suffixes consist of one vowel or consonant, as Hu. -*t* (-*tt*) locative: *Kolozsvár-t, Pécsett*; -*n*: *fán* = on a tree; -*é*: *mögé* = to behind, etc. These are older than the longer secondary suffixes, which are derived from independent roots, or compounded from combining primary suffixes e.g. -*ban/-ben*, -*nál/-nél*, etc.

Knowledge of phonology thus assists in relating grammatical elements which today differ considerably in form. The Hungarian present participial formative in *-ó/ő* (*szántó*, ploughing; *menő*, going) has various cognates. In Vogul and Ostyak it is *-γ* (Osty. *jawreγ* = twisted, cf. *jawrem* = to twist), in Votyak *-e*, in Zyryan *-ε* (Zyr. *munε* = going, he goes; *mun-ny* = to go), in Finnish dialectal *-k* (e.g. *puhek* = speech, cf. *puhu-* = speak), and in Samoyed *-χa* (Nen. *χāwa-χa* = fallen (tree)). In all these instances the starting-point is Uralic *-k*, to which the Finnish, Ob-Ugrian and Samoyed forms are closest. How then, does the Hungarian form come to be related to these? The Foundation Deed of Tihany Abbey (1055) contains the following phrase: *feheruuaru rea* meneh *hodu utu rea*, in modern Hungarian *Fehervárra* menő *hadútra* = the military road going to Fehervár. Thus in the eleventh century *menő* appeared as *meneh*. In an even earlier Greek document concerning the Veszprém Valley convent, the name of the Transdanubian village of *Szántó* is written as σαμταγ. *Meneh* was probably to be pronounced *meneγ*, with a voiced velar fricative at the end. This is indeed the development in Hungarian of medial or final FU *-k*. In a Latin transcription of a later version of the Greek document already mentioned the name of the village appears as *Zamtou*. During the eleventh century *-aγ* developed into a diphthong *-au > -ou*, which not long afterwards became *-ó*, as can be seen from the form *zamto* (*Számtó*), dating from the second half of the twelfth century. A similar development is postulated in the case of *meneγ* (*-eγ >* *-eü > -ő*). In the Permian (i.e. Zyryan and Votyak) languages final *-k* has likewise disappeared.

To sum up, it may be stated that the whole of Finno-Ugrian linguistic science is based on historical phonology. Without its aid, no investigation is possible in etymology, grammar or syntax – in short, it is impossible to prove relationship between the various languages.

PART I

Finno-Ugrian Prehistory

🔅🔅🔅🔅🔅🔅

SUBJECT AND METHOD

LINGUISTIC relationship does not necessarily imply ethnic relationship. While it is possible to demonstrate the former, it is far more difficult to trace connections in the realm of culture or anthropology. Linguistically the Hungarians are closely related to the Ob-Ugrians, but anthropologically and culturally there are wide differences. While the languages have retained their Finno-Ugrian characteristics despite all the changes that have occurred in them, the peoples have been changed out of all recognition by admixtures and foreign influences in the course of history. Thus although language may be an important factor in ethnology and on this basis it may be possible to talk of a relationship between Finno-Ugrian peoples as well as languages, for practical purposes it is necessary to make a distinction between the history of language and the history of ethnic groups. The former is the realm of the linguist, while the latter belongs to a different branch of science, known as prehistory.

The prehistory of a people concerns its earliest degree of development. Although it is essentially a branch of history, it is hardly to be identified with what is usually understood by historical science. This is not only because its sphere of investigation is different, but also because of the different methods used. Historical research depends upon written sources, but these are extremely rare in the study of prehistory. Results are obtained by using other branches of knowledge, the most important of which are linguistics, folklore, archaeology and anthropology.

In investigating the prehistory of a people known to speak a certain language but lacking written records, one of the surest methods of discovering events lost in the mists of time is to examine the language. Language develops over thousands of years; its structure outlives forms of society which have long since disappeared, for it is independent of many of the changes that affect them. The same linguistic system serves both new and old social and economic developments. Sudden changes are not typical of linguistic development; the very solidity and resistance to change offered by a language make it possible to deduce events and processes occurring thousands of years ago. This does not imply, however, that languages do not react to social and economic change. These naturally leave traces, more particularly in vocabulary, as can be seen from the technical words that have increased the stock of many languages in the present century.

Historic events have left their mark on language. By using scholarly methods, it has been proved that there are very many Turkic loanwords in Hungarian; these entered the language during contacts with Turkic peoples. These loanwords can be further divided into different strata, and can be shown to have come from different languages at different times. It has also been proved that a great number of them were taken over before the arrival of the Hungarians in present-day Hungary. Comparison of present forms, dialectal variants and historical data with the appropriate Turkic forms has led to the discovery that the oldest Turkic loanwords in Hungarian are derived from at least three Turkic languages of the Chuvash type.[1] Since these words are chiefly concerned with cattle breeding, agriculture and tribal organization, it may be deduced purely on linguistic evidence – for there are no written records – that the early Hungarians were in close and lengthy contact with folk who spoke a Chuvash-type Turkic, and that this contact brought about important changes in the economic and political life of the Hungarians.

Loanwords are not the only important factor in prehistorical research. The Finno-Ugrian origin of Hungarian is today a well-established fact. Certain words can be traced to a common Uralic or Finno-Ugrian language, and those which have appropriate forms in other modern FU languages are of supreme importance

1 The Turkic languages may be divided into two groups as follows: 'Chuvash' types show *r, l, š, š̌* where common Turkic has *z, š, j, s*. The early Hungarian borrowings are of the former type, e.g. Hu. *ökör* (=ox) ~ Chuv. *veger* (Osmanli *ökiiz*); Hu. *szél* (=wind) ~ Chuv. *šil* (Osmanli *yel*); Hu. *sár* (=mud) ~ Chuv. *šur* (Cumanian

in establishing the nature of the vocabulary of this language. This gives some idea of the social and economic factors which existed then, while linguistic palaeontology helps to determine the region in which this language existed. This science is based on the premise that it is possible to define with some accuracy the area in which certain plants and animals can live. Thus by collecting the names of plants and animals in common Uralic and taking into account the geographical extent of their habitat, it is possible to obtain some idea of the region in which this language was spoken.

An examination of geographical names may also prove extremely useful. A linguistic analysis of the names of rivers and settlements on the western slopes of the central Urals, for example, has led to the deduction that the area was once settled by Voguls, who are therefore not to be regarded as original inhabitants of Siberia where they are now to be found. But great care is necessary here. A handful of place names or river names is insufficient for prehistorical deductions to be made; but if all such material in a given region can be explained through a language no longer existing there, we may assume that this language was once used throughout that region or, in other words, that a people speaking the language once lived there.

As we have stated, archaeology, ethnography and anthropology have their part to play in prehistorical research. These branches of scholarship, however, serve to complete and support the results reached by linguistic methods. Archaeological finds are limited because they cannot be made to speak, and thus cannot be related to a definite people. Recent Soviet discoveries help to confirm many of the conclusions tentatively reached by linguists. Ethnography also has its part to play. The Hungarian word *ágy* (= bed) is of FU origin and can be traced back to common FU. This, however, does not mean that the piece of furniture now associated with that word was in common use among Finno-Ugrians. From ethnographical descriptions it is clear that a layer of hay covered with pelts placed along one of the sides of the tent served as a bed for certain primitive FU peoples who had either just turned to a settled mode of life or were semi-nomadic. This we may well picture as the typical FU bed.

Ethnographical data must needs be treated with caution, for objects, customs and superstitions may travel rapidly from one people to another. It would be quite wrong to observe certain phenomena and uncritically project them back some five or six thousand years. Moreover, proofs of relationship should not be sought in social and economic phenomena which are common to all peoples at a certain phase in their development.[1]

Anthropology may be of assistance in two ways. First, examination of physical characteristics of modern Finno-Ugrian peoples makes it possible to analyse common elements (which may be of identical origin) and to distinguish these from later miscegenation. Secondly, palaeoanthropology, which is particularly concerned with bone material discovered on ancient burial sites, reconstructs the physical structure of early inhabitants of the region. Anthropological research, however, requires a wealth of data and this cannot be expected in the case of primitive man.[2]

It should now be clear that prehistory is a complex science, using the results of several specialized branches of knowledge. Other branches may also be used as occasion arises, e.g. musical history, climatology, pollen analysis and even atomic research. For the moment their rôle is less significant, but together they help to complete the picture. Linguistic research, since it is the most exact, remains the most important factor in prehistoric research. It is for the historian, on the other hand, to collate the results of prehistorical scholarship and integrate them with the history of a people.

THE PRIMEVAL HOME OF THE FINNO-UGRIAN PEOPLES

Since the Finno-Ugrian and Samoyed languages have a common origin, they are the continuation of a more or less unified original

1 Traces of matriarchy have been noted among the customs of several FU peoples. Although this might be regarded as evidence that the FU people at one time lived in a matriarchal society, there is no proof here of relationship. Matriarchy is characteristic of many human societies at a certain stage of their development. Similarly, although both Lapps and Samoyeds are breeders of reindeer, this is no proof of relationship, for in given circumstances other nations also might have developed this occupation. But the surprising degree of similarity between certain Lapp and Samoyed sledge-types may at least be taken as evidence of early connections between them.

2 If twenty-five graves are discovered in the excavation of a burial-site, this may well be an important event for the archaeologist; the examination of twenty-five skeletons provides little data for the anthropologist.

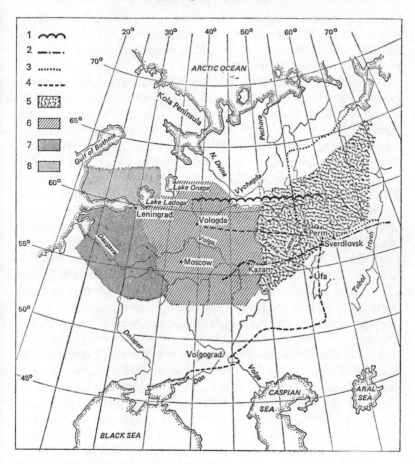

Map 1. The Primeval Home of the Finno-Ugrians

1. Northern limit of hedgehog

2. Southern limit of pinus abies

3. Western limit of the Siberian pine (pinus cembra)

4. Northern, eastern and southern limits of oak

5. - 8. Neolithic cultures of North East Europe in the 3rd millenium B:C.

    5. Kama-Ural culture

    6. Volga-Oka culture

    7. Baltic-Dnieper culture

    8. Sperrings culture

language. This presupposes that there was a human community which used it. Where and how did this community live, and when did the period of coexistence, which must have lasted for many thousands of years, come to an end?

Before answering these questions, it is necessary to clarify two terms which have been and will be frequently used. Both scientific and popular works dealing with the subject use the terms 'Finno-Ugrian' and 'Uralic' in connection with the common language (language-group and languages). In the strict sense, Finno-Ugrian languages are those related to Hungarian and Finnish, excluding the Samoyed languages. Thus the common Finno-Ugrian language is that from which the Baltic-Finnic, Lappish, Volga Finnic (Mordvin and Cheremis), Permian (Zyryan and Votyak) and Ugrian (Ostyak, Vogul, Hungarian) languages are all derived. The relationship of this group to Samoyed was a later discovery. Finno-Ugrian and Samoyed are themselves descendants of a common language called Uralic; the Uralic language-group thus includes both. The Samoyeds were the first to break away from it, and the period succeeding this is called the Finno-Ugrian period, when the language spoken was common Finno-Ugrian.

This is the distinction between the two terms. Chronologically it is significant, but the difference linguistically is not great; indeed, it is impossible to make a sharp distinction between them. Finno-Ugrian is the organic continuation of Uralic. In the final instance Samoyed belongs to the same language-group as Finno-Ugrian, and there is no obstacle to its inclusion in that term. The term 'Uralic' has not had an easy passage. Even specialists tend to use 'Finno-Ugrian' in an all-inclusive sense – indeed the title of this book was so conceived. In any discussion of the common language, however, it is necessary to distinguish between the Uralic and the Finno-Ugrian periods.

Any attempt to define the boundaries of the primeval home must be carried back to the oldest possible – i.e. Uralic – period. There was for a long time considerable uncertainty concerning this problem. In the nineteenth century it was commonly believed that the Finno-Ugrian and Samoyed peoples were of Asiatic origin, a theory which was supported by such well known scholars as F. J. Wiedemann of Estonia and M. A. Castrén, one of the great pioneers of Finno-Ugrian scholarship. This theory is really the logical result of belief in the linguistic and ethnic relationship of the Uralic and Altaic peoples. Both Wiedemann and Castrén firmly believed that both were descended from a common 'tribe'; since Mongol and Turkic peoples are first mentioned as inhabitants of Central Asia, it was natural that the home of the Finno-Ugrians was also to be sought in the same region, the Altai and Sayan mountains. This theory though once widely held is now outdated. Castrén's main contention that Altaic and Uralic shared a common ancestral language has been refuted. Comparative linguistic studies, developed since his day, have led to a clearer understanding of linguistic relationships. Moreover, the arrival of linguistic palaeontology at the end of the last century made it possible to deduce a more precise geographical location for the primeval home of the Finno-Ugrians.

The essence of this science has already been mentioned. The names of flora and fauna from a common word-list will give a fair knowledge of the plants and animals known to the speakers of the original language. The areas in which these flourished are plotted on a map, and the home of the speakers may be determined from the region in which all are to be found. One of the key words in FU research is that for honey (Hu. *méz* ~ Finn. *mesi* (*mete-*) ~ Mordv. *med'* Zyr. *ma* etc. < FU *mete*); another is 'bee' (Hu. *méh* ~ Finn. *mehi-läinen* ~ Mordv. *mekš* ~ Cher. *mukš* ~ Voty. *muš* etc. < FU. *mekše*). The FU people thus knew bees and honey and lived in an area where the honey-bee could be found. This, however, was unknown in Asia, until relatively recent times, with the exception of Asia Minor, Syria, Persia, Afghanistan, Tibet and China, none of which can be taken into account for our purposes. The bee was not found in Siberia, Turkestan, Central Asia and Mongolia; indeed, it was introduced to Siberia only at the end of the eighteenth century. On the other hand, the bee is found west of the Urals in Eastern Europe, mainly from the northern limit of the oak (see map 1), or from Latitude 57°–58° southwards. Moreover, the middle Volga region was known of old as a bee-keeping area. This is one of the clues to the original home of the FU people. Further proof can be found in other plant and animal names.

The Uralic languages have a rich assortment of names for

various kinds of fir. Map 1 shows the limits of the area in which *pinus abies* and *pinus cembra* are to be found. Although their original names have been lost in Hungarian, the other FU languages indicate that they are of Uralic origin: *pinus abies* = Finn. *knusi* ~ Nen. *χ̄ādy* etc.; *pinus cembra* = Zyr. *sus-pu* ~ Osty. *tɛγet* ~ Nen. *tydy* etc. From the map it can be seen that the southern limit of the former type follows Latitude 56° in Europe, and only in Siberia turns further north. The *pinus cembra*, on the other hand, is a typically Siberian tree, sometimes known as 'Siberian pine'; this does not mean that the primeval home must be placed in Siberia, for we know that its area extends westward over the Urals into Europe, where it is found in a fairly limited region round the Upper Kama and Pechora; here the climate is cold. Roast pine kernels from this tree are popular among the Ostyaks and Voguls, and the name for them appears to be FU in origin. It no longer exists in most languages, but may possibly still exist in Finnish apart from Ob-Ugrian. Here, however, it has undergone a strange change, for Finn. *nauris*, if indeed it is related to this root, has come to mean 'turnip', presumably because its shape resembles that of a pine kernel.

A further indication of the European home of the Finno-Ugrian peoples is found in the word for 'hedgehog' (Hu. *sün*, Hu. dial. *sül*, cf. Finn. *siili* etc.); this animal is unknown East of the Urals, but is to be found as far north as Latitude 61°.

The flora and fauna we have mentioned suggest that the Finno-Ugrian or Uralic ancestral home was located in N.E. Europe, not too far from the Urals. This theory is supported by other arguments. The Finno-Ugrian languages include not only a great variety of evergreens, but also several deciduous trees, of which a number, e.g. the elm (Hu. *szil*) are not found at all in Siberia. The northern location of the region is supported by the words in several languages for 'rowan' (Finn. *pihlaja*), whose southern boundary lies close to Latitude 57°. Finn. *muurain* and its cognates denote a type of berry (*rubus arcticus, rubus chamae-morus*) which grows in marshy land in the north. Hu. *fogoly*, now 'partridge', at one time certainly meant 'hazel-grouse' (*tetrastes bonasia*), a typical northern bird. There is a common FU, name for the reindeer, except in Hungarian, where the word was lost as a result of the migration to the south. Certain animals may also be brought into the investigation: the flying squirrel, ermine, mink, sable and pine-marten. We also know that the region included not only forests rich in wild animals, but also small rivers in which the Uralic people caught plenty of fish. There are astonishing varieties of pike common to the Uralic languages, and several other kinds of fish common in the rivers and lakes of northern Europe were also known, as for example the sturgeon and sterlet of the Volga river system. To these may be added the names of certain typically northern birds of forest and river; these preclude a search in Southern Siberia or Southern Asia for the ancestral home. The Uralic word for 'iron' (Hu. *vas*, Finn. *vaski* 'copper') also suggests that this cannot have been far from the rich ore deposits of the Ural mountains.

Further evidence is provided by the word for 'salt'. Hu. *só* may be of Uralic origin, but this has not been proved. It is certain, however, that another word with this meaning, Finn. *suola* and its cognates, is an Indo-European loanword dating from the FU period. It appears therefore that the Finno-Ugrians came to know this important article through the agency of Indo-Europeans. The route by which they received it is presumed to have been the River Volga, since there are numerous salt lakes by the Caspian Sea round the Volga delta, and these without doubt provided salt for the lands to the north.

Thus from the data supplied by flora and fauna it may be concluded that the Finno-Ugrian peoples were based in the middle-Volga and Kama region. The precise boundaries of this ancestral home cannot of course be determined by linguistic palaeontology; indeed, different views have been expressed on matters of detail. Those scholars who have tried to reach more precise definitions have come to varying conclusions. One disputed problem, for instance, is whether the River Oka, a tributary on the right bank of the Volga, was included in the region; another is whether the Urals indeed form the Eastern boundary of it. The proper answer is that the question of boundaries must be considered with extreme caution. There are many indications that the Ural mountains are not to be regarded as an impenetrable natural barrier. Even today they do not prevent communication between peoples on either side; indeed, work, hunting and commerce have always provided sufficient stimulus for such intercourse. Journeys of very great length are often undertaken by hunting peoples, particularly those with reindeer, and the network of streams and rivers in the northern Urals, together with the easy passes through them, make their passage easy. It is probable that the Uralic and Finno-Ugrian peoples were familiar with Western Siberia.

Archaeological discoveries support this theory. The neolithic culture of the Kama region differs little from that of North West Siberia. On the other hand, the Mesolithic and Neolithic culture of the Oka valley varies considerably from that of the Kama-Ural region, which makes it appear likely that the Oka valley was not inhabited by Finno-Ugrian peoples before the third millennium BC.

All these factors suggest that we must search for the Uralic-Finno-Ugrian ancestral home in the wooded region between the great Volga bend (the mouth of the Kama) and the Ural mountains i.e., along the Kama and Vyatka rivers and their tributaries.

Recently a further divergent view has gained considerable support. This originates from the proposition that linguistic palaeontology, although providing a useful method of research, is not entirely satisfactory unless the *former* areas of fauna and flora are considered. These change in time with climatic changes; thus it is by no means certain that the present-day habitat of the hedgehog, for example, or the pine, gives a true picture of conditions 6,000 years ago. There is undoubtedly much truth in this theory, but at the same time it is certain that wherever possible such changes have been taken into account. The *pinus cembra*, for instance, now extends for about 200 km. into Europe on the west side of the Urals, whereas several thousand years ago it penetrated much further, to a depth of some 400–500 km. Moreover, the greatest climatic changes occurred in this area immediately after the last ice age, when the northern boundary of the pine forests reached the Arctic Ocean, whose shores at that time were much further south. It is doubtful, however, whether these circumstances have much bearing upon the quest for the Finno-Ugrian homeland, since the earliest traces of the Finno-Ugrians can be dated only as far back as the fourth millennium BC, which leaves a gap of some six to seven thousand years between them and the ice age. The difference between the Finno-Ugrian period and today does not make it necessary to alter greatly the theoretical area of the region already proposed by linguistic palaeontology. There was a period of drought in the second half of the third millennium BC and later, when the boundary of the southern steppe lands was extended much further north than it is today, but the only resulting difference in the forests of the north was that life there became much more tolerable.

Naturally such considerations should induce caution, but they do not imply the rejection of the older method and its results. Those who favour the latest theories, notably E. Itkonen, recognize the results already obtained and do not refute them; they attempt to bring the discoveries of archaeology into harmony with those of linguistic science. Moreover, many archaeologists have long emphasized that the neolithic culture characterized by comb-decorated earthenware, which stretches eastwards from the Baltic and the White Sea to Western Siberia, is to be ascribed to the Finno-Ugrians.

Others have come to the conclusion that the ancestors of the Baltic Finns were living in the Baltic area many thousands of years before Christ. It would be possible to resolve these contradictions by extending the area of the Uralic ancestral home in a broad zone from the Baltic to the Urals. But is it likely that such a small community lived in so large an area, the western and eastern bounds of which are separated by fifteen hundred to two thousand kilometres? It is customary to cite the case of the Nenets in reply; this community of 25,000 people lives in an area 4,000 km. from east to west, scattered over the tundra from the mouth of the North Dvina to the Yenisei in groups of different sizes. There is a great difference between the way of life of the nomadic Nenets who breed reindeer and that of the old Finno-Ugrian peoples who fished and hunted. On the tundra there is nothing to prevent the reindeer herds and their guardians from wandering hundreds of kilometres; indeed, this way of life compels the Nenets to occupy a vast stretch of land. The nomadic life led by hunters and fishermen is quite different in character. Their peregrinations are restricted to a much smaller area. True, they frequently reach distant parts while hunting, but they do not cover such enormous distances as the inhabitants of the tundras. The hunting routes of the Finno-Ugrian peoples were also restricted by the dense forests surrounding their homeland; in this country travel over long distances must have meant following the rivers. But to keep alive it was unnecessary for the Finno-Ugrian hunter to roam from the Kama region as far as the Baltic to hunt down his quarry. Moreover, fishing, which was also practised together with hunting, kept the Finno-Ugrians to a relatively fixed base, for from hunting expeditions long and short they would return from time to time to their more permanent fishing quarters.

Thus their manner of life offers no reason for extending their homeland as far as the Baltic – indeed it refutes this argument. Nor do archaeological discoveries support it. While it is true that comb-decorated pottery culture extends from the Baltic to the Urals (and indeed beyond them), recent research has shown that despite its many common characteristics it is by no means so unified that it represents one single ethnocultural zone. Analyses made by M. E. Foss and other Soviet archaeologists show that the wooded zone of Eastern Europe containing comb-decorated earthenware of the third millennium BC may be divided into three or four independent cultural regions, i.e., the Volga-Oka central region, the Ural-Kama region, and the so-called Western region which may be more precisely divided into the East Baltic and the Baltic-Dnieper groups. Undoubtedly P. N. Tretyakov is right when he affirms on the basis of this division that the Neolithic inhabitants of the wooded zone of Eastern Europe were not ethnically unified. The boundaries of these varying ethnic areas were naturally not permanent; indeed, they changed from time to time. Traces of a migration from east to west can be found from the Mesolithic or early Neolithic period onwards, but extensive variations in the boundaries of the different ethnocultural regions occur only later.

The original Finno-Ugrian inhabitants of the wooded region of N.E. Europe may be seen in the Ural-Kama cultural zone and its comb-decorated earthenware. According to archaeological data, this culture extended as far west as the confluence of the Kama and the Volga in the third millennium BC, but did not spread any further. Nevertheless, it is interesting that the Sperrings culture of the Eastern Baltic and other discoveries connected with this (e.g. the Olenyeostrov burial ground dating from the late fourth or early third millennium BC) display characteristics shared with the Ural-Kama culture. Perhaps this connection may be explained by the breakaway of one branch of the Finno-Ugrian people at a very early date and its peregrination to the White Sea area or possibly even further west, where it became isolated from the other Finno-Ugrians. Thus there is a possibility that certain Finno-Ugrian groups lived early in the Baltic region, but it must be added that the ethnic composition of the people of the Sperrings-culture requires further investigation. It is however probable that the hunting and fishing inhabitants of the Volga-Oka region in the third millennium BC differed from those of the Baltic and the Kama, so that we have every reason to assume that the inhabitants of the Volga-Kama region were not Finno-Ugrians.

Archaeological evidence shows great migrations and complicated ethnic changes at the end of the third millennium and in the early second millennium BC. At this period the Volga-Oka culture extends northwards, penetrating along the left-bank tributaries of the Volga to the White Sea. This thrust was the result of increasing population and tribal divisions. As their numbers grew, these folk filtered into the sparsely populated territories to their north, where fish and game were plentiful. Side by side with this slow and peaceful migration there are traces of another, more warlike transfer of population. Round about 2000 BC the Finno-Ugrians of the Ural-Kama area invaded the Oka region in large bands, subduing the inhabitants of the eastern part of the Volga-Oka cultural area and incorporating them to produce the so-called Volosovo culture. Thus the Finno-Ugrians appear at the beginning of the second millennium BC along the lower and middle Oka valley, on the Klyazma and even further north of it. They penetrated westward not only along the Volga but also along another Northern route via the Upper Kama and Upper Vyatka towards the North Dvina, whence the disintegrating Finno-Ugrian groups were able to follow the banks of the Suhona and reach the White Sea.

By the middle of the second millennium BC the Finno-Ugrian speaking Ural-Kama peoples had reached the north-western lake region, and at the end of it had arrived at the White Sea. This territorial conquest was associated with changes in the ethnic boundaries of North-East Europe. As a result of this process, the fusion of the existing and the westward-penetrating cultures, the second millennium BC saw the creation of a virtual ethnic unity in the wooded zone between the Eastern Baltic and the Urals, which territory was later inhabited also by Finno-Ugrians. This relative unity, however, is not primeval and is not to be explained by postulating an original settlement of Finno-Ugrians from the Urals to the Baltic, but, as we have seen, is the result of several centuries of westward penetration by the inhabitants of the Ural-Kama region.

This expansion of the Finno-Ugrian hunting and fishing culture and its modification and unification of other types of culture are not synchronic phenomena. It thrust forward at different times and places until it eventually occupied the wooded territory of northern Europe. These archaeological findings, most recently summed up by Tretyakov, support the linguistic theory that the original home of the Finno-Ugrians lay between the Urals and the Kama; they also agree with the chronology – likewise based on linguistics – of their disintegration, which began in the fourth and third millennia BC, and continued into the following era.[1]

CONNECTIONS BETWEEN THE ORIGINAL LANGUAGE AND OTHER LANGUAGES

The Uralic or Finno-Ugrian peoples did not live in a vacuum. Archaeological discoveries show that at this period the population of North and East Europe was not ethnically homogeneous. Thus we must assume that non-Finno-Ugrian speakers lived near them or among them in North-East Europe.

What is the linguistic evidence? There are traces of very old and important connections with several other languages and language-groups.

Much is made of the connection between Uralic and Indo-European. Since Samoyed does not show this so unequivocally as

1 The Soviet archaeologist V. N. Chernyetsov holds a different view of the origin of the Finno-Ugrians. He believes that the neolithic culture of the Ural-Kama region is derived from the Kelteminar culture, basing his theory upon the similarity of the earthenware. Citing the discoveries of S. P. Tolstov, he concludes that the primeval home of the Finno-Ugrians must be sited in the area of the Kelteminar culture, beside the Aral Sea. A. P. Smirnov and other Soviet archaeologists reject this hypothesis. In their opinion the similarities in earthenware vessels merely prove that the inhabitants of the Ural region learnt their manufacture from their neighbours in the south. Chernyetsov's theory is also refuted by research into place names. Not long ago A. P. Dulzon demonstrated that the geographical names of the southern part of Western Siberia are not Ugrian in origin, and that the Ugrians of the Ob can only have arrived in their present habitat from the west.

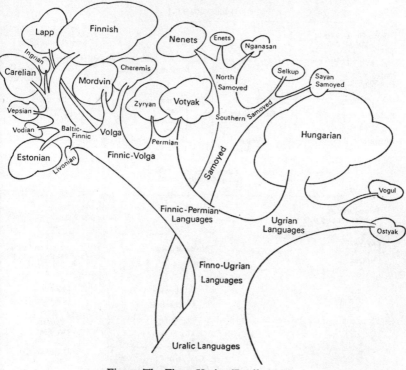

Fig. 1. The Finno-Ugrian Family Tree

the remaining languages, it is more correct to talk of the connection between Finno-Ugrian and Indo-European. It has long been known to linguists that cognates exist, some of which cannot be explained by later contacts between separate languages.

The following words show this connection:

Hungarian	Finnish	< FU root	~ Indo-European	English
méz	mesi	*mete	*medhu	honey
név	nimi	*nime	*nōmn-	name
ház	kota	*kota	*koto-	house
—	jyvä	*jɛva	*jevo	seed
vezet	vetä-	*wetä-	*u̯edh-	lead, pull
visz	vie-	*wīke-	*wegh-	carry, take

A further group of words shows that the Finno-Ugrians were still more or less unified when Proto-Indo-European had broken up.

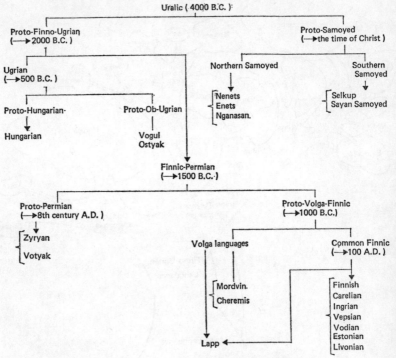

Fig. 2. The Division of the Finno-Ugrian Languages

Certain FU etymologies show a connection not with this language, but with one of its descendants, Proto-Iranian:

Hungarian	Finnish	<	FU *root*	~	Proto-Iranian	English
száz	sata		*śata		*šata-m (IE *kmtom)	hundred
szarv	sarvi		*śorwa		*šrva (IE *krwo-)	horn
arany	—		*sarńa		cf. Avestan zaranya-	gold

The two language-groups show further similarities in certain pronouns and grammatical elements, such as the accusative in *-m* and the ablative in *-ta/-tä*; these also exist in Samoyed. Such linguistic similarities, however, are not confined to Indo-European;

42

Turkic or Altaic elements may also be cited. Here, too, there is agreement between certain pronouns and grammatical elements (the ablative suffix, the genitive in *-n*, the lative in *-k* etc.), as well as formatives and vocabulary:

Hungarian	Finnish	<	FU	~	Turkic	English
al-ja	ala-		*ala		al	bottom
em-ik	ime-		*ime-		äm	suck
(obsolete)						
nyal-	nuole-		*ńolo-		jala-	lick
tő	tyvi		*tüŋe		tüŋ-gek	base

In addition there are numerous syntactical similarities between Uralic and Altaic.

Recently the most surprising development has been the connection between the Uralic languages and Yukagir, a language spoken by some three hundred folk along the Kolyma and Indigirka rivers of North-East Siberia. Yukagir is normally included among the so-called Palaeo-Siberian languages, chiefly for geographical reasons: the generic term covers such languages as Yukagir, Ket, Chukcha, Koryak, Kamchadal and Gilyak, whose linguistic relationships were not clarified until quite recently. Apart from Yukagir, whose position is still not entirely clear, these languages have not been classified. Yukagir may be the survival of some ancient Arctic language, but it may well have close connections with Uralic; indeed, it may be related to this group. There are many grammatical similarities; several suffixes and formatives are similar in form and usage, and pronouns and vocabulary show surprising likeness:

Hungarian	Finnish	Yukagir	English
eme, emse	emä	emei	mother
kéreg	keri	χar(=skin)	bark of tree
lélek (soul)	löyly (steam)	lūl	breath
nyuszt	— Est. nugis	noχšo	marten
al-	ala	-āl	bottom
ho- (hol)	ku-: kuka(=who?)	hon	where
mond	manaa	mon-	say
név	nimi	neve, nim	name

Similar syntactical constructions may also be noted.

Investigations have yet to be made into the connections

between Uralic, Indo-European, Altaic and Yukagir. If it were merely a question of vocabulary, the task would be simple: we should be able to regard certain words as loanwords and try to determine the time of the borrowing. But as we have seen, pronouns, grammatical elements, suffixes and formatives must also be considered. Grammatical elements are not so easily taken over by one language from another. At most the process involves a lengthy period of coexistence and a connection so close that it results in bilingualism, and the number of such grammatical loans is very limited. How then can the structural similarities between the four groups be explained? If we regard the formal similarity of the grammatical elements as accidental, then we may well go on to consider that lexical similarities are due to borrowing from one or other of the languages (it is often difficult to determine the parent language in such cases). In this case we may also apply the term 'accidental' to similarities which, indeed, occur as a result of the relatively small number of vowels and consonants available to form short suffixes and formatives (i.e. those consisting of one or at most two phonemes). The same epithet must also apply to other similarities of suffix and formative which are based on the expressive characteristics of certain sounds.

Nevertheless, agreement among grammatical elements may also be the result of very early relationship. Many linguists have considered this possibility – indeed, there are those today who champion the cause of Uralic-Indo-European and Uralic-Altaic unity. As for the relationship between Yukagir and Uralic, there are many who believe that the former, now moribund, language was once closely connected with Proto-Uralic. Others would include Yukagir in the Uralic group, assuming that it broke away from its parent in primeval times.

Confronted by all these possibilities, even the most unbiased expert finds it difficult to pronounce judgement on these highly complicated relationships, but it is worth while trying to size up the present situation. Is it probable that the structural agreements between the Uralic, Altaic, Indo-European and Yukagir languages are not accidental? Naturally it is. Then does it follow that the explanation is to be found in a common origin? Here the answer must be more guarded. In principle there is no obstacle to such a theory, but it is impossible to prove in practice, since there are not sufficient structural and lexical similarities for this purpose. It would be impossible to reconstruct from them, even in the most fragmentary way, their common basic language. If there was indeed some form of relationship between Uralic and the other languages, this must have preceded Proto-Uralic by several thousand years, and the present state of linguistic knowledge makes it impossible to make realistic deductions about such a distant age. So for the present it seems wisest to regard lexical similarities as the traces of early connections or borrowings. This statement is necessary even when we are dealing with Indo-European and Finno-Ugrian: some of the words involved may be explained from basic Indo-European forms, while others came into Finno-Ugrian only after the disintegration of Indo-European, at a time when we cannot talk of relations between the two language-groups, but only of borrowings based on contact between them.

The decisive factor in the problem is that linguistic relationship can be proved only by comparing the entire language systems and several hundred etymologies. Such comparative material does not exist in Uralic-Altaic, Uralic-Indo-European or even in Uralic-Yukagir connections. With the best will in the world, the number of Uralic-Indo-European etymologies does not exceed thirty-seven, of which only some ten to twelve are unexceptionable. The situation is similar in the other two cases, although the number of etymologies is greater. In the case of Yukagir, for example, those who believe in the relationship with Uralic have discovered over one hundred words and several dozen suffixes and formatives which they regard as common. Yet the majority of these are based on exterior factors – phonetic similarity, for instance – and are not proved by regular agreements based on sound laws firmly backed by historical linguistic knowledge. Naturally it would be difficult at present to fulfil these requirements, since our knowledge of Yukagir is scanty and its history little-known.

Thus we are still far from being able to prove the relationship of Uralic with these other languages, but one thing is certain: Uralic and Finno-Ugrian society did not exist in isolation. Around them and perhaps in their midst lived speakers of other languages. To the south there were certainly Indo-Europeans, while to the east and north-east, perhaps on the Siberian slopes of the Urals, ancient sub-Arctic peoples may have had their homes. Just as the Indo-European and Proto-Iranian loanwords in Finno-Ugrian are explained by this contact, so too perhaps the similarities noted in Yukagir may have come about through contact between sub-Arctic hunting peoples and the Uralians. Many other theories might be propounded here; each one might be considered a good idea, but would be equally difficult to prove.

Of all the peoples in contact with the Finno-Ugrians, the best known in history are the Indo-Europeans. For this reason the contacts between them are important, particularly in determining the place and era of the ancestral home of the Finno-Ugrians.

We have already noted that the Samoyed languages possess no Indo-European loanwords. Thus in the Proto-Uralic period the Indo-Europeans had no contact with them, or else the effect of any contact did not reach the groups whose descendants were to become the Samoyeds. Therefore the end of the Uralic period, i.e., the separation of the Samoyeds from the parent language, occurred while the Indo-European language was still unified to a greater or lesser degree, for there are certain Indo-European loanwords of the Finno-Ugrian period whose source is Proto-Indo-European. The Finno-Ugrians remained together after the disintegration of Indo-European, as shown by the Proto-Iranian loanwords found in FU. The time of this disintegration is the subject of various theories. Indian, Hittite and Greek possess written records from the middle of the second millennium BC, which show both that these three languages existed then and that they differed from each other and from Proto-Indo-European. It is clear that their emergence was a lengthy process. Although there is no doubt that the breakaway of certain groups did not imply the complete disintegration of the parent language, we may well adopt the view that the unity of Indo-European was so loose by the fourth millennium BC that certain independent languages were already beginning to emerge then. Using this as a basis, if not entirely firm, at least we have a starting point from which it is possible to postulate the dates of the Uralic and Finno-Ugrian periods. The ancestors of the Samoyeds had either loosened or broken their connection with Proto-Uralic before the fourth millennium BC, and during that millennium only the ancestors of the Finno-

Ugrians maintained a relatively unified language, which was in existence when Proto-Iranian came into being. Recalling the archaeological statement that the settlement of Northern Europe in the neolithic period gathered momentum in the middle of the third millennium BC and gained this from the Volga-Oka region, we are justified in holding the view that the dispersion of the Finno-Ugrians took place at this time. Research into the history of these peoples and their languages supports this theory.

The last word has yet to be spoken concerning the original habitat of the Indo-Europeans. Opinions here are sharply divided. The steppes of Central Asia, the plains of Southern Russia, the Baltic, Central Europe, the Caucasus – all these have been proposed. But wherever it was sited, it is certain that in the second millennium BC members of this language-group were to be found both in Europe proper and outside her boundaries. The contacts between Finno-Ugrian and Indo-European, Finno-Ugrian and Proto-Iranian, and those later developed between Finnic and Balto-Slavonic, Finnic and Germanic, Ugrian and Iranian etc. support the theory that from the fourth millennium onwards the Finno-Ugrian peoples lived to the north of the Indo-Europeans. The Indo-European names of rivers in Europe show that various groups of this family had settled large areas of Europe in the first millennium BC; they may well have covered the area from the Baltic to the Volga and thence to the Urals, where they made contact with Finno-Ugrians, partly as a unified community and partly in the process of dispersal.

THE DISPERSION OF THE FINNO-UGRIAN PEOPLES

Why did the parent language divide into several separate groups? Why did these further develop into the present related languages? Why was Finno-Ugrian not preserved intact?

It would be sufficient to consider what has happened to other language-groups and call them to witness to the differentiation of languages, but this would not explain the reasons for the dispersion and development of separate languages. These may be found in the parent language itself.

When we speak of the 'unity' of the parent language and 'unified' Finno-Ugrian peoples, we are using these terms in a relative sense. The basic language was not as unified as those we know today, with their written records, developed literatures and standard spoken and written languages. The unity of modern Hungarian is also relative. It is divided into dialects, class and group languages, which differ from each other in phonetics, vocabulary, morphology and syntax to varying degrees. Some languages, like German and Finnish, may include dialectal differences so great that comprehension is difficult. In these languages a process of unification occurred at the same time as their speakers discovered a national identity, leading to a national literature and a standard language which rose above dialects, class and group-languages. The use of such literature and language, and their unifying force are fostered by compulsory schooling, television, radio, press, film and theatre, which assure their growth. This unity is preserved by education in one's mother tongue, orthographical and grammatical rules and dictionaries.

A much more variegated picture is shown by the Proto-Finno-Ugrian of several thousand years ago. At that time there was no standard language with its unifying influence, nor did writing exist; thus linguistic rules which could be formulated in writing did not exist either. There is an enormous difference between the unity of a modern language and that of Finno-Ugrian, which was much less concrete. We have already noted that its speakers lived in a vast area at the earliest era discernible through the science of prehistory. No realistic estimate of their numbers is possible. It seems probable that they were not to be counted in millions, but rather in tens of thousands. These few folk, whatever their number, lived scattered over many thousands of miles. Thus the density of population was low, even if we include speakers of other languages living in the same area. The settlements were based on tribes, and not on villages. Each tribe, consisting of several families, set up its own settlement on the banks of a river in the dense forest. Great distances separated them, and although they doubtless made contact with each other during their hunting trips, the tribes lived virtually self-contained lives, thus bringing into being dialectal differences. Is there, then, any justification for talking of a 'unified' original language? There is, in the sense that the vocabulary, grammatical system and main linguistic tendencies and developments throughout this widely dispersed community remained virtually identical for a long period of time, except for minor variations.

Similar dialectal distinctions may be noted now among the Ostyaks and Voguls who live in comparatively small communities, well isolated from each other, along the River Ob and its tributaries. In this area, each settlement has its own dialectal variants, some of which are so great that different groups may find it difficult to understand each other. We must then expect to find dialects in the original parent language. Naturally this is theoretical, for comparative linguistic studies have not reached the stage of being able to produce examples of such dialectal variations. But if we assume their existence, the reason for the disintegration of the parent language is more easily explained. After a certain time these variations became so great that two communities separated by a great distance gradually ceased to understand each other. Then these dialects would begin to develop independently as the common features assuring the unity of the language ceased to be effective. New sounds developed in individual dialects, grammatical constructions assumed new forms, new modes of expression arose, the vocabulary was extended with elements unknown to other dialects: in brief, dialectal differences slowly reached a stage where the requirements for a new language were present; and this itself had dialects of its own. Thus the process of disintegration was caused partly by internal factors, but other external forces affected it also.

One of these was the natural increase in population of the various tribes. Sometimes this was so great that the area occupied by a particular tribe proved too small. In this situation there were two ways of assuring material welfare: either the population migrated to an area richer in game and fish, or it altered its economy by switching to animal breeding or agriculture. These changes, however, are possible only at a certain stage of social development.

Migration may also have played an important part in the creation of new languages, and here we must assume that foreign pressure made this necessary from time to time. Parts of the original community may well have been isolated as the result of foreign conquests.

These are the factors which help to explain the disintegration of the Uralic language. The people occupied a large area, so that there was no hindrance to widespread dispersal. Speakers of foreign languages also lived in the vicinity, and their influence doubtless assisted the process.

The first evidence of this disintegration is the separation of the ancestors of the Samoyeds from the Finno-Ugrians in the fourth millennium BC. After this the latter lived in relative unity until the following millennium, when the Ugrians began to draw away, forming a separate branch in the second millennium. The two new languages were Ugrian and Finnic-Permian. The former embraced the later Hungarians, Voguls and Ostyaks; the remaining Finno-Ugrian languages were in the Finnic-Permian group. This was by no means the end of the process; the result is shown in Figs. 1 and 2.[1]

URALIC AND FINNO-UGRIAN SOCIETY

Linguistic knowledge may be used not only to determine the region of the original home and the time limits of its occupation, but also to give some idea of the life of the inhabitants. The evidence here is not based on historical sources, but on the etymological material gained from comparing the vocabularies of related languages.

Common elements in the Finno-Ugrian and Samoyed vocabulary show objects and ideas expressible in the parent language, so

1 Recent experiments in glottochronology, an attempt to show how long it takes for changes to occur in vocabulary, have been applied to Finno-Ugrian. According to its practitioners, a basic stratum of 100 words is reduced to 86% in 1,000 years; thus some 74% of two related languages (86% of 86%) will remain identical after 1,000 years. After 2,000 years this is reduced to 55%, after 3,000 to 41%, after 4,000 to 30%, after 5,000 to 22%, after 6,000 to 16% and after 7,000 to 12%. Applying this scale to Finno-Ugrian, it has been shown that of 100 basic words 27% have remained in Hungarian and Finnish, 31% in Finnish and Zyryan, 36% in Mordvin and Cheremis, and an average of 13–15% in Finno-Ugrian and Samoyed. Translated into time, this would mean that more than 6,000 years have elapsed since the division between Finno-Ugrian and Samoyed, and 4,500 years between Hungarian and Finnish. Interesting as these results are, glottochronology is to be treated with the utmost caution, since preparation of suitable word-lists is highly complicated and the omission of a few vital etymologies may result in significant errors of several thousand years.

that it is possible to trace the outlines of material culture and social organization. Complete detail is impossible, since we shall never know the extent of the original vocabulary. The few hundred etymologies known to science are sufficient to characterize the main features of society in the Uralic and Finno-Ugrian period, and may thus be regarded as valuable historical evidence.

It is from the vocabulary that we know Uralic society to have consisted of hunters and fishers. The importance of fishing can be seen in the Uralic origin of such words as Hu. *hal* (fish), *tat(hal)* 'tench', *háló* (net) and their equivalents in the other related languages. Life on the water can be seen in the following: Hu. *ár* (current, formerly 'flood'), *hab* (foam, formerly 'wave'), *halad* (to progress, formerly 'float, travel by water'), *jó* (now obsolete, formerly 'river', preserved in certain river names e.g., *Sajó, Berettyó* < *Berek-jó*), *láp* (marsh), *tó* (lake), *úszik* (swim) *víz* (water) and perhaps *mart* (dip), also Finn. *souta-* (row). As for hunting, we may cite Hu. *íj* (bow), *nyíl* (arrow), *ín* (bowstring), *ideg* (sinew) and Finn. *noutaa* (hunt, trail), all of Uralic origin.

Food was thus supplied mainly by fish and game. Unfortunately we have no detailed evidence of Uralic cuisine, but some methods of preparation and serving can be deduced. It is probable that both fish and flesh were eaten raw, since this custom still exists today among certain peoples. Raw meat may well have caused illness, particularly worms, as can be seen from the Hu. *nyű* (worm). Hu. *főz* (cook), Finn. *sysi* (charcoal), *tuli* (fire) suggest that cooked meat was also known. It was cooked in a pot (Hu. *fazék*) and doubtless the flavour (Hu. *íz*) came in for praise or criticism.

Considerable variety of meat was available, as can be seen from the names of fish, birds and animals. Hungarian retains only *nyúl* (hare), *fogoly* (partridge), *holló* (crow), *kígyó* (serpent) and possibly *evet* (squirrel); but reindeer, sable, marten and other furred animals were also known, together with numerous woodland birds and waterfowl, such as wild geese and wild duck. The menu was completed with different types of berry and eggs (Old Hu. *mony*) discovered in birds' nests (*fészek*).

For transport in the summer there was the rowing boat, as the Finn. *souta-* (row) betrays, but in the lengthy snowy seasons (Hu. *hó* = snow), snowshoes were in use (Finn. *suksi*), and their quarry was pulled on sledges (Finn. *ahkio*). Their clothes were made from the skins (Hu. *bőr*) of the animals they hunted. Sewing was presumably the task of the women; Finn. *äimä* (needle) shows that this craft was known. It was made not of steel, but of bone (Finn. *luu*), probably fishbone. The clothes were gathered in at the waist by a belt (Hu. *öv*).

They knew the gimlet (Hu. *fúró*) and were able to carve (Hu. *farag*) with implements which possessed some sort of blade (Hu. *nyel*). These implements were made either of stone (Hu. *kő*) or of bone. Of the latter they also made glue (Finn. *tymä*), with which to stick things together. The Uralic origin of Hu. *fon* (weave) probably refers to the twisting of thread out of animal sinews (Hu. *ideg*) and perhaps to the making of nets (Hu. *háló*). As for metals, only Hu. *vas* (iron) can be traced back to Uralic times, but this does not prove that ironworking was then known. It is probable that this name was given to the brown layers of iron to be found in the marshes and lakes surrounding their settlements, or to the surface ore of the Ural region, but that no use was made of it.

They knew neither animal breeding nor agriculture. Their dwellings were not permanent, for hunting demands frequent changes of place. For shorter trips they passed their nights in shelters dug out of the snow, providing some protection from the wind. They also had more effective protection against the forces of nature in dwellings well-dug into the ground, as the word for tent-pole (Finn. *vuoli*) attests.

The tribe was an important factor, and the number of words expressing various degrees of kinship suggest that blood-relationship was strongly maintained: Hu. *ős* (now 'ancestor', originally 'father'), *eme* (obsolete: 'mother'), *feleség* (wife), *meny* (daughter-in-law), *vő* (bridegroom), *nap(a)* (mother-in-law), *rokon* (relation), Finn. *setä* (uncle), *nato* (sister-in-law).

The Finno-Ugrian period does not display any great material changes from those of the Uralic era. Thus the picture already given applies largely to this period too: the vocabulary available allows us to fill in further details.

The fishing vocabulary, for example, is enlarged by the addition of the word for a fish-trap made of net (Hu. *fal*, now 'wall'), Hu. *vejsze* (fishweir), *para* (cork), Finn. *onki* (hook) and a number of species of fish e.g., Hu. *ón* (bream), *keszeg* (bream). Hunting continued to be important; new words appearing at this time include Hu. *lő* (shoot), *öl* (kill), *ravasz* (now 'cunning', formerly 'fox'), *fajd* (grouse), *lúd* (goose), *vöcsök* (grebe), *nyuszt* (pine-marten), *nyest* (beech-marten) and perhaps *hölgy* (now 'lady', originally 'ermine').

The word now used in Hungarian for 'black cherry' (*meggy*) was then applied to an edible berry found in the woods and marshes, which formed an important part of the diet. So collection of food was added to hunting and fishing, as can be seen in the words for 'bee' (Hu. *méh*) and 'honey' (Hu. *méz*). The bee-keeping of those days must be presumed to have been primitive: honey was found in hollow trees, but the fate of the swarm and the preservation of the bees were not considered. The appearance of words such as Hu. *ház* (now 'house') and *lak* (dwelling) does not imply a break with earlier conditions. These expressions continued to mean a primitive, easily constructed tent covered with animal skins or birch bark, or a hut half-dug into the ground. It was equipped with a bed (Hu. *ágy*) consisting of skins spread out on the ground and a doorway (Hu. *ajtó*), merely a simple opening in the dwelling. Domestic equipment was increased by the use of the knife (Hu. *kés*), awl or punch (Hu. *ár*) and the axe, all of which continued to be made usually of stone and bone, and were used to fashion these materials together with wood, bark and skins: from them vessels, clothing and other necessities were made.

In the Finno-Ugrian period other metals appear, e.g., gold (Hu. *arany*) and lead (Hu. *ón*), but we know little of their use. Hu. *arany* is derived from Proto-Iranian, which suggests that it first became known through foreign traders as an article of merchandise. A certain form of trading, and in particular the 'silent trading' mentioned by Ibn Battuta[1] was in existence at this period, for we have the evidence of Hu. *ár* (price) to support this view. Counting was known, and is attested by several numerals: Hu. *két* (2), *három* (3), *négy* (4), *öt* (5), *hat* (6), *húsz* (20), *száz* (100). The Finno-Ugrians were also able to orientate themselves in space and time, e.g., Hu. *jobb* (right), *bal* (left); Hu. *év* (year), *hó* (month), *ősz* (autumn), *tél* (winter), *tavasz* (spring).

1 See his description below, p. 125.

The question of agriculture and animal breeding at this period has evoked much discussion. From the various names for reindeer surviving from the Uralic and Finno-Ugrian periods, some scholars argue that the breeding of these animals took numerous forms. But the names might well have applied to different kinds of wild deer, since there is nothing to suggest that in either period they were domesticated. Against this argument, these scholars cite certain, mainly Lappish and Samoyed, etymologies which are now used as specialized terms in reindeer breeding, e.g., words for 'winter pastures', 'guarding the herd', 'harness' and 'reins'. These however are not sufficient to prove that reindeer were bred in those distant times. Archaeological and ethnological researches point unequivocally to the fact that reindeer breeding is one of the newer forms of animal breeding; it cannot be traced back to palaeolithic or neolithic (Finno-Ugrian) times, and the oldest records of it on the Amur, Baikal, Irtysh and Yenisei, consisting of rock drawings depicting reindeer pasturing and the riding of reindeer, date from the bronze and iron ages. It is true that rock and cave drawings of the palaeolithic age show reindeer, but only as the hunted quarry. Zoological researches also support the view that reindeer breeding is of no great age. There is very little biological difference between the domesticated and the wild reindeer, while the horse, dog and cat, for example, show wide differences. It should also be noted that in certain areas horse breeding led to reindeer breeding. These arguments suggest that Uralic or Finno-Ugrian reindeer breeding was extremely unlikely.

The wild reindeer, however, was well-known as one of the most important prizes for the hunter; hence the variety of names for it. There were different terms for the bull, calf and probably for various types of colouring and antler. How then can we account for the technical terms already mentioned? Winter pastures are necessary for wild as well as domesticated animals, and 'guarding' or 'watching' the herd in all probability referred to the hunter, who from his hiding place observed the movements of the deer. As for 'harnessing' and reins, there is no need to suppose that they were restricted to reindeer. The Uralic people, as we have seen, were familiar with the sledge, preserved in Finn. *ahkio* and its cognates. This was probably hollowed out of a tree-trunk and shaped like a boat; it had no ribs and no runners, and was pulled by hand in the manner used today by certain Samoyeds, who drag their prey home on them. It is pulled either by the hunter or by his dog and on occasion by reindeer. (This type of sledge has been modified by the Lapps into a travelling sledge for use with reindeer.) In the Uralic period it was first drawn by man, who later taught his dog to perform this task. Thus harness and reins and straps (Hu. *szíj*) were needed for this mode of transport, whether pulled by man or dog.

It is also possible that the wild reindeer were not only hunted for their own sake, but also used as decoys. One of the methods of hunting observed among reindeer hunters is to use a bull as a decoy on the approach to a wild herd. As it draws near to the herd, the bull sees the cows, becomes excited and utters a mating call with a characteristic coughing sound. Hearing this the bull from the wild herd rushes in anger and fear towards the decoy as it covers the huntsman, whose task is now simple. The deer, which normally gives human beings a wide berth, approaches him from an angle which makes it easy for him to kill it.[1]

It is not unlikely that the Finno-Ugrians used this method of hunting wild deer. It may even have existed at an earlier period. All that was needed was to catch a young wild deer and tame it to some degree. This is the first stage of taming and breeding, but it does not imply that anything further was known. Horses and cattle were unknown at this time. The word for 'butter' (Hu. *vaj*, Finn. *voi*) might suggest that cattle were kept, but in the related languages it has preserved the original meaning of 'fat'. Finn. *uuhi* and its cognates show that sheep were known (Hu. *juh* is problematical, owing to phonetic problems). In the absence of further evidence it is impossible to decide whether they were kept as domesticated animals or whether they were known simply through other animal breeding peoples. It is easier to decide the case of the pig. Finn. *porsas* (sucking-pig) and its cognates in Mordvin, Cheremis and Permian show that it was known in the Finnic-Permian period. It was once believed to be a loanword from Proto-Iranian at that time, but more recently it has been suggested that *porsas* may be one of the oldest borrowings from Indo-European. If we accept this view, we may suppose that the Finno-Ugrians, or at least some of them, came to know the pig

1 See also Nganasan methods, p. 228.

through their Indo-European neighbours, but pig breeding became regular only during the Finnic-Permian period, if the evidence of vocabulary is taken into account.

There remains the dog. This was known from the Uralic period (Obsolete Hu. *fene* ~ Finn. *peni*), and since it is one of the earliest animals to be domesticated, it may be supposed that the Uralic – Finno-Ugrian word implied the *canis familiaris*. There is no point in attempting to estimate when the dog was set to serve man, but ethnological research testifies that the process of domestication was begun by a fishing and hunting society. Here again the boat-shaped sledge must be mentioned; realization of the ability of the dog to draw this instead of a man probably led to its use in this sphere, and it was certainly known in the time of the parent language. From this there was later developed the breeding of dogs for harnessing to the sledge, which in its turn grew into a passenger vehicle. Although there is no proof that the Finno-Ugrians reached this stage, it is at least probable. Moreover, dog breeding began much earlier than reindeer breeding, and was known throughout the sub-arctic regions of Europe and Asia.

Thus the Finno-Ugrians did not develop into an animal breeding people proper; only the rudimentary traces of this activity can be seen among them.

The situation in agriculture is similar. All experts agree that there is no sign of agriculture during the Uralic period, but there are differing opinions concerning the Finno-Ugrian age. Some say that agriculture was already an important supplement to the other means of production, while others see it only in a very elementary form. These divergences arise from the imprecise nature of the etymological evidence available. Among the basic words in the argument are Finn. *jyvä* (seed, grain, grain of corn) and its cognates, which are old Indo-European loanwords. All this can prove is that the Indo-Europeans shared their knowledge of corn with their northern neighbours; it certainly does not imply the growing of corn by the Finno-Ugrians. Perhaps Hu. *kenyér* (bread) may be regarded as Finno-Ugrian, although its origin is disputed, and we may also cite Zyr. *piž* (flour), Cheremis *šädänge* (wheat) and Zyr. *rok* (gruel); but none of these can be used as convincing evidence of agricultural activity. The Votyak cognate of Hu. *kenyér* can mean 'millet' or 'gruel'. The Ostyak equivalent of

Cher. *šädäŋge* is similarly used for both foods. This uncertainty of meaning suggests that the Finno-Ugrian original words were used not for a certain type of wheat, but only generally for some sort of grain or the food prepared from it. In any case, there is no evidence here for advanced agriculture, but rather the opposite. Nor is it certain from the evidence of these words that they ever meant food milled from wheat. They may also have been applied to some form of pulp made of roots or berries with a floury content or to the food made from it, either baked on embers or boiled in water. This is like the food called by the Ostyaks 'wild cherry-bread'; they chop up wild cherries, knead them together and bake them in loaves, all without the addition of flour. Similar 'bread' made of berries and flour is known also to the Zyryans. These expressions may also have been used to denote fish-flour, made of dried fish, a popular food in the north; it is easy to preserve and to make up into soup by merely throwing it into water and boiling it. The most weighty evidence against the existence of agriculture in the Finno-Ugrian period is seen in the lack of names for implements and processes connected with it; all are of foreign origin. Not a single word for sowing, reaping, the scythe or the hoe can be traced back to Finno-Ugrian.

Thus there is no justification for the view that agriculture was beginning to develop in this period. It is not improbable that corn was known through neighbouring peoples, but no attempt was made to cultivate it among the Finno-Ugrian people. It is possible that when they began to disperse, certain groups acquired a knowledge of primitive agricultural processes, but the only evidence of this comes from the later Finnic-Permian period when signs of development appeared. Hunting and fishing remain the characteristic modes of life during the Finno-Ugrian era.

As for internal social relationships, all the signs indicate that they lived in tribal communities. Both for the individual and for society as a whole the tribe was the focus of life. The preservation of words for 'tribe, nationality' through the ages is a witness to this: FU **kunta* still exists in a changed form and sense in the Hu. *had*, which now means 'army', but has also meant 'war' and earlier came closer to its original meaning, as can be seen in the *hadas* (i.e. tribal) settlements of the Nagykunság area. In Ostyak the word has now come to refer to the whole nation (*Chanti*), while in Finnish it has been degraded to a collective suffix, as in *perhe-kunta* ('family community': *perhe* = family) and *maa-kunta* ('province': *maa* = earth). Thus the once-important word has changed considerably in meaning as the tribal concept has altered. Some languages have lost it completely.

The tribe was then the most important community. To the individual at this primitive period it assured a livelihood, for most work in the chief branches of production, hunting and fishing, was performed collectively by tribal groups. The spoils of the hunt were also common tribal property. It was necessary for the tribe to have a leader, who would organize fishing, hunting, division of spoils etc., and would also represent the tribe when, for example, it was involved in barter.

The problem of whether this society was patriarchal or matriarchal has often been raised, but it remains open. The Finno-Ugrian peoples which still preserve some form of tribal organization are all patriarchal, but in the social life of certain peoples there are traces of matriarchy. Of these we may note the honour paid to the founder of the tribe – a mother-figure, usually in the form of an animal. The more important spirits and deities frequently take the forms of women. These indications, however, do not allow us to conclude that matriarchy was practised in prehistoric times.

The beliefs and religious practices of the Finno-Ugrians may also be mentioned here. Man living in primitive surroundings depended much more on the forces of nature and was more troubled by the whims of climate and natural disasters than were later generations. He explained the incomprehensible by attributing it to the interference of higher beings. It is probable that worship of gods believed to exist in natural phenomena or in certain objects was known in Uralic and Finno-Ugrian times. Ancestor worship is also typical of tribal society and this doubtless had its place among them. Concrete proofs can be found in a number of words. Hu. *hagymáz* (typhoid) is a compound of which both members are Finno-Ugrian: the first element *hagy* probably meant 'evil spirit', cf. Vogul *χūl'-ōter* (*ōter* = prince) 'the lord of the underworld' and Finn. *koljo* (giant). The second element of the Hungarian word, now obsolete, *máz ~ mász* meant 'illness, trouble'. This group of words suggests that animism was prevalent. The same is suggested by Hu. *lélek* 'spirit', while Hu. *révül* 'fall into a trance', although incapable of being traced right back to the FU period, points to the form of animism known more commonly as shamanism. Shamanistic peoples offer sacrifices to avoid illness and catastrophe, and to cure sickness. The ritual includes the shaman's trance, in which he may come forward as the intermediary between humans and the spirit world.

The form of shamanism preserved up to the present century among certain Finno-Ugrian peoples cannot be regarded as the direct descendant of the Finno-Ugrian type, since various later influences have been at work among them; etymological evidence, however, shows that there was some form of shamanism in existence then. It was primitive and simple, based on the worship of ancestors and the dead in general, and on the superstitious cult of natural phenomena. The beginnings of a priestly order, i.e., the separation of the shamans from the rest of the tribe, must also be traced back to this period. Finn. *noita* 'magician' and its cognates witness to this.

The picture of Uralic and Finno-Ugrian society based on the evidence of common vocabulary is by no means complete. Unfortunately our knowledge of the structure and vocabulary of the basic language is fragmentary, so that the life of its speakers is known only in part. But at all events we can trace the outlines of a larger picture and distinguish many essential characteristics of life several thousand years ago.

Further light can be shed if we set the anthropological view against the relatively uniform linguistic scene. The results of palaeoanthropological research have so far shed no light on the characteristics of the Uralic type, so that the problem must be approached from our knowledge of present-day FU peoples.

Anthropologically the Finno-Ugrian and Samoyed peoples present a very mixed picture. Comparison between representatives of Vogul, Zyryan, Mordvin, Cheremis, Finnish, Lapp and Hungarian types reveals marked differences even to a layman. Experts, however, basing their conclusions on thousands of measurements, distinguish three basic types that can be found in various groups of Finno-Ugrian and Samoyed peoples, and are not restricted to single ethnic groups.

The first of these is the Uralic type (otherwise known as

Europo-Sibirid or Ugrian). According to Pál Lipták and Cheboksarov, its characteristics are: a mesocephalic head, thin straight hair of black or dark brown colour, skin not as dark as the mongoloid, brown or varicoloured eyes, rare or medium facial hair. The face is fairly broad, the nose somewhat prominent and either straight or turned-up; the cheeks are relatively flat and the jawbone not unduly wide; the epicanthus is not often found; the lips are narrow or moderately full and the general stature is short or below average. This type developed from a mixture of Europid and Mongoloid elements; taking an intermediate place between them. It is most frequently found among the Ob-Ugrians and, with certain modifications, among the Samoyeds; but particular characteristics can also be observed in the physiognomy of the Permian and Cheremis peoples, as well as among various Turkic peoples of Siberia, Chuvash and Bashkirs.

It is interesting from the Hungarian prehistorical viewpoint to note that Pál Lipták's investigations into graves dating from the occupation[1] have revealed an occurrence of 21 per cent of the Uralic type among the Hungarians of those days. They occupy second place to the Turanid type, which accounts for 48 per cent.

The White Sea-Baltic (East Baltic, East Europid) type is widespread among the Finno-Ugrians. It is strongly Europid, and is characterized by a fairly short head, straight or gently wavy hair of a blonde colouring, light skin and eyes, fairly dense facial hair and a nose, either straight or snub, with a moderately high bridge; this is of medium, or less than medium, stature. It is generally found among Baltic Finns, the Volga Finno-Ugrians and the Permians, but may also be traced among the Latvians, Lithuanians, Northern Russians and the Poles. Recent research indicates that it was not so common among the early Hungarians as was once believed, although it is fairly widespread among modern Hungarians.

The third type to be found among the Finno-Ugrians is the Atlantic-Black Sea (Atlanto-Pontus) type, which has dark and somewhat wavy hair, thick facial hair, dark or varicoloured eyes, a long face and high-bridged nose, either straight or slightly hooked; this type, with mesocephalic or moderately brachyce-

---

1 896 AD is the traditional date of the occupation of the central Danube valley by the Hungarians.

phalic head-structure, can be seen among the Permjaks, Votyaks and Moksha-Mordvins, also among the southern Voguls. Similar characteristics may be seen among various Tartar, Balkan and Caucasian races.

Besides these main types, mention must be made of the characteristic Lappid or Lapponoid type, whose name links it with the Lapps. In the Ural district there is a mixed variant known as the Uralo-Lapponoid.

These types have developed as a result of lengthy historical processes and frequent mixtures, so that it is impossible to state whether any one of them can be regarded as identical with a Finno-Ugrian anthropological type. It is, however, certain that the Atlanto-Pontus type was introduced among the Finno-Ugrians through southern (possibly Iranian or Turkic) influence. The White Sea-Baltic type is characteristic of a large number of Finno-Ugrians – indeed of practically the entire Finnic-Permian branch, while the eastern Finno-Ugrians (Ob-Ugrians, Samoyeds, and the early Hungarians, to a certain extent) represent the Uralic type or its main characteristics. These facts have led some to conclude that the anthropological characteristics of the Finno-Ugrian age are continued in the Uralic type, while others favour the White Sea-Baltic type as their successor.

But we cannot decide the problem so simply. It seems likely that we must not search for any particular prototype among the Finno-Ugrians. The majority of anthropologists agree that all peoples, even at an early stage in their development, were composed of a number of racial elements. Thus the population in Finno-Ugrian period certainly displayed a mixture of racial characteristics; at first they were perhaps only Europid, and later Europid and Europid-Mongoloid in character. Development from the earliest Europid basis led to considerable diversity. The eastern wing of the Uralic peoples, the ancestors of the Ugrians and Samoyeds, came under strong and repeated Mongoloid influence, and this at a very early period – perhaps even before the dispersion of the Finno-Ugrians – led to the creation of the Uralic type.

This Mongoloid influence did not touch the western wing, or if it did, it was limited and came much later; then this group moved westwards and, after some further mixture of races, was joined by elements from the Baltic area. The mingling of various Europid elements brought into existence the White Sea-Baltic type that is characteristic of them.

It is difficult to trace these complicated movements, and it is quite certain that from anthropological arguments alone it would never be possible to prove the relationship between the Finno-Ugrian peoples.

Thus, however probable it is that the society which spoke a unified Finno-Ugrian language formed a unified and genuine ethnic community, only one general deduction may be made concerning its anthropological characteristics – that at first the Finno-Ugrians were of the Europid type. This theory naturally has still to be verified by new and reliable palaeoanthropological material.

THE UGRIAN PERIOD

The dispersion of the Finno-Ugrians resulted in the linguistic separation of two large groups. There came into existence the common Ugrian language, which is the predecessor of Hungarian, Vogul and Ostyak; and Finnic-Permian, the source of the other Finno-Ugrian languages.

In this instance linguistic separation certainly implied geographical changes also. It is probable that the Ugrians populated the area between the Kama and the wooded country of the Urals, while some of their groups gradually moved southwards towards the tree-lined steppes. Their home was to all intents and purposes on the boundary of these two areas.

The Ugrians came into contact with foreign tribes. They undoubtedly maintained lively connections with certain Iranian-speaking folk of indeterminate origin. Proof can be seen in Hu. *hét* 'seven' and *tegez* 'quiver' and their Ob-Ugrian cognates, which are of Iranian origin.

In recent times the suggestion has been mooted that the Ugrians also made contact with Turkic peoples. Certain Ugrian words of indistinct origin, such as Hu. *hattyú* 'swan', *hód* 'beaver' and *szó* 'word', may possibly be of Turkic origin. The argument concerning the origin of these words and the possibilities of Ugrian-Turkic contacts has not yet been resolved.

We must also bear in mind that the Ugrians, or at least some of them, had connections with groups speaking related languages after the dispersion of the Finno-Ugrians, who had settled west of them. Considerable research has been devoted in recent years to the links between Ugrians and Permians, but the linguistic significance of such connections has been overrated by some authorities. Taken in isolation, the fact that the Ugrians and Finnic-Permians, and later the Ugrians and Permians, did not break their connections completely is nothing unusual. The only disputable point is whether these links could have been so close that they caused identical developments in language. There has also been the question of an ancient link between the Ugrians, or their more northerly groups, and the Proto-Lapps; here, too, we can rely only on suppositions, not on demonstrable facts. There is much more to be said for the co-settlement of the northern Ugrians and one of the hunting peoples of Western Siberia, to which we shall return. First, however, we shall examine the differences between the Ugrian period and its predecessor, with particular reference to social and economic conditions.

The Ugrian period demonstrates a more developed society, and this can most easily be measured by changes that took place in its economic basis. The most important factor to be deduced from a study of the vocabulary is that the Ugrians came to keep horses. Proof of this horse-culture can be found in the words for 'horse' (Hu. *ló* ~ Vogul *lū*, Osty. *law*), 'saddle' (Hu. *nyereg* ~ Vogul *ncwrä*, Osty. *noyer*), 'bridle' (Hu. *fék* ~ Osty. *pēk*) and possibly 'whip' (Hu. *ostor* ~ Vogul *ōšter*). Here it should be noted that the Hungarian word for 'stirrup' (*kengyel*) came into existence during the Proto-Hungarian period that followed the Ugrian period. Although today it is felt to be a root incapable of analysis, linguistic examination reveals that it is in fact a compound, of which the first element *kengy*- no longer exists in Hungarian; its cognates in the other Ugrian languages, however, Vogul *kĕńś*, Osty. *kenč*, mean 'shoes (of reindeer skin)'. The second element is Hu. *al*, 'bottom', which has become *el* by assimilation, the first element having a front vowel. Thus the compound means 'shoe-bottom', and is an important record of ancient Hungarian horse-culture. We may also include among Ugrian horse breeding records such adjectives as Hu. *másodfű* (second-grass, i.e. two year old) and *harmadfü* (three year old), which have their counterpart in the horse vocabulary of the Voguls, e.g., *kit pum lü* (Hu. *két-fü-ló*), 'two grass horse' = two year old.

In addition to any linguistic arguments, it must be remembered that the Hungarians appeared on the historical scene as horse-riders, and this activity can be traced back to the Ugrian period. Further proof is that the horse plays an outstanding rôle in Ob-Ugrian folk tradition. The greatest gods in their poetry, for example the so-called Man who watches over the World and the Gods of the Source of the Ob or the God of the Pelim, travel mainly on horseback, while the Heavenly Father possesses great herds, according to their songs. One of the sacrifices most favoured by the gods was a horse, and this tradition was known to Ostyaks and Voguls alike.

Comparative ethnographers have discovered an important relic of Ugrian horse-culture. The bow, the ancient hunting weapon, was in use among the Ob-Ugrians until the beginning of the present century. The arrows belonging to it were carried in quivers, of which two types were known. One of these was an oval-shaped sack with two straps to be worn on the back. This type was normally used by the inhabitants of the northern wooded areas (Samoyeds, Kets, Yukagirs, Chukchas etc.), and its use spread to the Ob-Ugrians only after they had settled finally in the north. There was a second type of quiver, however, used by equestrian peoples; this was a rhomboid type to be fastened to a belt. For a horseman this is a natural method of carrying it, but it is not natural for a hunter in the northern forests, where it would hinder his movements, whether he were walking or skiing. So this second kind of quiver attached to the belt is for the Ob-Ugrians a relic of the past which, with the cessation of horse breeding, was gradually superseded by the more convenient back-quiver. Thus it is probable that the quiver (Hu. *tegez* and its Ugrian cognates) referred in its earliest Ugrian form to the first type, whose existence in the Kama region in the first millennium BC has been proved by archaeological discoveries.

Such are the most important proofs of the existence of horse-culture among the Ugrians. There are, however, certain related problems to consider. In particular it must be stressed that the Ugrians, encamped in wooded countryside, treated the horse differently from the horse-breeding nomads of the steppes. The huge herds of the latter found rich pastures on the plains; forests and wooded steppe country do not provide unlimited possibilities for horse breeding. For the nomads of the steppes, animal husbandry was the basis of economic life, but in the forests hunting and fishing still retained their leading rôle. So the Ugrians may be described most aptly as equestrian hunters, or more precisely equestrian trappers. Horse breeding and hunting, the use of the horse and at the same time the continuation of forest ways of life, are not contradictory concepts, even though horse breeding is generally characteristic of desert nomads.

Here a genuine historical source is worth quoting. Herodotus (*c.* 484–425 BC) writes as follows in the section of his history devoted to the neighbours of the Scythians:

When one crosses the River Tanais,[1] one is no longer on Scythian territory; the first zone belongs to the Sauromatae,[2] who inhabit the region fifteen days' journey from the end of Lake Maietis[3] to the north; there are no woodland or fruit trees throughout their land. Beyond these the second zone is inhabited by the Budini,[4] whose entire territory is everywhere covered by thick forests. Beyond the Budini towards the north there are first two days of desert land, while after the desert, in a more easterly direction, there dwell the Thyssagetae, a separate and numerous nation who live by hunting. Immediately next to them and in the same country live those they call Jyrkae. They also live by hunting in the following way: they climb a tree (of which there are many throughout the land) and lie in wait; each has his horse (which has been taught to lie on its belly so that it appears smaller) and his dog at the ready; when from the tree he espies the quarry, he gives chase, shooting arrows and mounting his horse, while his dog accompanies him.[5]

Many suspect that the names 'Thyssagetae' and 'Jyrkae' refer to Ugrian tribes, but this is by no means certain. They may well

1 Don.
2 Sarmatians, an Iranian tribe.
3 Maeotis, the Sea of Azov.
4 These are identified by commentators as Permians.
5 Herodotus, IV, 21-22.

cover other ethnic groups also. But apart from linking the Budini, Thyssagetae and Jyrkae of Herodotus with certain descendants of the Finno-Ugrians, this description is chiefly important to us as a reliable report of a people who in the first half of the first millennium BC pursued a way of life which involved trapping on horseback. It is probable that the description given by Herodotus reflects more or less the Ugrian type of equestrian hunting. According to early Mongol sources a similar mode of life was followed by the Mongolians who inhabited the forests on the shores of Lake Baikal, and there are other hunting peoples in forest areas who also kept horses, e.g. the ancient Buriats.

How did the Ugrians become acquainted with horse-breeding? This is a much-disputed yet basic problem. The theory is often advanced that the Ugrians (or the Hungarians) learnt this from some foreign source; Turkic and Iranian peoples are most frequently mentioned in this connection. It would certainly be unwise to deny the influence of foreign elements in the development of horse breeding in the Ugrian period, but whether the Ugrian form of horse breeding is completely foreign in origin is a different problem. Here it seems right to uphold the view that it was a native development. The influence of foreign elements is to be seen first of all in that their knowledge of the horse and perhaps its name also were adopted from some unidentifiable foreign source; they did not have to tame and domesticate the animal. But their breeding methods may well have developed along lines best suited to their native needs. At all events it is noteworthy that horse breeding has almost completely disappeared among the Ob-Ugrians; its traces are preserved chiefly in their folk poetry. The Hungarians, however, both before and after their occupation of their present homeland, appear as a typically equestrian people.

The Proto-Hungarians, as they separated from the Ugrians, moved southwards through the wooded steppes to the plains of Southern Russia. Here there were already equestrian nomad peoples, whose presence, together with natural conditions, offer a logical explanation for the rapid development of horse breeding. Meanwhile the ancestors of the Ob-Ugrians remained for a time in their original habitat and continued to hunt on horseback. It is possible, however, that these northern Ugrians were not so closely acquainted with equestrian life as the southern groups who are to be regarded as the ancestors of the Hungarians. Yet we must assume that they knew the horse and its use until they moved further north and east and possibly came under foreign influences which gradually led to the disappearance of this form of animal husbandry. From this time onwards it remained only a memory.

The development of animal husbandry meant an important change from the hunting and fishing of the Finno-Ugrian period, though in its Ugrian form it did not represent a complete break, as we have already seen. Nevertheless it initiated a process of change in the whole structure of society, leading to its stratification. Society in Ugrian times did not yet display the patriarchal tribal organization common to nomadic animal breeders, divided into several strata according to wealth and social rank, but the process of stratification and tribal development in certain places may well have begun at this time.

The separation of the Ugrians from the other Finno-Ugrian peoples began towards the end of the third millennium BC. From this time onwards there occurred in their language changes which cannot be demonstrated in other Finno-Ugrian languages. These changes may be noted in phonetic modifications, grammatical developments, including the formation of new grammatical elements, and above all in words which exist only in the three Ugrian languages. It is nevertheless surprising that the number of specifically Ugrian changes and developments is not great. Apart from a comparatively large number of new words, they may be summed up as one or two phonetic changes, three grammatical suffixes of common origin, a few Ugrian formatives and possibly the beginnings of a common 'objective' verbal conjugation.

How can the relative unimportance of these Ugrian linguistic developments be explained? It is certainly not due to the brevity of the period, for the end of the Ugrian period is usually put in the first half of the first millennium BC, which implies that the ancestors of the Ugrian peoples lived in one linguistic community for at least 1,500 years. Although the periodization of Finno-Ugrian prehistory and the determination of the extent of these periods are subject to alteration if new evidence is forthcoming, the rarity of characteristic linguistic peculiarities in the Ugrian period would not of itself be a reason for supposing that this period did not last as long as is generally supposed. The key to the problem is to be sought in the form of the Ugrian community. It seems probable that the Ugrian groups were relatively loosely related to each other; indeed, it may be postulated that the Ugrians split very early into two groups which gradually became separated from each other. There was a southern group containing the ancestors of the Hungarians, and a northern one consisting of the predecessors of the Ob-Ugrians. Linguistic similarities witness to the contact between the two groups, but they also betray that this contact was not strong and uninterrupted.

The modern Ugrian peoples came into existence after lengthy and complicated processes of intermixture and are not the direct descendants of these Ugrian groups. First of all, the southern Ugrians detached themselves and slowly pulled away southwards towards the steppes, reaching the area of modern Bashkiria. They were encouraged by natural conditions to develop animal husbandry quite rapidly. It may be assumed that this region was where they first came into close and lasting contact with Turkic peoples. The great migrations that began in the fifth century AD then swept the Proto-Hungarians, who by now had become a firmly established nomadic tribe among these Turkic folk, towards the grassy steppes of Southern Russia and thence westwards. During their migration, after long contact with Turkic and other, mainly Iranian, languages, the Hungarian language developed the form which, with certain modifications, is still in use today.

After the departure of the predecessors of the Proto-Hungarians, the other Ugrians continued to live together. Not long after the final break certain important events occurred in their life, and these had a decisive influence on the development of the present Ob-Ugrians. In the middle of the first millennium BC, as the bones discovered in the burial grounds of the Kama region testify, a mongoloid-type people crossed the Urals from the east and settled in the Kama area, intermingling with the europid type settled there. This archaeological and anthropological discovery implies that after the departure of the southern Ugrian group, those who remained settled in the Kama region lived alongside a hunting people from Western Siberia. The two races became mingled, as can be seen in the anthropological characteristics of the Voguls and Ostyaks and in their northern, sub-Arctic culture. These foreign hunters, whose identity cannot be determined and who are usually

68

termed 'Palaeo-Siberian', acquired the language of the Ugrians and completely lost their own native tongue. The result of the intermingling of these peoples was thus a victory for the Finno-Ugrian type of language over the Western Siberians' own characteristic tongue.

This all-important development in the ethnogenesis of the Ob-Ugrian peoples is reflected in the division of the Vogul and Ostyak peoples into two great fraternities. Each of them can be shown to be divided into two large groups, bigger than the family or tribe. This division into fraternities called *por* and *mōś* has remained a tradition among the Voguls and Ostyaks virtually to the present day, and the relationship between them is thus described by Vogul scholars: members of the *mōś* fraternity look down upon the *por*; in Vogul folk poetry *mōś* is used in connection with heroes who represent the nobler and higher culture, while *por* is applied to mythical figures of evil intent. The *mōś* fraternity regards *Numi-Tōrem*, the greatest god, as its ancestor, while the *por* fraternity is descended from the devil called *mēŋkw*. The bear cult is preserved in the *por* tradition, and the horse in that of the *mōś*.

It should be noted here that the name *mōś* is derived from an earlier form *mańś'*, which is connected on the one hand with the Voguls' name for themselves, *man'si*, and on the other with the first element (*magy-*) in the name *magyar*.[1] Thus the significance of the two fraternities becomes clearer: if the modern Ob-Ugrians are compounded of two elements, one Ugrian and one foreign, the names for these preserve the traces of their origins. There is every reason to assume that the name *mōś* was applied to the original Ugrians, and *por* to the hunters from Western Siberia who became fused with them.

THE FINNIC-PERMIAN PERIOD

Finnic-Permian is the name given to the western branch of the Finno-Ugrians after the separation of the Ugrians, and is derived from its most widely divergent elements, Finnish and Permian (Zyryan and Votyak).

[1] There are several explanations for the second element *-ar*. The most probable one is that *-ar* or *-eri* (as in Old Hu. *Mogyeri*) is derived from a FU word meaning 'man, human' (cf. Finn. *yrkō*, Cher. *erye*).

The Finnic-Permian period cannot be described in satisfactory detail, since historical sources still cannot shed sufficient light upon it. It is probable, however, that the western and eastern boundaries of the region inhabited by these peoples were far apart, with a central point somewhere in the area of the confluence of the Volga and Oka, or the Volga and Kama.

The results of the Finnic-Permian period are to be seen in the linguistic innovations which divide these languages from Ugrian. The system of adverbial suffixes began to increase, as can be seen by the number of identical secondary adverbial suffixes in Finnish, Lapp, Mordvin, Cheremis and the Permian languages. New elements enriched the vocabulary, proving that the society of the Finnic-Permian period reached a higher stage of development; agriculture and animal husbandry made great strides alongside hunting and fishing, and in the following centuries these new modes of production took precedence, a process doubtless encouraged by the existence in that neighbourhood of Iranian peoples who already practised them. It is certain, however, that the existence of an agricultural and stockbreeding vocabulary does not imply a sudden change from one to the other means of livelihood, nor should it be inferred that all the Finnic-Permian peoples were equally affected by it. For the Finnic-Permian period was a relatively short one and the population was scattered thinly over a wide area. Linguistic links within this branch are commonly assumed to have been broken by the middle of the second millennium BC. Thus around 1500 BC this hitherto unified branch split into two new groups, Permian and Volga-Finnic. Nevertheless, Herodotus writes thus of the Budini, usually regarded as Permians:

The Budini, a numerous and powerful nation, all have blue eyes and red hair. There is in their territory a town built of wood and called Gelonus; both dwelling houses and temples are of wood, and the high wooden wall around it is thirty furlongs each way. Here there are temples to the Greek gods, adorned after the Greek fashion with statues, altars and shrines of wood. Every three years there is a festival in honour of Dionysus, with Bacchic revels. The reason is that the Geloni were originally Greeks, who emigrated from the commercial towns and settled among the Budini; their language is half Scythian and half Greek. The Budini, however, use a quite different language from the Geloni, and their way of life is also different. For the Budini have always lived here and are nomads; alone of the people here they eat pine-kernels. The Geloni on the other hand cultivate the soil, eat corn and keep gardens and resemble them neither in stature nor in complexion. It is true that the Greeks call both of them Geloni, but they are wrong to do so. The whole region is covered by forests. In the most densely-wooded part there is a huge lake surrounded by marshes and reed beds; here they catch otters and beavers and another creature with a square face whose skin they use for making edgings for their coats; its genitals are good for afflictions of the womb.[1]

If it is true that the Budini of Herodotus are the Permians, this description is of considerable value. First, it adds historical weight to the deduction that amongst or alongside the Finno-Ugrian groups there lived folk who spoke a different language (the Scythians of Herodotus are Iranians). Secondly, the account makes it clear that the changes in their economic life took place over a long period. The Budini still made hunting an important part of their life, although the Permian vocabulary testifying to a knowledge of agriculture and animal husbandry was already in existence. This contradiction can be resolved only if we conclude that the Finnic-Permian period saw the beginnings of the more advanced processes of agriculture and stockbreeding, but that they became the general basis of the entire economy among the national groups only much later. This process began with the acquisition of knowledge about the various grain-crops, types of corn and domestic animals from neighbouring, more developed societies with whom the hunters and trappers bartered goods. Later, however, these new economic methods began to spread among the hunting population. The extent and intensity of this development depended on a variety of factors and its geographical spread was uneven.

Thus in the middle of the second millennium BC there emerge two new separate Finno-Ugrian groups. Of these the Permians were probably settled towards the east, as is to be deduced from the present distribution of the Permian languages. Their home

1 Herodotus, IV, 108-9.

seems to have been to the north and north-east of the Volga bend, along the middle stretches of the lower Vyatka and Kama. Apart from reflecting their knowledge of agriculture and animal husbandry, the language shows other important changes. The vocabulary and grammatical system of the Permian language show characteristic developments during its 2,000 years of unity which can easily be seen by any layman who glances at modern Zyryan and Votyak. The most important event of the period was the influence on the southern Permians of the Chuvash-speaking inhabitants of the Volga-Bulgarian empire of the seventh and eighth centuries AD. This left its traces mainly in the countless Chuvash words which occur chiefly in the Votyak vocabulary; their influence on Zyryan is slighter. This fact leads to the deduction that Chuvash influence from the south mainly affected the southern dialect of Permian which gave rise to Votyak; the northern dialect, the basis of Zyryan, was less susceptible to it. This fact is relevant to the further development of the Permian language, for the influence of Chuvash reached it towards the end of the Permian period, when the bonds between its northern and southern constituents were wearing thin. Taking certain other factors into consideration, we may put the final rupture between the Permian languages in the ninth century AD.

The life of the Volga-Finnic period was by no means as lengthy as this. The ancestors of the Baltic Finns, Lapps, Mordvins and Cheremis had broken their ties in the first millennium BC. The vocabulary of the period reveals not only a knowledge of agriculture and animals, but certain social developments also. Evidence is found in the words for 'weave', 'grind', 'plough', 'weed', 'mortar', 'wheat', 'cow', 'pig' and 'slave'. The word 'pay' tells of the development of trade, while 'threshold' and other words give some idea of the progress of culture.

The Finnic-Volga period still shows the continuation of Iranian influence, while links with the Balto-Slavonic peoples (Lithuanians, Latvians and the extinct Old Prussians) can be traced to the end of the period or the beginning of the succeeding one. These links continued after the separation of the Baltic Finns from the Volga peoples (Mordvins and Cheremis); in these latter languages, and particularly in Mordvin, there are Baltic elements which have no counterpart in the Baltic-Finnic languages.

During the short Volga-Finnic period, contact between its constituent groups appears to have been relatively loose. This is explained by the vast area in which they lived: the ancestors of the Baltic Finns were to be found at this time in the Baltic region, while the Volga Finno-Ugrians, the ancestors of the Mordvins and Cheremis, did not extend so far west; they remained in the regions nearer the right bank of the Volga, somewhat to the west of their present habitat. Modern Mordvin and Cheremis do not show many similarities as, for example, the two Permian languages. Mordvin displays closer links with the Baltic Finnic languages than does Cheremis. We may therefore argue that contacts between the Volga languages after the end of the Volga-Finnic period were not particularly close, and that the Mordvins settled in the western part of the region, nearer to the Baltic Finns, while the ancestors of the Cheremis were further to the east of them.

This argument is supported by an examination of the Chuvash loanwords in the Volga languages. Since there is a great number of them in Cheremis and there are considerably fewer in Mordvin, it can be postulated that Chuvash influence reached them when these two languages were already separated. The final rupture between these languages must be assumed to have taken place in the sixth and seventh centuries AD, for it is in the following centuries that the Chuvash influence became strong.

The other group to emerge from the period of Volga-Finnic unity is represented by the Baltic Finns. The Baltic Finnic languages remain relatively close to one another today, since it is not long since they broke away from the linguistic unity of the so-called Common Finnic period. This cannot be divided sharply from the Volga-Finnic period, a problem which has given rise to many varied opinions. In our opinion, the beginning of the Common Finnic period may be put at the commencement of the first millennium BC, though this does not imply a complete and final break in the links between the Baltic Finns and the Volga peoples. Links with the Baltic languages, whose traces are found first of all in the Baltic Finnic vocabulary, began in the fifth century BC; Mordvin was also affected, partly by direct contact, and partly through Baltic Finnic transmission – a fact which implies that the western branch of the Volga group and the Baltic Finns were still in contact during the early Common Finnic period, and in addition shows the impossibility of dividing this latter period sharply from its predecessor.

The earliest age of the Common Finnic period is sometimes called the Finnic-Lapp period, because at this time, the first half of the first millennium BC, the Lapps, whose origin is something of a mystery,[1] were living to the north of the Baltic Finns with whom they had close contact. Differences between their languages had not yet developed; the most we can assume at this time is that there were dialectal variations. Close contacts between them ceased in the fifth century BC, a deduction supported by the evidence of Baltic loanwords. In the Baltic Finnic languages there are some three hundred loanwords, while in Lapp there are altogether twenty, which entered the language through Common Finnic. This shows that the Lapp language had become separated from Common Finnic at the time when contact with the Balts was in its early stages.

After the Lapps had moved northwards, the Finnic peoples continued to live beside the Baltic Sea, more or less in the area of modern Estonia. The population were engaged chiefly in agriculture and animal husbandry. Their long and peaceful contacts with the Baltic peoples helped to raise their social and economic standards. Words for 'pea', 'gruel', 'garden', 'shepherd', 'wheel', 'wall', 'bridge', 'room', 'lamb', 'goat', 'ram' and 'wool', together with other similar loans from Baltic, reveal the development of a settled life and economic activity.

Further evidence of such development is to be found in the Germanic loanwords in Finnic. The Common Finns first made contact with Germanic tribes at the time of Christ, when the influence of the Baltic languages ceased. The entire vocabulary of the Common Finnic dialects may be said to have been reformed by Germanic loanwords of Proto-German, Gothic or Scandinavian character. They are several hundred in number, and may be divided into categories concerning agriculture, stockbreeding, building, domestic economy, trade, communications and a well-developed social life, e.g., 'plough', 'cheese', 'earth', 'rye', 'oats', 'hoe', 'hen', 'cattle', 'barn', 'staircase', 'floor', 'nail', 'hook'

---

1 The disputed origin of the Lapps is treated on pp. 205–8.

(on which to hang cooking-pots), 'dough', 'joist', 'arch', 'wages', 'measure', 'thief', 'lock', 'guard', 'lead', 'gold', 'prow', 'saddle', 'oar', 'prince', 'king', 'power', 'fine', 'festival', etc. The acceptance of such words suggests considerable social and economic development.

There are numerous Russian loanwords in all the Baltic Finnic languages. In addition to these recent words adopted by the separate Finnic languages, there is a stratum of Common Slavonic loanwords to be found in Baltic Finnic. These words probably came from Old Slavonic and Old Russian during the period from the sixth to the ninth century AD, when the linguistic unity of the Common Finnic age was disintegrating. The oldest Slavonic stratum is not as important as that of the Germanic or Baltic groups; it does, however, include the first words related to Christianity and some concerning agriculture, fishing and building, e.g., 'priest', 'cross', 'pagan', 'rye porridge', 'barley porridge', 'sickle', 'yoke', 'goods', 'fish-trap', 'anchor', 'stable', 'stove'.

The dispersal of the Common Finnic tribes and their linguistic and physical separation began during the first century AD, and had reached an advanced stage by the eighth and ninth centuries. Some of these tribes settled finally to the south or east of the Gulf of Finland. Others began to populate the south and south-west shores of Finland. Centuries of migration and intermingling resulted in the development from Common Finnic of the modern Finnish, Carelian, Vepsian, Vodian, Estonian and Livonian languages.

PART II

Finno-Ugrian Languages

࿘࿘࿘࿘࿘࿘

PROTO-FINNO-UGRIAN

In the previous chapters we have discussed the concept of the Finno-Ugrian family of languages and the primeval history of this group. Here we shall give a brief description of the linguistic characteristics of the Finno-Ugrian languages and their common ancestral tongue.

First we must consider the Proto-Finno-Ugrian language, since this was the source of all the others; a description of its characteristics will illuminate the immense developments that have taken place in Hungarian and other Finno-Ugrian languages, enabling them to become artistic instruments of expression of the abstract ideas of literature and the sciences, and of the great ideals of life as well as its small incidents. Here, however, we must add a note of caution. We do not know, and never shall we be able to know, this primeval language as fully as modern spoken languages or dead languages whose written records have survived, where there are dictionaries and grammars at our disposal. Proto-Finno-Ugrian existed before the age of written records and has left no texts for our guidance, so that neither its vocabulary nor its grammatical structure can be known in detail. This does not, of course, imply that we are completely ignorant of it; indeed, in many respects we can gain an excellent impression of its main features and of the tendencies which caused it to develop as it did.

There is no need to discuss the methods used to unlock the secrets of this language, since the main one – comparative linguistics – has already been described in the previous chapter. One of the main aims of comparative study is to acquire as extensive a knowledge as possible of the common ancestor of languages which are related. It may be postulated that features common to them have preserved characteristics of the basic language; these form a mosaic which, when properly pieced together, will give a general but consistent and connected picture of the language used by the Finno-Ugrians many thousands of years ago.

What, then, was this language like, used as it was six or seven thousand years ago? Phonetically it varied in many ways from Hungarian and the other modern Finno-Ugrian languages. One of its peculiarities was that there were no voiced plosives (*b, d, g*), although unvoiced plosives (*p, t, k*) were frequent. Another characteristic was that it contained three sibilants: *s, ś* (palatalized *s*) and *š* (*sh*). Affricates occurred chiefly in the medial position (*č=ch* and *ć*, palatalized *ts*). It is interesting, however, that there are no traces of voiced affricates or voiced sibilants. Voiced consonants were not entirely absent from the language; there were four nasals – *m, n, ń* (palatalized n) and *ŋ*, which exists in modern Hungarian before *g* and *k*, as in *hang* 'sound'. There were also *l* and its palatalized form *l'*, *r, j* and *w*.

It should be added that combinations of consonants were not rare in Proto-Finno-Ugrian, especially groups of the nasal + plosive variety (e.g., *nt, ŋk, mp*). These occurred in the medial position; there are no examples of initial consonant groups. (Modern Finno-Ugrian languages have no liking for consonant groups in this position.)

The number of vowels during this period was smaller than in modern Hungarian, which contains fourteen; short and long vowels were distinguished. The rule of vowel-harmony, common to most Finno-Ugrian languages, can also be traced back to this early period. This postulates that in one word only back (e.g., *a, o, u*) or front (*ä, e, i*) vowels might be found, and that this principle applied to suffixes and formatives also; these latter had two forms, one back-vowel and one front-vowel.

The acoustic effect of this language must have given the impression of a large number of unvoiced plosives and harsh sibilants balanced by softer liquids and nasals and frequent vowels. It was a musical language, made so by the law of vowel-harmony, and rhythm was added to its melodious flow by the regular accentuation of the first syllable.

It would be interesting to support these statements by examples, but, as we have seen, no original words or sentences have survived.

At most we can attempt to reconstruct a hypothetical FU text, using all the results achieved by linguistic research. (1) *wete patana peje*: 'The water in the pot boils'; (2) *lunta pesänä elä*: 'the goose lives in the nest'; (3) *mekše metem anta*: 'the bee gives honey'; (4) *ńomala utkona pukta*: 'the hare runs along the road'. These, we must stress, are artificial sentences created over 6,000 years after the disintegration of the original language, from reconstructed elements. They do not reveal the language as it really was, but are merely an attempt to give the layman some idea, however imperfect, of Proto-Finno-Ugrian.

Having established that this language was not a confusion of unarticulated sounds made expressive by movements of the face and body, but was composed like modern languages of words and sentences, let us now consider these latter.

Two large groups of words may be distinguished in this period: there were monosyllabic and disyllabic words (these last, when suffixed, became trisyllabic). This distinction is important, and not merely from the formal standpoint; different word types are involved. The monosyllabic words were personal, interrogative and demonstrative pronouns and interjections, while the disyllabic words were so-called 'noun-verbs'. This term is used to denote those words which are used either as nouns or as verbs without any distinction in form, whatever their function. Today there are sharp distinctions between nouns (and adjectives) and verbs. The former are concerned with objects, properties or abstract concepts, the latter with action, existence and occurrence. At an early stage of development, however, one and the same root could express the concepts of, for example, object and action: thus one word represented 'fire', 'burning' and 'to burn', another 'rain' and 'it is raining', and another 'wave' and 'to undulate'. Such 'noun-verbs', relics of this early stage, are still to be found in most modern Finno-Ugrian languages. Hungarian, for example, has such words as *fagy* 'frost' – 'it is freezing', *les* 'ambush' – 'lie in wait' and *nyom* 'trace, track' – 'press, oppress, weigh'.

A fagy elvitte a termést Frost destroyed the crop.
Semmi nyom nem maradt utána No trace remained after him, he left no trace.

In these examples *fagy* and *nyom* function as nouns. In the following they appear as verbs:

Kékre-zöldre fagy He turns blue with cold. ('He freezes green
and blue.')
Mennyit nyom? How much does it weigh?

The original language contained a large number of such words, which later gradually took on nominal or verbal functions. Differentiation between the two types was the result of usage; some words were more frequently used to denote objects, and others were concerned with action. At the same time this meant that certain words were more appropriately used as subjects of sentences, while others acquired a more predicative rôle. Thus the crystallization of the differing semantic character of these words and their rôle in the sentence initiated the separation of noun from verb. This process was later accelerated by the development of different suffixes to modify nouns and verbs – the difference between declension and conjugation – so that the distinction came to be measured not only by the function of the word in the sentence, but also by the use of different grammatical elements.

The process of separation of noun from verb, the two most important categories of word, took a considerable time. The statement that the disyllabic words in Proto-Finno-Ugrian were noun-verbs does not imply that they remained unchanged throughout the period. It would be wrong to imagine that this stage of development was characteristic for several thousand years. Comparative studies do not support such a static view of language – indeed, all the evidence points to the rapid pace of linguistic development.

The origin of several case-suffixes can be traced back to the original language, as can certain characteristic signs of tense and mood. This shows that the process of separation of noun from verb had already begun in the Uralic period; it continued at an increasing pace during the Finno-Ugrian period, and reached the peak of development in the independent Finno-Ugrian languages. Nevertheless there was no sharp division between these two main categories for a very long time, as is shown by the continued existence in Hungarian, Finnish and several cognate languages of certain archaic noun-verb types.

As for structural, grammatical elements, Proto-Finno-Ugrian displayed a relatively advanced system; it was, however, more primitive and less complicated than those used by modern Finno-Ugrian languages. Words functioning as nouns developed a fairly extensive system of suffixes. The basic or nominative form had no suffixation, nor has it today. The possessive relationship (genitive) was expressed either without suffixation (as in modern Hungarian *a ház teteje* 'the roof of the house' and Vogul *lū puŋkä* 'the horse's head') or by using the suffix *-n*. This has disappeared from Hungarian, but has been preserved in Finnish, Cheremis, Lapp and the Samoyed languages, e.g., Finn. *isä-n hattu* 'father's hat'. There were also two methods of denoting the object (accusative); the indefinite object remained unsuffixed, while definite objects took the suffix *-m*. In Hungarian and several cognate languages the unsuffixed object is frequent today, e.g., Hu. *veszem a kalapom* 'I take my hat' (where *kalap*, 'hat' has a possessive suffix *-m*); it is also found in common constructions which include an accusative relationship, e.g., *szemlesütve* 'with downcast eyes', literally 'casting down the eyes' and *favágó* 'woodcutter'. In Hungarian the old Uralic *-m* accusative suffix has been lost, and in its place a newer *-t* suffix is used. On the other hand, Hungarian retains traces of the Uralic locative suffix *-na*, *-nä*, which was a general suffix of place in answer to the question 'Where?'; it can be seen in the *-n*, *-nn* termination of such adverbs as *otthon*, 'at home', *kinn* 'outside', *fönn* 'up above' etc., and in the suffix *-on/-en/-ön*, denoting 'place on which' (superessive), e.g., *fán* 'on a tree', *vízen* 'on water', *lovon* 'on horse(back)'. It is also found in the final element of the suffix *-ban/-ben* 'in'. All the Finno-Ugrian languages have preserved this suffix: e.g. Finn. *ulkona* 'outside' (*ulko* = exterior), Vogul *tāl* 'winter' *tāl-ne* 'in winter', Ostyak *χat* 'house' *χat-na* 'in a house', Votyak *gurt* 'village' *gurt-yn* 'in the village'. Another locative suffix was also used in Proto-Finno-Ugrian; this was *-tt*, which occurs chiefly in the Ugrian languages. In modern Hungarian, however, its use is confined to certain adverbs and postpositions, e.g. *alatt* 'under', *felett* 'above', *együtt* 'together', *itt* 'here', *ott* 'there', and to a few place-names which may still be found with this locative suffix, e.g., *Pécsett* 'in Pécs', *Fehérvárt* 'in Fehérvár'. Other languages show this in e.g., Vogul *jā* 'river' *jā-t* 'in the river', Ostyak *ko-* 'who, what?' *kot* 'where?', Finn. *ny-t* 'now'.

Ablative relationship was expressed by the suffix *-ta, -tä*. This has been preserved chiefly in the northern languages, e.g., Finn. *siel-tä* 'from there', Mord. *tolga* 'feather' *tolga-da* 'of feathers', Nenets *sal'l'e* 'promontory' *sal'l'e-d* 'from the promontory'. Apart from these, at least two suffixes existed to denote 'direction to which' (lative), *-k* and *-ń*. The former can be traced in Hungarian *-é, -á, -e, -a*, e.g., *felé* 'towards', *mellé* 'to near', *mögé* 'to behind', *alá* 'to under' *haza* 'homewards', *oda* 'thither'. In Proto-Hungarian FU *-k* lost its plosive quality and became a voiced fricative *γ*; this form is preserved in several cognate languages, e.g., Vogul *sis* 'back' *sis-yγ* 'backwards'. This Proto-Hungarian *γ* later formed a diphthong with the final open vowel of the root, e.g., *-eγ > -ei*, afterwards giving rise to a long vowel (*-é*). In certain instances this might be shortened (*-e*). That the original form was *-k* is shown by the languages which have preserved this, e.g., Selkup *üt* 'water' *üt-qo* 'to/for water', Lapp *dei-ke* 'hither', Cheremis *pel* 'side', *pel-ke* 'towards', Finn. dial. *ympäri-k* 'around', *ala-k* 'to under'.

These examples show that there was in Proto-Finno-Ugrian a developed case-system which served as a basis for further developments in the separate Finno-Ugrian languages. Naturally this did not exist throughout the Uralic period, but came into being through a long period of time. Here we may ask what elements in the language were suitable as bases for suffixes. No precise answer is possible, since the language itself is reconstructed from comparative study of the cognate languages. It must also be recognized that there may have been several methods of development. Recently, however, the theory has been advanced that at least some of the suffixes, including the locatives *-na/-nä* and *-tt*, were derived from demonstrative pronouns; there is much to support this view. At first sight this may seem surprising, even when we learn that there was a back-vowel demonstrative pronoun *to, ta*, used for distant objects, and in addition a front-vowel equivalent *te, ti* for near objects. Its traces can be seen in the Hungarian *tova* 'away, forth', *tél-túl* 'here and there' and *tétova* 'faltering'. There was a further demonstrative with an initial *n-* (cf. Finn. *nuo* 'those'). The similarity between these and the two locative suffixes is striking, but how can the development from demonstrative pronoun to suffix be satisfactorily explained?

It is interesting to pursue this problem, not only for itself, but for the reasoning involved. First we must try to visualize conditions as they were some ten to fifteen thousand years ago. This was in the pre-Uralic period of the thirteenth to twelfth millennium BC. The speech of this period did not include what might be termed 'case-suffixes'. The unsuffixed form of any word must have performed several functions, and these were clarified by the position of the word in its context. If asked to describe his everyday life, a man of this period might well have said something like the following, 'I forest go. Bear cave see. Bear cave run. I bear kill spear. Meat take house. Woman bear-meat cook pot. Skin sew clothes . . .' From this we should understand that he had been *in* the forest and had seen a bear's cave. The bear ran *out of* the cave, but he had killed *it with* his spear. He had taken the meat home, and his wife had cooked this *in* a pot, while she would make clothes *out of* its skin. The meaning can be gleaned from the simple sentences, but it is clear that the language cannot express thoughts and feelings in precise and accurate terms. For example, a sentence like 'Father son see' could well be misunderstood, since there is nothing to denote which is the subject of the sentence. Perhaps word-order (as in English), intonation and stress played a part here, or the actual physical situation may have showed the relationship of the speaker to his subject. This is the time of so-called 'unsuffixed adverbs', where one word in the same form designated different adverbial relationships, the accusative or the possessive. For example, the word 'water' would originally mean 'in water', 'on water', 'out of water', 'with water', etc. Attempts to express different shades of meaning and to give more precise definition gave rise to these later modifications, but the process was very gradual and lengthy. The first step in this development was to distinguish between the subject of the sentence and those words which had some different relationships in the sentence. The subject remained as it was, but a demonstrative pronoun followed the latter type of word, thus the primitive sentence 'Bear cave lives' would later become something like 'Bear cave *that* lives', where the demonstrative pronoun of the *t*- or *n*- type was used for this function. The effect was to define the rôle of the word for 'cave' more precisely. Although this may seem peculiar today, similar kinds of construction can be found in modern Finno-Ugrian languages, so that this theory is by no means mere speculation. In Hungarian there is a well-known folk song that begins thus:

Erdő, erdő, erdő,	Forest, forest, forest,
Marosszéki kerek *erdő*	Round forest of Marosszék,
Madár, lakik *abban*	Birds dwell therein,
Madár lakik tizenkettő . . .	Twelve birds dwell (there) . . .

These lines could be equally well expressed in modern prose thus: 'A marosszéki kerek erdő*ben* lakik tizenkét madár' 'In the round wood of Marosszék dwell twelve birds'. But the text of the song, instead of using the suffix *-ben* (in) to define the relationship of the word *erdő* (forest) to the rest of the sentence, takes instead the demonstrative pronoun *az* (that), to which it adds this suffix (*az* +*-ban* = *abban*); this refers back to the unsuffixed *erdő* and defines its relationship to the rest of the sentence. A further example is seen in the folk ballad beginning

Diófának három *ága*,	Three *branches* of a nut-tree,
Az alatt űl három árva . . .	Under *those* sit three orphans.

Here the prose rendering would be 'Under the three branches of a nut-tree sit three orphans.'

These Hungarian examples differ in one important respect from the Proto-Finno-Ugrian type; Hungarian uses a suffixed form of the demonstrative itself (*abban*, *az alatt*), while the original language contented itself with the demonstrative alone, since suffixes did not exist at that time. This in turn means that the simple demonstrative pronoun following a word had not one, but a variety of adverbial functions. So the noun + demonstrative construction (as in *wete-tä* or *weet-nä*:*wete* = 'water') had almost as many meanings as the earlier unsuffixed noun it replaced. Yet this first step led very gradually to the more specialized use of the construction. This process was aided by the existence of more than one demonstrative pronoun in the language. We may assume, therefore, that the demonstratives in *t-* and *n-* came to be used after words to express a spatial relationship in answer to the question 'where?'. Although this is a considerable advance, we cannot yet talk of a locative case or locative suffix, since the two elements, unsuffixed noun and pronoun, were still separate and preserved their own identity. But through frequent use the demonstrative sooner or later lost its independent existence and was no longer felt to have any pronominal connections. It then adhered to the preceding noun and became a suffix. This last and important step may have been speeded by other circumstances – for example, that certain pronouns acquired certain permanent functions, and were adapted to denote a particular relationship; at the same time there were phonetic modifications in their form when they performed such functions, and indeed some emphatic elements may also have been added to them.

This process may well have been only one of many in the development of suffixes. The formation of suffixes and postpositions is a phenomenon that can be observed in more modern times, and proof can be shown of suffixes developing from independent words – personal pronouns, formatives or even the final syllables of other words. It cannot be assumed that these methods were unknown in Uralic times.

From these arguments, it appears that the case-system in Proto-Finno-Ugrian, as deduced from a comparative study of the cognate languages, was the result of a development which certainly continued for several thousand years. The same is true of other structural elements in the language.

It can be shown that both plural and dual forms existed. This latter has disappeared from most modern Finno-Ugrian languages, and today is used only in Lapp, the Ob-Ugrian languages and the Samoyed group. The dual was expressed by a suffix -*ka*, which is derived, like Hu. *két* 'two' and Finn. *kaksi*, from a form **kakte*. This, of course, is a theory, but a very probable one; if it is true, it is yet another proof of the lengthy period needed for the development of structural elements in language. The plural -*t* of the original language is preserved by many modern Finno-Ugrian languages, e.g., Finn. *kala* 'fish' pl. *kala-t*, Vogul *lū* 'horse' pl. *lūt*, Mord. *tolga* 'feather' pl. *tolgat* etc. It does not exist in Hungarian, and its origin remains a mystery as yet unsolved.

The possessive pronoun suffixes, on the other hand, are relatively easy to follow. All the Finno-Ugrian and Samoyed languages have a system of possessive pronominal suffixes, and there are so many common features that they provide an excellent guide to its growth. Let us first consider the first, second and third persons singular in Hungarian and certain cognate languages. In Hungarian the forms are:

kéz	hand	*szem*	eye
kezem	my hand	*szemem*	my eye
kezed	thy hand	*szemed*	thy eye
keze	his/her/its hand	*szeme*	his/her/its eye.

The first person suffix is generally *-m*, e.g., Vogul *säm-em*, Ostyak *sem-em* 'my eye'; Mord. *ked'-em*, Cheremis *kid-em* 'my hand'. In the second person *-t* and *-d* are found, e.g., Votyak *sinmy-d*, Cheremis *sinzä-t* 'thy eye'; Mord. *ked'-et* 'thy hand'. In the third person, languages other than Hungarian show *-z̧*, *-s*, *-š*, or *-t*, e.g., Ostyak *sem-et*, Votyak *sinmy-z̧*, Zyryan *sinmy-s* 'his eye'; Cheremis *kit-še* 'his hand' etc. In the first two persons, the similarity is striking, while in the third person Hungarian is apparently very different. Comparative research, however, shows that an original *-s* in the third person suffix has disappeared in Hungarian, while in the Ob-Ugrian languages it has become *-t* and in the other related languages it has either remained *-s* or further developed into *-š* (Cheremis) or *-z̧* (Votyak). Thus all these suffixes have a common origin.

The characteristic signs of the first three personal possessives are then *-m*, *-t* (or the later voiced form in *-d*) and *-s*. These, however, must be set alongside the Uralic personal pronouns **me*, **te* and **se* for further clarification. It is clear that the original language chose the simplest solution to the problem of designating personal possession, and merely added the appropriate personal pronoun to the object possessed. The connection between them was doubtless relatively loose at first; later the pronouns became abbreviated, lost their independent status and gradually developed into possessive suffixes. Primitive forms of these suffixes existed in Proto-Finno-Ugrian, and the languages which developed from this modified them considerably, so that today there are numerous differences between their forms in Finno-Ugrian as a whole. They have a common origin, and the germ of future development was there before they began their separate existence.

No complete system of verbal conjugation can be traced back to Uralic times. The category of verb came into existence and began to develop away from the noun. Moreover, modifications were made to distinguish commands and wishes from statements. To form the imperative mood a suffix *-k* was used, while the conditional or optative was formed with *nek*. In Hungarian, the former became *-j*, as in *ad* 'he gives' – *ad-j* 'give!', and the latter the conditional *-ná/-né*, e.g. *ad-ná-m* 'I should give (it)', *men-né-k* 'I should go'.

The relationship of the action of the verb to time was also to be found. Originally the aspect of time was probably expressed only through the verb roots themselves; the verb, through its very meaning, could express the length or frequency of an action, or its completion. These qualities are best seen in the Nenets language, e.g., *madā-* 'cut off' expresses a momentaneous action already completed at the time of speaking, so that the simple root + first person suffix *madā-m* automatically produces a past tense form 'I cut off'. (In order to express the present tense, the quality of the action must be changed; this is done by using a frequentative suffix: *madā-śety-m* 'I keep on cutting, I cut'.) A verb which indicates a long, continuous or frequent action refers automatically to present time, e.g., *nū-m* 'I stand, I am standing'.

The concepts of past and present time were also expressed by participles, which occur frequently in Finno-Ugrian languages. The participle of a verb indicating continuous action referred to the present, while the past participle was derived from verbs indicating completed action. Apart from these usages, there are other signs that distinction began to be drawn between these two tenses in the original language.

Here we may well consider the question of verbal conjugation and its development at this period. Any careful study of the modern Finno-Ugrian languages reveals very great differences between them; the development of their systems of personal suffixes must therefore be regarded as having taken place during the separate existence of these languages. Nevertheless, there are two characteristics common to them all. First, in every language it is possible to find first and second person suffixes (though there are several varieties in certain languages) which are identical with the suffixes used to denote first and second person possession, e.g., Hu. *ház-am* 'my house' *ad-om* 'I give (it)'; *ház-ad* 'thy house' *ad-od* 'thou givest (it)'; Cheremiss *kidem* 'my hand' *widem* 'I lead'; *kidet* 'thy hand' *widet* 'thou leadest'; Lapp *akkum* 'my grandmother' *viegâm* 'I run'; *akkud* 'thy grandmother' *viegâk* 'thou runnest'. This does not lead to the conclusion that the verbal suffixes were adapted from the personal possessive system; they are the result of denoting the performer of an action by placing the appropriate personal pronoun after the verb. This word-order seems all the more strange when all indications point to the normal word-order in Uralic being of the 'Subject-Predicate' type, and this would suggest that the pronoun preceded the verb. Nevertheless, the development of the personal pronoun into a suffix demands the reverse order. The explanation may be that the two existed side by side at one time, the difference between them being one of emphasis: when the verb came first, this was stressed more than the pronoun, and vice versa. The verb + pronoun construction underwent virtually the same development as the noun + personal pronoun, resulting in a system of personal suffixes. The differences between the verbal suffixes now used by Finno-Ugrian languages indicate that the development of the personal pronoun into a verbal suffix probably began during the Uralic period, but did not end there. The process of agglutination was completed during the separate life of each language.

The second common feature of verbal conjugation inherited from Uralic is the use in the third person of unsuffixed forms which are originally of a nominal type. In Hungarian the past tense (*ő*) *hallott* '(he) heard', *adott* 'gave', *nézett* 'looked' and their plurals (*ők*) *hallottak* '(they) heard', *adtak*, *néztek* are merely the past participles of the verbs *hall*, *ad* and *néz* respectively, which form their plurals with -*k*, as do nouns, e.g. *ház* 'house' *házak* 'houses'. This -*k* suffix originally had no personal connotation whatsoever; cf. Hu. (*ők*) *hallottak* 'they heard' *a hallottak után* 'after what had been heard', lit. 'after the heard things'. The obsolete form of the verb 'to be' – *vala* 'he was' – is etymologically identical with the present participle '*való* 'being'. Similar examples can be seen in other Finno-Ugrian languages. In Finnish, the older and dialectal form of *laulaa* 'he sings' is *laulavi*; this is historically identical with the participle *laulava* 'singing'. The third person plural form is *laula-vat* 'they sing', where -*vat* is today felt to be a verbal suffix; its origin, however, is in the participial -*va* to which has been added a -*t* plural (cf. *laulava-t linnut* 'singing birds').

This phenomenon can be traced back to Uralic, in which, as we have seen, the predicate was originally a 'noun-verb'. The separation of verb and noun was a gradual process, as each developed certain semantic and syntactical functions. The verb became semantically associated with action and syntactically it acquired the rôle of the predicate, while the noun, becoming associated with objects, began to play the part of the subject. This difference, however, was slow to appear in their forms, for the complete verbal conjugational system had not yet developed. The number of noun-verbs was still quite large, so that one and the same root might appear in both functions. As the verbal category developed, it became necessary to show how the subject – the initiator of the action – was related in time to the action itself, hence the need for the concept of tense. The problem was solved by the use of participial formatives, both continuous (for the present) and perfective (for the past). These forms, however, again emphasized the nominal character of the embryo verbs. The result was that until the personal endings of the past and present tenses had become established and crystallized into a conjugation-system, the third persons singular and plural were expressed by noun (participial) forms.

Thus Uralic used not only unsuffixed noun-verbs in a predicative rôle, but also participles, and the use of the latter gradually increased. When it became necessary to define the subject of the verb more precisely, the first and second personal pronouns were brought into use. There was no need for a third-person suffix, since the absence of the other pronouns was in itself sufficient indication of the subject. At this time the plurality of the subject was not indicated; only the verb showed this (so that a singular subject would be used with a plural verb), hence the use of the plural form of the participle to denote a third person plural verb. Traces of this linguistic state can still be seen in the modern Finno-Ugrian languages, although with the emergence of complete conjugational systems the participial origin and nature of the third-person forms have largely been forgotten.

This brief sketch of the grammatical elements of Uralic would be incomplete without some reference to formatives of which very many can be traced back to this period. They are of considerable antiquity, and may even be older than the suffixes already mentioned. There would be little point in listing them here, for virtually all consonants in the original language and numerous combinations of them can be demonstrated to have been used as formatives. We shall confine ourselves to certain points of interest.

Modern grammars list formatives according to their function; distinctions are made between noun and verb formatives, and within these two main groups there are subdivisions indicating whether they are used to create verbs from nouns, verbs from verbs, etc. Then there are the special functions of the formatives themselves; in Hungarian, for example, the formative *-ság/-ség* creates noun from noun, but also has a collective rôle (*rokon* 'relative' – *rokonság* 'relatives en masse'), while *-ás/-és* creates noun from verb (*tanul* 'learn' – *tanulás* 'study'). The formative *-ódik/-ődik* has a reflexive function and is added to verbs (*ír* 'write' – *íródik* 'is written', lit. 'writes itself'), while *-z* forms verbs from nouns (*levél* 'letter' – *levelez* 'correspond'). These main and subsidiary divisions are usually kept in comparative linguistic studies. But if the history of these various formatives is traced back to Finno-Ugrian or Uralic times, we find that identical formatives are used to fulfil different functions. In Hungarian there are several *l* or *ly* formatives, now mainly obsolete. One is denominal (i.e., creates noun from noun), e.g., *körtvély*: *körte* 'pear', and *személy* 'person': *szem* 'eye'. Similar instances can be found in other Finno-Ugrian languages, e.g., Est. *peial* 'thumb', Votyak *iskal* 'cow', Ostyak *sosel* 'lizard', etc. There is another *-l/-ly* formative which is deverbal (i.e., creates nouns from verbs); Hungarian examples are *lepel* 'cover': *lep-*, *kötél* 'rope': *köt* 'tie', *födél* 'cover': *föd* 'cover', *fogoly* 'captive': *fog* 'seize'; other FU languages also show this formative, e.g. Finn. *askel* 'step' ~ Vogul *ūsil*: *ūs-* 'to step'. The suffix *-l* is also used in Hungarian to form verbs from nouns, e.g. *szó* 'word': *szó-l* 'speak', *munka* 'work': *munkál* 'work', *ének* 'song': *énekel* 'sing'; similar instances occur in Zyryan: *pemyd* 'dark': *pemyd-ly-* 'grow dark', and in Vogul: *tūlmax* 'thief': *tūlmax-l* 'steal'.

Apart from these, there is an *-l* frequentative in Hungarian, e.g., *rom-l-ik* 'decay', *dob* 'throw': *dob-ál* 'toss about'. This is found also in Finn. *anta-* 'give': *antele-* 'keep giving', Mord. *kando-* 'carry': *kańt'l'e-* 'convey', and elsewhere. It is then no surprise to discover an *-l/-ll* instantaneous formative, as in Hu. *szök-ik* 'leap':

szök-ell 'gush forth', *szól* 'speak': *szól-al* 'speak out'; Nenets *ŋam-* 'eat': *ŋowo-llá* 'begin to eat'; Lapp *kerte-* 'fly': *kertle-* 'fly up'. Finally there is an *-l* causative: Hu. *asz-ik* 'go dry': *asz-al* 'dry', *nő* 'grow': *nevel* 'bring up', *forr* 'seethe, boil': *forr-al* 'boil' (trans.); Vogul *tōs-* 'grow dry': *tōsl-* 'dry'; Selkup *yty-* 'hang' (intrans.): *ytäl-* 'hang up' (trans.).

All these formatives are derived from Uralic *-l*, and since the functions mentioned above are to be found in the majority of the Finno-Ugrian languages, whether obsolete or still in use, the existence of six *l-* formatives must be postulated in Proto-Finno-Ugrian. The first created noun from noun, the second noun from verb, the third verb from noun, the fourth was frequentative, the fifth instantaneous and the sixth causative. It is customary to make these practical distinctions of function in Proto-Finno-Ugrian, but it is extremely unlikely that there were significant differences between them at that period. It is much more rational, and much more in keeping with what we have deduced of conditions at that time, to assume that all these *-l* formatives are derived from one single Uralic *l*, which even then was used to fulfil various functions which are not now capable of closer definition. The historical linguist finds no difficulty in accepting such a solution. We know that for a long time there was no distinction between noun and verb. During the centuries or thousands of years that these separate categories took to evolve, there must have been considerable confusion. With this in mind, it does not require much explanation to understand why all the *-l* formatives may be regarded as having a common origin: while there was only one word-category and during the slow process of evolution, formatives were added without distinction to what later became nouns and verbs. Naturally at this period the rôle of formatives was much more vague and comprehensive, and probably also more haphazard, than it is today. This helps to explain why the same formative developed in different ways in the separate languages. Their function in many cases may well have been influenced not only by their original rôle, but also by the meaning of the original word from which they have been derived.

Such are the main grammatical features of Proto-Finno-Ugrian. One feature, however, still demands consideration: the structure of the Uralic sentence. Again, it must be emphasized that many changes took place during the long period from the original language to the formation of the separate Finno-Ugrian languages. The sentence naturally became less primitive and more complicated, as the necessity grew for clearer, more precise linguistic expression.

The investigation of this problem begins before the Uralic period, when man had the ability to speak, but the linguistic form of his speech was extremely primitive, as was his thought. His speech consisted of brief, ejaculatory sounds which might be termed 'words', referring to visible, audible and other sensory objects or phenomena e.g., water, snow, fire, wood, fish, bear, man, woman, etc. Sentences did not exist at this period; speech consisted simply of independently uttered shouts and interjections, doubtless accompanied by gestures, to attract attention. These sounds were accompanied by strong feelings, various shades of intonation and mimicry. How many ways, for example, could the word 'bear' be uttered – as a shout of fear, accompanied by defensive gestures as the animal suddenly attacked, or as a quiet, cautious word of warning from one hunter to another as he pointed out the direction in which the animal could be found; it could also be a shout of triumph as the animal's corpse was dragged back to the cave. These few examples show how one word alone – or a one-word 'sentence' – can express such emotions as fear, joy, caution, warning, and resignation. This one-word sentence could not be analysed; it contained no subject, predicate, adjective or qualified noun.

The development of the sentence from the speech of primeval man is one of the most remarkable achievements of mankind, for it made possible the communication of knowledge as thought-processes evolved. The sentence of the subject + predicate type probably developed from the fusion or synthesis of two primeval one-word sentences. Originally the sight of a bear merely conjured up the instinctive cry 'Bear!'; then the experience came to be analysed. At this stage, the sight of the quarry brought to the hunter's mind the appetizing meal that it would make; he therefore shouted 'Bear! Meat!'. These two thoughts were originally separate, but later fused with each other; the linguistic expression followed this development, thus forming a sentence analysable into two elements: 'Bear – meat'. Modern analysis would regard this as an adjectival phrase of the type adjective (bear)+noun (meat), and this was probably the most primitive type of sentence. It is, however, possible to regard this as a predicative construction, the first element representing the subject and the second the predicate. (Here it should be noted that the Finno-Ugrian sentence does not require a verbal predicate, e.g. Hu. *A ház magas* 'The house (is) tall'.) Thus, for example, the two elements 'Blood! Red!' would form the sentence 'The blood (is) red' and the previous example would result in 'The bear (is) meat'.

Whichever explanation is more probable, the Pre-Uralic age was doubtless familiar with relatively well-developed sentences of this type. Other elements were also familiar, so that – in modern terminology – subject and predicate, adjectival, adverbial and accusative relationships were known. At first there were no distinguishing elements to denote these relationships, but during the Uralic period, as we have seen, the more important adverbial, accusative and possessive ideas began to acquire grammatical means of expression. The division of words into nouns and verbs was evolving, and the outlines of verbal conjugation began to be seen. Speech at this time consisted chiefly of simple sentences; parataxis and not subordination was the rule, since subordinate clauses and their appropriate conjunctions are all of much later origin.

The following characteristics of Uralic sentence-construction deserve particular mention:

1 Subject and predicate did not agree in number. Only the predicate showed a dual or plural suffix.
2 Adjectives did not agree with nouns.
3 The subject preceded the verb, and the adjective the noun.
4 Noun declension showed singular forms only.
5 Both noun and verb (or participle), as well as the older noun-verbs, could be used as the predicate of a sentence.
6 Optative-conditional and imperative sentences existed in addition to statements.

Other minor characteristics might also be mentioned, but sufficient has been said to show that Proto-Finno-Ugrian was a form of language which evolved continuously towards a more perfect form of expression. In its last phase it had reached a comparatively advanced stage of development.

THE MODERN FINNO-UGRIAN LANGUAGES

After describing the main characteristics of Proto-Finno-Ugrian, it would be useful to continue the history of the various separate languages that evolved from it, but this is beyond the compass of the present work. Instead we shall discuss certain characteristics of the modern languages which shed light on the way in which linguistic phenomena already noted in Uralic developed further. This naturally includes a number of traits common to these languages today.

The phonetic system of the original language has undergone many changes and transformations in the separate lives of the Finno-Ugrian languages. Least change is shown by *l*, *r* and the nasals *m* and *n*. The other consonants show great diversity; some languages, for example, preserved the three sibilants of Uralic (the Permian group), others, like Mordvin, displayed its traces, while in others they have been lost entirely (e.g., Hungarian, Vogul, Ostyak and Finnish). Thus in some cases the sounds of the original language have either changed considerably or disappeared in the later course of history. But at the same time new sounds have developed, some from the original system, like the voiced *b*, *d*, *g* of Zyryan, Votyak and Hungarian, and some as a result of close contact with foreign languages, like the Hungarian *zs*, *c* and *dzs*.

These divergences make it impossible to give a general description of the phonology of the modern Finno-Ugrian languages. There remain, however, a few traits which are common to most, if not all, of them. One of these is their dislike of initial consonant groups (except in Mordvin); thus when loanwords are found with such groups, attempts are made to break them down. Thus Slav *stolъ* > Hu. *a-sztal* 'table', Latin *schola* > Hu. *i-skola* 'school', German *Schnur* > Hu. *zsinór* 'cord', French *clinche* > Hu. *kilincs* 'latch'; so too Swedish *skola* > Finn. *koulu* 'school', Lithuanian *briaunà* > Finn. *reuna* 'edge', Latvian *sluōta* > Finn. *luuta* 'broom', Russian *svobodъ* > Finn. *vapaa* 'free', Russian *kraj* > Finn. *raja* 'boundary', Russian *vnuk* > Carelian *vunukka* 'grandchild', etc. This also accounts for the appearance of the Russian *sluzhitъ* in Vogul as *lusiti* 'serve', Russian *starshina* as *istārsin* and Russian *zdorovo* in Nenets as *torowa* 'strong'.

Although it is particularly confined to the Finnic languages and Lapp, consonant gradation is regarded as a general Finno-Ugrian phenomenon. The essence of it is that certain consonants (in Finnish *k*, *t*, and *p*), when used at the beginning of a syllable within a word, appear in different forms according to whether the syllable is closed or open. For example, in the Finnish *kukka* 'flower' long *kk* appears when the syllable is open, but short *k* when it is closed, as in the plural form *kukat*. The open syllable contains the so-called strong grade, the closed the weak grade. The phenomenon of consonant gradation is not confined to mere length; in certain cases there may be a change of quality also. For example, *-p-* appearing as the strong grade at the beginning of an open syllable alternates with *-v-* in closed syllables, as in *tupa* 'room' ~ *tuvat* 'rooms'. At one time it was believed that consonant gradation in Lapp and Finnic was a feature derived from Uralic, and attempts were made to demonstrate traces of its existence in other Finno-Ugrian languages and particularly in Samoyed. It can be argued, however, that consonant gradation in these languages is not of common origin, but the result of independent development; not every linguist is now prepared to subscribe to the theory that it is a Uralic phenomenon (hence it was not mentioned in the previous chapter). It is nevertheless characteristic of certain Finno-Ugrian languages.

Most of the modern Finno-Ugrian languages still preserve the rule that the main stress falls on the first syllable of a word. In the Permian languages, Cheremis and to a certain degree in Mordvin also, other factors have militated against this tradition.

Vowel-harmony is another common feature which has continued more or less intact in all the languages except for Lapp and the Permian group. Certain developments have taken place; in Finnish the simple distinction between palatal (front or high) and velar (back or deep) vowels has been maintained, but in Hungarian, the eastern dialect of Cheremis and Selkup a further distinction has been added. This differentiates between labial and illabial vowels; the rule is that labial or rounded vowels (*o, ö, u, ü*) may not occur in the same word as illabial or unrounded vowels (*e, é, i, a, á*). The result of this can be seen in the Hungarian noun suffixes; some, like *-ban/-ben* 'in', have back and front vowel forms only, while others, like *-hoz/-hez/-höz* 'to', have two front-vowel forms, one illabial and the other labial. Roots containing an illabial front vowel take the form *-hez*, e.g. *kéz* 'hand' ~ *kézhez*, but those containing a labial vowel require the form *-höz*, e.g., *bőr* 'skin' ~ *bőrhöz*, *tű* 'pin' ~ *tűhöz*. In the case of back vowels, there is only one form *-hoz*, for both labial and illabial roots (*úr* 'gentleman' ~ *úrhoz*, *vár* 'castle' ~ *várhoz*). This development is probably the result of Turkic influence on the languages concerned.

Of the many changes in the vowel-system, one is of particular significance. The disyllabic (and possibly trisyllabic) words of the original common language which ended in an open vowel have become shortened in most Finno-Ugrian languages. The final open vowel disappeared in the course of time. Finnish is the most conservative language in this respect, cf. Finn. *kala* 'fish' ~ Mord. *kol* ~ Cher. *kol* ~ Vogul *kul* ~ Hu. *hal*.

Several important changes may also be noted in the structural elements of the languages. As for nouns, the most striking feature is the development of the case-system. In Proto-Finno-Ugrian there were certain general suffixes of place, denoting where, whence and whither the action was directed, but within these categories there was no more precise definition. In modern Hungarian the place where an action occurs can be defined as 'on' (*-on/-en/-ön*), 'in' (*-ban/-ben*) or 'at' (*-nál/-nél*). These distinctions were not made in the original language. Most Finno-Ugrian languages felt the need to specify these spatial relationships more precisely, and to provide for abstract relationships also. Attempts to meet these newer needs have resulted in the creation of new suffixes, so that today Hungarian possesses over 20 'cases', Zyryan 17, Votyak 16, Finnish 15, Cheremis 13 and Mordvin 9.

What is the relationship of the original suffixes to the new systems? The simple suffixes of the Uralic age have rarely retained their original forms. It is true that Finnish has *-na/-nä*, which is identical in form with the original locative, but its function has changed, and it is now used to express state, e.g., *opettaja-na* 'as a teacher'. The original primary suffixes can be discerned chiefly in the terminations of old, suffixed noun or pronoun derivations, where their significance is lost to modern speakers; these have crystallized into independent adverbial or postpositional forms, as in Hu. *ala*tt 'under' (postposition), *aló*l 'from under' (postposition), *i*tt 'here' (adverb), *hol*? 'where?'; Finn. *koto*na 'at home', *ny*t 'now'. These primary suffixes may also be found as elements of later compounded suffixes. Thus the Uralic locative *-na/-nä* can be seen in the *-n* of Hu. *-ban/-ben* 'in' or in Finn. *-ssa/ssä* 'in' from an earlier **-sna/-snä*; it also forms the second element of the Nenets locative *-χana*.

Various methods were used to create new suffixes capable of expressing the finer shades of adverbial relationships. The original suffix may still exist, but has acquired a special meaning; in Finnish, for example, the original ablative *-ta/-tä*, either unchanged or in a shortened *-a/-ä* form, is now used to express a partitive object, e.g. *maa-ta* 'part of the land' (acc.). Functional distinctions were also assisted by the fusion of the primary suffix with the final open vowel of the root to create new forms. This happened in the case of Hu. *-on/-en/-ön* 'on', which is derived from the Uralic locative *-na/-nä*; the present vowels, however, were not originally part of the suffix, but developed from the final open vowel of the root to which it was added. For example, modern Hungarian *út* 'road' is derived from an earlier form *utu* (as can be seen in documents of the eleventh century); this gave the suffixed form *utu-n*. Later, when the final open vowel disappeared, a process which was completed before the Tatar invasion of 1242, the root became *út* and the suffixed form *utun* became *uton*; the final root vowel was felt to be part of the suffix, and the root was now analysed as *ut + on*. There came into existence a new suffix in *-on/-en/-ön*, which became separated from the old general place-suffix *-n* and took a specific function, that of denoting a superessive relationship, i.e., 'on the surface of, on'.

Compounding of suffixes is a frequently used device to create new ones, as is the addition to the simple primary suffix of other formatives or emphatic particles. Hungarian *-nál/-nél* serves as a good example of the former method; it is compounded of *-n* locative + *-l* labative. In Nenets the ablative suffix *-χad* is compounded of *-d* < Uralic ablative *-ta/-tä* and the so-called coaffix *-χa-*, which is usually identified as a Finno-Ugrian formative occurring in other languages. In the Finnic-Permian languages, the external and internal spatial suffixes arose from a fusion of the old case-suffixes with an element denoting these relationships; the elative suffix (in answer to the question 'where from, out of what?') is in Finnish *-sta/-stä* 'out of', Mord. *-sto*, Cheremis *-štö* and in the Permian languages *-št-*, where the *s, š, s* element denotes internal relationship and *t* (+vowel) is the old ablative. The external equivalent to the elative, the ablative, is in Finnish *-lta/-ltä*, where *-l* denotes the external relationship. These examples are typical of the development of case-suffixes in Finno-Ugrian.

There is, however, another method of creating new suffixes found in Finno-Ugrian. They may develop from independent words. The Hungarian group of suffixes *-ban/-ben* 'in', *-ból/-ből* 'out of', *-ba/-be* 'into' is none other than the noun *bél* 'the inside, intestines', Old Hu. *bele* with *-n* locative, *-l* ablative and *-á/-é* (< Uralic *-k*) lative suffixes respectively. In Old Hungarian the modern *házban* 'in a house' was expressed by the possessive construction *hazu belen* (*belne*), i.e., 'in the inside of a house', as in the modern *ház belsejében*. The forms *belen, belne* gradually lost their independence and became postpositions, then frequent usage eventually reduced them to suffixes after various phonetic changes. At first only the form *-ben* existed; the back-vowel *-ban* was a later development in accordance with the rules of vowel-harmony. Similar examples can be cited from cognate languages. In Nenets the word *ńä* 'friend, companion' has become a comitative suffix ('with'). Livonian *-ks* and Estonian *-ga*, also comitative suffixes, were derived from an independent root which in modern Finnish appears as the postposition *kanssa* 'together with'; it is to be connected with the noun *kansa* 'people'. In Finnish no abbreviation of the root has occurred and the word remains a postposition; in Livonian and Estonian the process has gone further, and the result is a suffix.

Such development of the case-system is characteristic of the Finno-Ugrian languages, and particularly of Hungarian, the Finnic languages, Mordvin, Cheremis, Zyryan and Votyak. There are, however, certain languages where little change has occurred. Lapp is a prime example; here there are only seven suffixed cases. If a further six suffixes, to be found in the adverbial system, are included, this simplification of the case-system would appear to be a relatively recent development. The Samoyed languages also show the creation of new suffixes, but the number of cases (some six or seven) hardly exceeds that of Uralic. In Vogul and Ostyak there has been a general simplification of the case-system; the former retains five, the latter only two cases. The question may therefore arise whether the Finno-Ugrian languages in Siberia show some kind of regression when their meagre case-systems are compared with the considerably larger systems of their relatives in the west. The answer is a firm negative. In spite of their apparent deficiencies, these languages can express spatial relationships adequately by means of postpositions, of which they all possess an unusually large number (though other Finno-Ugrian languages are by no means lacking in postpositions). These are usually the suffixed forms of some noun, linked to the noun they qualify by means of a possessive construction, e.g., Finn. *veden alle* 'to under the water', consisting of the genitive form of *vesi* 'water' + *alle* 'to the bottom', i.e., 'to the bottom of the water' or Nenets *jïd ʔ ŋylna* 'under the water', where *jïd ʔ* is the genitive of *jï ʔ*, 'water' and *ŋylna* the locative of *ŋyl* 'the bottom' which has become a postposition, i.e., 'on the bottom of the water'. It is possible that if the roots of these postpositions die out and their form is simplified, they may well become suffixes in the course of time.

Another characteristic of the Finno-Ugrian languages is their system of personal possessive suffixes, a feature unknown in other European languages with which they are in contact, e.g., 'my house' = Hu. *házam*, German *dein Freund* = Hu. *barátod*. The basis of this development can be traced back to Uralic, but the separate languages evolved different systems, hence the various differences between them today. In most Finno-Ugrian languages the second person possessive suffix developed from the pronoun in *t-*, but in the Ob-Ugrian languages the continuation of a second person in *n-* can be traced. Finnish does not distinguish between singular and plural possession in the nominative; thus *talomme* is either 'our house' or 'our houses' (cf. Hu. *házunk* 'our house' – *házaink* 'our houses'). But when further suffixes are added, the difference is shown, e.g. *talo-ssa-mme* 'in our house' *talo-i-ssa-mme* 'in our houses', where *-ssa* = 'in' (inessive), *-i-* denotes plural possession, and *-mme* is the first person plural possessive suffix.

Plural possession is denoted in different ways in other Finno-Ugrian languages, though -*n*- is frequent, e.g., Mord. *tolga-ʒo* 'its feather' *tolga-n-ʒo* 'its feathers'; Vogul *sāli-n* 'thy reindeer' *sāli-än-en* 'thy reindeer' (pl.). While this plural -*n*- appears to be very old, the Permian languages and Cheremis use plural formatives of more recent origin in the same position, i.e., between the root and the personal possessive suffix, e.g., Cheremis *kid-em* 'my hand' *kid-wlä-em* 'my hands'; Votyak *val-dy* 'your horse' *val-jos-ty* 'your horses'. Other variations also occur in the personal possessive suffixes. Certain languages indicate dual as well as singular and plural possession, a feature that is seen at its most complete in the Ob-Ugrian and Samoyed languages. The following comparative table shows the formation and variety of the first person possessive suffixes in Vogul, Ostyak and Nenets. The noun used is the word for 'skin', in Vogul *sow*, in Ostyak *soχ* and in Nenets *χōba*:

Possession	Possessor	English	Vogul	Ostyak	Nenets
	Singular	my skin	*sowem*	*soχem*	*χōbam*
Singular	Dual	the skin of the two of us	*sowemēn*	*soχemen*	*χōbamï?*
	Plural	our skin	*sowūw*	*soχew*	*χōbawa?*
	Singular	my two skins	*sowäyem*	*soχŋelam*	*χōbaχajün*
Dual	Dual	the two skins of the two of us	*sowäyemēn*	*soχŋetamen*	*χōbaχajüñi?*
	Plural	our two skins	*sowäyūw*	*soχŋetew*	*χōbaχajüna?*
	Singular	my skins	*sowänem*	*soχtam*	*χōban*
Plural	Dual	the skins of the two of us	*sowänemēn*	*soχtamen*	*χōbañi?*
	Plural	our skins	*sowänuw*	*soχtew*	*χōbana?*

This table shows only the first person forms, nine in each language. The total number of possessive suffixes in each is therefore twenty-seven. This, however, refers only to the nominative case. In Nenets there are a further six cases, which brings the total number of possessive forms to one hundred and eighty-nine! The order of the suffixes is not identical in all the languages. In Hungarian and Ob-Ugrian the order is: Root + Possessive suffix + Case suffix, e.g., Hu. *hàʒ-am-ban* 'in my house', Vogul *kwol-en-nel* 'out of thy house'. In Finnish, Lapp and Mordvin this order is reversed, i.e., Root+case suffix+possessive suffix: Finn. *kirja-ssa-ni* 'in my book', Mord. *kudo-sto-nʒo* 'out of his house'.[1] In the Permian languages and Cheremis there is some vacillation. On the whole they incline to the Finnish order, e.g., Zyryan *kar-śy-s* 'out of his town', but at times the Hungarian order is followed, e.g., Zyryan *mort-yd-lɛn* 'with thy man, to thy man'. Cheremis shows similar variations, e.g., *tule-šte-ʒo* 'in its fire' but *tule-m-lan* 'to my fire'. The case used determines the order; some case-suffixes may only follow the possessive suffix, while others must precede it.

This relatively detailed description of possessive suffixation has been necessary to demonstrate how the systems used in the various languages, inseparable as they are from their Uralic antecedents, developed on different lines in the course of history. The basic unity of the possessive suffixes and their obvious diversity in modern times can thus be explained.

Another peculiarity of the personal possessive suffixes in Finno-Ugrian is that they are used not merely to denote possession, but also to function as a definite article. There is no definite article as such in Finno-Ugrian; in Hungarian *a/az* 'the' is an independent development from the demonstrative *az* 'that'. In other languages the noun is suffixed, as in Nenets *χāl'ē* 'fish' *χāl'ē-da* 'the fish', where -*da* is a third person possessive suffix.

Similar general conclusions can be reached concerning the development of verbal conjugations. Like the possessive suffixes, they have evolved from a common origin, but show independent growth. Proof of this is to be seen in one distinctive phenomenon. Unlike Indo-European and other language-groups, Hungarian, Vogul, Ostyak, Samoyed and Mordvin have all developed a type of conjugation which relates to the object of the verb. In Hungarian the distinction is drawn between *alanyi* 'subjective' and *tárgyas* 'objective', the former applying to all verbs, whether transitive or intransitive, while the latter applies to transitive verbs only; the verb *lát* 'see' thus has the forms *lát-ok* 'I see' and *lát-om* 'I see him (her, it, them)'. This 'objective'

---

1 In both Hungarian and the Ob-Ugrian languages there are traces of this type of order. It is to be found in postpositions, e.g. *mell-ett-em* 'beside me', *mell* 'breast (but *mell-em-en* 'at my breast'), *alatt-am* 'beneath me', etc. It is also true of suffixes with pronominal endings, e.g. *től-em* 'from me', *ról-ad* 'about thee', *hoz-zá* 'to him'.

conjugation is not identical in all these languages. Mordvin has developed it in its most advanced form, where it shows separate forms for e.g., 'I teach thee', 'I teach you', 'I teach him', 'I teach them' etc. This is much more comprehensive than can be found in Hungarian, which designates the third person object, singular or plural, by using the same form; there is also a form for use when the second person object is used with a first person singular subject, e.g., *lát-lak* 'I see thee (you)'. The only conclusion is that the 'objective' conjugation developed during the life of the separate Finno-Ugrian languages that possess it.

The common identity of formatives in the original language has already been discussed. Here it must be stressed that these elements are very numerous and varied in the Finno-Ugrian languages. Those inherited from Proto-Finno-Ugrian are partly still in use, while some have become obsolete. Their numbers have been increased considerably by the addition of new formatives, many of which are the result of fusion of various elements. Modern Finnish contains over 150 productive formatives. In Hungarian the verb *ad* 'give' has produced some 200 derivatives.

Word-formation is not confined to the admittedly very varied possibilities offered by the use of formatives; compounding is frequently found. Among the compounds typical of the Finno-Ugrian languages certain 'comprehensive' compounds deserve special mention. They may be either abstract or concrete collectives, and are compounded of two characteristic or even opposing elements, e.g., Vogul *āyi-pȳ* 'child' (girl + boy), *nē-χum* 'married couple' (woman + man); Ostyak *nē-χo* 'human being' (woman + man), *ńot-sem* 'face' (nose + mouth); Zyryan *jaj-ly* 'body' (flesh + bone); Votyak *ym-nyr* 'face' (mouth + nose); Estonian *suu-silmad* 'face' (mouth + eyes); Finnish *maa-ilma* 'world' (earth + air); Hungarian *orca, arc* 'face' (nose + mouth: *orr* 'nose', *száj* 'mouth'), *szemfüles* 'alert' (eye + eared). As for the frequency of compounds, the Finnish scholar Ravila discovered 50 of them in a Finnish text of 800 words, while a French text of 7,000 words revealed only 20.

One of the common characteristics of the Finno-Ugrian languages is their general preference for participial constructions instead of subordinate clauses, e.g., Hungarian *madárlátta kenyer* lit. 'bird-seen bread', i.e., bread brought home again from work in the fields, *szú-ette fa* 'worm-eaten wood', *jövet is menet is mindig arra járok* 'on my way there and on my way back I always use that route' etc. In Hungarian such constructions are slowly being replaced by subordinate clauses, but other Finno-Ugrian languages use them in profusion. In Nenets subordinate clauses are unknown, participial constructions being used in their place, e.g., *χāptōna? pōd' ermana? mal'eŋgana ńe? m̃ādō χawadajdo?*, lit. 'in the midst of the unharnessing of our reindeer the women set up the tents', i.e., 'while we unharnessed the reindeer, the women set up the tents.'

In Finno-Ugrian the predicate can be nominal as well as verbal: 'nominal' includes both nouns and adjectives, e.g., Hu. *Az ember boldog* 'the man (is) happy', where the function of the predicate is fulfilled by the adjective *boldog* 'happy'. Such sentences in Indo-European (though with the exception of Russian) generally require an appropriate form of the verb 'to be'. In Mordvin and Samoyed the predicative use of the noun is so extensive that verbal suffixes may be added to nouns, e.g., Nenets *χāsawa* 'man' gives *χāsawa-m* 'I am a man' (*-m* is the first person singular verbal suffix), *χāsawa-n* 'thou art a man' (*-n* is second person singular), and *χāsawa* (unsuffixed) 'he is a man'. Nor is this usage confined to the present tense; the past tense sign may be added, e.g., *χāsawa-m-ś* 'I was a man', *χāsawa-n-ś* 'thou wert a man', *χāsawa-ś* 'he was a man' etc. This is a relic of the time when there was no distinction between noun and verb. Today subject and predicate normally agree in number, but this is a recent trend. There are still traces of the time when only the predicate designated the plural, e.g., Finnish *lintu lentävät* 'birds fly', where *lintu* 'bird' is singular and the verb plural. The subject, incidentally, still normally precedes the predicate.

The qualifying adjective also precedes its noun, but does not agree with it in number or case, as is customary in other languages, e.g., Hungarian *a nagy ház* 'the big house' – *a nagy házak* 'the big houses' – *a nagy házakban* 'in the big houses'. Finnish is an exception to this rule: adjectives are declined like the nouns they qualify. This is presumably due to foreign influence.

One further unusual characteristic of Finno-Ugrian is that plural numerals are not followed by plural nouns, e.g., Hungarian *a tojás* 'the egg' *tíz tojás* 'ten eggs'.

This sketch of the development of the Finno-Ugrian languages may be completed by a brief examination of their place in the linguistic world.

The extensive system of suffixes and postpositions clearly betrays a different type of language from that to which Indo-European languages belong; the distinction can be seen in the phrase 'in the houses', German *in den Häusern*, Hungarian *a házakban*, where the Indo-European languages use prepositions. But this difference is not confined to such usages alone. In Hungarian, the plural 'houses' is formed by a simple suffix *ház-ak*; in German the quality of the root vowel is altered, e.g., *Haus-Häuser* (cf. *Satz-Sätze*, and English *foot-feet*). Such changes in the root vowel are not characteristic of Finno-Ugrian.

The verbal systems show similar divergences. In Finno-Ugrian it is the suffixes which distinguish the various verb forms; in Indo-European, although the importance of suffixes is not to be underrated, the root vowel again plays a significant rôle, e.g., I see – I saw; German *ich trete* 'I step' – *ich trat* 'I stepped'; Hungarian *lát-ok* 'I see' *lát-tam* 'I saw'. Here Hungarian forms the past tense by adding its characteristic sign *-t-* and a personal suffix, while the Indo-European examples demand a change of vowel in the root.

Such differences as these lead to the classification of Indo-European as 'inflected' and Uralic as 'agglutinating'. Other languages of this latter type include Turkic, Manchu-Tunguz and a number of African languages. Naturally this kind of division has its dangers, among which is the idea that such groups should be regarded as widely differing and incompatible with each other. In reality the division is made only on the most general grounds; in practice it is often found that an essentially agglutinating language shows features typical of an inflected one and vice versa. The case-system of Indo-European, for example, with its characteristic endings, has much in common with the Uralic system (as any Latin noun with its case-endings will show).

Thus the agglutinating Uralic languages may be expected to show features which call to mind other language types. Hungarian *alszik* 'sleep' ~ *olt* 'extinguish', *halott* ~ *holt* 'dead' display vowel-alternation in the first syllable; Lapp *doalvom* 'I lead' ~ *dolvum* 'I led' shows the same feature, here related to tense;

Nenets *jā* 'land' ∼*jō* 'lands' (acc.) again uses vowel-alternation to distinguish between a nominative and accusative plural. Such alternation is one of the characteristics of inflected languages. And perhaps such Hungarian forms as *legmegelégedetlenebbektől*, which in English or German can only be translated by the use of a phrase 'from the most dissatisfied persons of all' 'von den am allermeisten unzufrieden Seienden', may be said to have the polysynthetic characteristics of Eskimo, Basque and the American Indian languages. It is generally true that languages rich in formatives show certain similarities to the polysynthetic types. As a fearful example, Artturi Kannisto, the Finnish linguist, created the following unused and unusable Finnish word, which must be the longest in any Finno-Ugrian language: *kumarreksituteskenteleentuvaisehkollaismaisekkeedellisenneskenteluttelemattomammuuksissansakkaankopahan*. This giant of 103 letters is based on the verb *kumartaa* 'bow', to which have been added various verbal, noun and adjectival formatives, deprivative suffixes, plural inessive, third person possessive and emphatic suffixes, and an interrogative. A translation of this colossus is virtually impossible: suffice it to say that it has about as much significance as the Hungarian 83-letter word *visszahajladozgattatástalanulhatmányoskodékonyítványszerűbbecskéselősdíjeitekképpen*. The majority of such words naturally owe their existence to jocular linguists; although they demonstrate the riches of the language and its ability to create new words, they do not prove that Finnish or Hungarian should be regarded as polysynthetic.

What is the 'social' position of Finno-Ugrian languages in the world today? In other words, how do they compare in usage and extent with other language groups?

Certain romantically inclined scholars of earlier times – notably the Hungarian István Horvát at the beginning of the nineteenth century – proved to their own satisfaction that Hungarian was the oldest language in the world, and that it was spoken by the ancestors of the Hungarians back to the time of Adam and Eve. Although this theory was scorned at the time, a somewhat different, more scholarly and highly chauvinistic idea had its adherents in the first half of the present century. This was the so-called 'Turanian' theory, built on the somewhat naive and confused belief that Finno-Ugrian, Turkic, Manchu-Tunguz, Korean and Japanese were all related languages. This was linked with a Turanian (or earlier Hunnish-Scythian) racial theory, and the whole was set up to oppose Pan-Germanism; its slogan 'From Dévény[1] to Tokyo' was doubtless used to serve Fascist ideology. But languages cannot be classified according to ideas of value or importance. Naturally there are less developed languages without written records, and for the present they cannot act as vehicles of more abstract ideas. Here a primitive state of society is indicated by the rudimentary state of the language, yet potentially it has the same chance of development as those which have become world languages today.

All languages possess the means to express hitherto unknown concepts; they merely need the society which uses them to master developments in the cultural and technical fields. In the Soviet Union great opportunities have been offered to the smaller nations to develop in this way, and these have responded remarkably, with new literary languages to match developments in the social, economic and political sphere. Another example of the equality of languages may be cited from America. The American Indian languages have no literature, and are customarily listed among the 'primitive' languages of the world. During the Second World War the US Army enlisted into its signals service Navajo Indians, native speakers who translated messages into their own language, thus confusing the Japanese who did not know this 'code' and had no key to it. This particular language was deliberately chosen, because it had somehow escaped the attention of the Germans who had made detailed investigations into the Indian languages before the war. The Navajo Indians had no words to express such ideas as 'jeep', 'radar' and 'air force', but succeeded in creating terms for them. So a 'primitive' language played its part in modern warfare communications. The use and development of Navajo Indian for these purposes demonstrates the truth of the statement made above – that languages possess the means to express previously unknown concepts. It would be even more impressive if literary development could also be shown.

In estimating the importance of a language, its geographical extent and number of speakers must be taken into consideration.

---

1 The traditional westernmost point in Hungary, now Devín, Slovakia.

Recent estimates suggest that some 2,796 languages are spoken in the world. Since there are roughly three milliard human beings, if they were proportionately divided, each language would be spoken by about a million folk. This, however, is not the case. Numbers of speakers vary from a mere handful to hundreds of millions. Chinese is the first in the list, spoken by some 620 million, followed by English (300 million), Hindustani and Russian (200 million each). Then follow Spanish (140 million), German (100 million), Japanese and Arabic (90 million), Malay (80 million), French (75 million), Bengali and Portuguese (70 million) and Italian (60 million). Thus two thirds of mankind use these 13 languages. At the other end of the scale there are some 1,200 American Indian languages, many of them used by only a few hundred or thousand speakers, and similar figures can be quoted from Australia, New Guinea, Oceania and many parts of Africa.

The situation of Finno-Ugrian in the light of these figures is not particularly encouraging. There are some 20 million speakers, but they share 19 languages between them. Hungarian, the largest of the Finno-Ugrian languages, is spoken by some 15 million people (and is among the 29 languages of the world spoken by more than ten million).

It is likely that the languages spoken now by only a few hundred people will gradually die out. The number of languages will therefore decrease; all the signs point to a process of integration in favour of the great world languages. Yet it would be premature to talk now of the disappearance of the Finno-Ugrian languages, at a time when there are many encouraging signs of new development among the smaller members of this group in the Soviet Union.

PART III

Finno-Ugrian Peoples

𝕊𝕊𝕊𝕊𝕊𝕊

The Ugrians

The Hungarians

THE Hungarians or Magyars form the largest of the Finno-Ugrian peoples in the modern world. Established in the northern Pannonian basin since the end of the ninth century AD, they also possess the longest settled history. The Hungarian People's Republic has an area of 93,030 square kilometres and a population of about 10,200,000 (1967), the overwhelming majority of whom speak Hungarian as their native language. Since the frontiers of modern Hungary were established only in 1919, it is no surprise to discover large numbers of Hungarian speakers in the surrounding countries. In Slovakia there are about 400,000, in the Sub-Carpathian Ruthenia district of the USSR 155,000, in Rumania over 1,500,000, mostly in Transylvania, in Northern Yugoslavia about half a million, and in the Burgenland district of Austria some 15,000. Emigration from Hungary during the last century has resulted in the creation of a large enclave in the United States of America, and there are smaller groups in Canada, South America, Australia and various parts of Europe. The total number of Hungarians in the world is estimated at fifteen million.

Hungary is a compact country, divided effectively by the Danube which flows approximately from north to south after forming the north-west frontier. Western Hungary, or Transdanubia, has the more varied, hillier landscape; much of the east of the country consists of vast plains. A chain of low hills, forming a link between the eastern Alps and the Carpathians, crosses Hungary from south-west to north-east, reaching its highest point, 1,015 metres, in the Mátra mountains. The country is fertile, well-

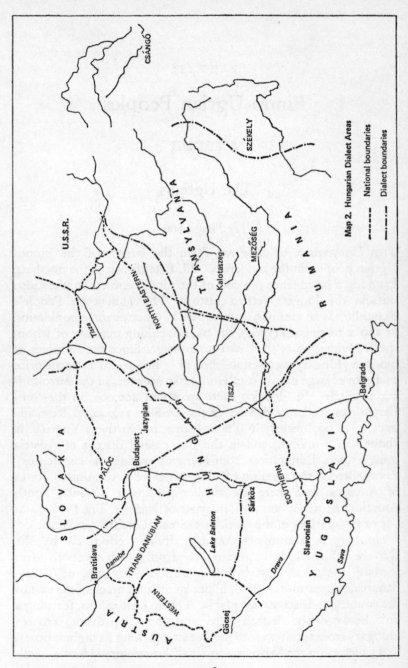

Map 2. Hungarian Dialect Areas

National boundaries
Dialect boundaries

CSÁNGÓ

SZÉKELY

TRANSYLVANIA

MEZŐSÉG

Kalotaszeg

RUMANIA

U.S.S.R.

NORTH EASTERN

Tisza

H U N G A R Y

TISZA

Belgrade

Jazygian

PALÓC

Budapest

SLOVAKIA

SOUTHERN

Sárköz

Lake Balaton

Drava

Slavonian

Y U G O S L A V I A

Sava

Bratislava

Danube

TRANS DANUBIAN

WESTERN

Göcsej

A U S T R I A

suited to agriculture and animal husbandry, which have long been followed there. The soil and climate are more favourable in the west; the great plain suffers from extremes of temperature, as well as periods of drought and floods. There is a constant battle to regulate the main river of this area, the Tisza, and its tributaries, which here meet the first large expanse of flat land in their courses. The contrast between western and eastern Hungary is not entirely due to natural causes. When the Turks occupied Hungary after the disastrous battle of Mohács in 1526, they advanced along the Danube and quickly secured control of the plains, while Transdanubia, though a border area, remained relatively free from their depredations. After 160 years of Turkish rule, the plains were devastated and depopulated, and the few villages that remained grew into immense 'market-towns', separated by large distances, the land between them being studded with isolated farm colonies known as *tanyas*. In the west there are smaller but more frequent villages and evidence of longer and more settled agricultural traditions. There are few large towns in Hungary. Budapest, the capital, has a population of over two million; the next largest town is Miskolc, with 175,000 inhabitants. Only Debrecen, Pécs and Szeged of the other towns have a population of more than 100,000.

The Hungarian language-area is customarily divided into eight dialect regions. (This division does not, of course, include the now well-established enclave in North America which has many distinctive features.) None of these is far removed from the standard literary language, nor is this unexpected, since the Hungarian Academy of Sciences, founded in 1830, has been instrumental in the stabilization of the language and its orthography, and its decisions have been implemented throughout the educational system of the country. The dialect-regions are: Western, Transdanubian, Southern, Palóc, Tisza, North-Eastern, Mezőség and Eastern (or Székely and Csángó). Most of them are further subdivided. The distinctions between them are by no means clearcut, and with the frequent movement of population the validity of this traditional division is being increasingly questioned. The following examples show the extent of the problem:

1 The standard pronunciation of the digraph *ly* is *j*, e.g., *folyik* 'it

flows' = *fojik*. Two dialectal variations are found, *folik* (*follik*) and *fol'ik*, as follows:

fojik	*folik* (*follik*)	*fol'ik*
Transdanubian (W)	Western	Palóc
		(Central)
Southern (Baranya, Szeged)	Transdanubian (S)	Csángó
Tisza	Southern (Somogy)	
Palóc (S and E)	Palóc (W)	
North-Eastern		
Mezőség		
Székely		

2 Variations on the standard suffix *-ból/-ből* 'from inside, out of', e.g., *a házból* 'out of the house':

-ból/-ből	North-Eastern (Füzér)
-bó/-bő	Palóc (W and Central)
-bol/-böl	Western (N), Mezőség, Eastern
-búl/-bűl	Tisza (partial), Palóc (S and E), North-Eastern, (Hajdú, Szabolcs/Szatmár)
-bú/-bű	Transdanubian (N), Southern (Baranya, Szeged), Tisza (partial)
-bu/-bü	Transdanubian (S), Western (S), Southern (Somogy).

3 In standard Hungarian the indicative mood has been reduced to three tenses: present, past and compound future. The easternmost dialects, Mezőség, Székely and Csángó, preserve an old perfect indicative and a compound pluperfect, the former expressing immediate past action, e.g., *most harangozának* 'they have just been ringing the bells'.

Since the Second World War, the Székelys of Bukovina have been resettled in the southern part of Transdanubia, in the Southern dialect region, adding a new dimension to the dialect problem.

There are considerable variations in vocabulary; the results of modern research into this aspect are now appearing with the publication by the Academy of a comprehensive dialect atlas (*A magyar nyelvjárások atlasza*, Vol. I, 1969, Vol. II, 1971, Vol. III, 1973).

Like the majority of the Finno-Ugrian peoples, the Hungarians are known by two names, one used outside the country and the other, Magyar, by themselves. The former, in a number of variants, is derived from a Slavonic root *ǫg(ъ)r-*, e.g.: Russian *venger-*, Polish *węgier-*, Czech *uher-*, Rumanian *ungur-*, Serbo-Croat *ugar-*, Bulgarian *vъgr-*, German *ungar*, Latin *hungarus*, *hungaricus*, French *hongrois*, English *Hungarian*. This in turn is from Bulgar-Turkic (Chuvash) *onogur*, the name of a Turkic tribe or tribal federation, compounded of *on* 'ten' + *ogur* (< *ok*) 'arrow', cf. Priscus Ὀνόγουροι, Jordanes *hunuguri*. The initial *h-* found in Latin, French and English is doubtless due to confusion with *Hunni*.

The name *Magyar* first appears as that of a 'Hunnish king' Μουάγερις, in a tenth-century copy of a document dating from the sixth century. Constantinus Porphyrogennetus uses it in the form Μεγέρη. Its origin has already been discussed (p. 69 above); the meaning of the compound is 'a man of the tribe', and it may be compared with the Vogul name *Man'śi* and the Ostyak fraternity *mōś*. The old Hungarian form *mogyeri* developed according to the rules of vowel-harmony either into *mogyor* > *magyar* or into *megyer*; this latter form is found today in place-names, e.g. *Békásmegyer*.

The history of the Hungarians between the end of the Ugrian period and their arrival in the Danube valley at the end of the ninth century AD is obscure. After breaking away from the other Ugrians, they certainly moved southwards; they may also have crossed the Urals into Central Asia. In the course of time they became an equestrian people like the Turkic tribes with whom they came into close and lasting contact. The name *onogur* suggests that they were a federation, but whether they kept themselves separate from their Turkic neighbours cannot be determined. To outside observers they were no different from them. During this long period they were affected by repeated invasions from the east; in 460 Priscus mentions them as having been driven from their homeland by the Sabirs. The language shows that they came into contact, presumably in the North Caucasus region, with the Ossetes, from whom they acquired certain loanwords, e.g., *asszony* 'woman'. By the beginning of the ninth century they were living in the Lower Don and Dnieper valleys, organized in a loose clan and tribal federation.

In 892 their leader, Árpád, was allied with the Eastern Frankish chieftain Arnulf against the Moravian Svatopluk. Although the expedition was unsuccessful, Árpád was encouraged to raid the Danubian basin and loot the area of Pannonia. Meanwhile their former homeland had been occupied by the Petchenegs, and they established themselves at very little cost in their present habitat.

For the first half-century of their history in Europe, the Hungarians used their new homeland as a base for sudden and lengthy raids on the richer lands further west. They reached Bremen, Nîmes and the coast of Italy on various occasions, and kept their western neighbours in a state of constant terror. Only when Otto the Great defeated them on the Lech in 955 were they effectively restrained.

Meanwhile Christian missionaries from both the eastern and western churches succeeded in gaining a foothold among the pagan Hungarians. The coronation of Stephen as king in 1000 AD represented a victory for Rome and at the same time linked Hungary firmly with the fortunes of Western Europe, politically and culturally alike. But Hungary remained on an exposed flank, and her history has been full of misfortune and tragedy. It says much for the tenacity of the Hungarian people that they have always been able to recover from the most appalling disasters. The first of these occurred in 1241–42, when the Tatars, who had been threatening eastern Europe since the early part of the century, overran and devastated the country. Two centuries later the Turks, who had been slowly but surely advancing into Europe, were effectively checked at Belgrade by János Hunyadi in 1456. There was a brief period of glory under Matthias Corvinus (1458–90) when the arts flourished and the court was amongst the most brilliant in Europe, but after his death there was a rapid decline. The year 1514 saw a violent peasant revolt under György Dózsa and equally violent reprisals on the part of the aristocracy. At this time the codification of customary law was being drawn up, and the resulting volume, known as the *Tripartitum*, contained the savage aftermath of the insurrection, a law which condemned virtually the whole of the peasantry to perpetual servitude.

The Turks struck again and in 1526 routed the Hungarian army at Mohács. The country was then divided; a small part of West Hungary came under rule from Vienna, the Turks established themselves in the central plain, and Transylvania became an autonomous principality under Turkish suzerainty. To add piquancy to the situation it was now that the Reformation began to spread in Hungary. The Turks remained until the end of the following century, leaving a trail of destruction and depopulation. Peace was not fully restored until the end of the insurgent war of Rákóczi in 1711.

The eighteenth century was a time of slow and uneven recovery. On the one hand the aristocracy were able to build fine late baroque palaces and extend their holdings of land, while at the other end of the scale the agricultural population became increasingly poverty-stricken. Towards the end of the century, new ideas began to take root; these, together with the attempted reforms of Joseph II and the after-effects of the French revolution, prepared the way for the rise of nationalism in the succeeding century. Intense intellectual and political activity preceded the revolution of 1848, its collapse in the following year and the compromise with Austria in 1867, which opened the door to foreign investment in Hungary and the rapid growth of industry. The First World War saw the disintegration of Austria-Hungary and a brief taste of communism under Béla Kun in 1919. In this same year Hungary was reduced almost to her present size. The inter-war period was one of continual economic and social uncertainty. Then came the ruin and defeat of the country in the Second World War, followed by the absorption of Hungary into the Soviet sphere of influence.

This chequered history has left indelible traces on the language. The vocabulary in particular reflects the numerous and lasting contacts of Hungarian with other languages. There are many Turkic loanwords, for example, from before 896 AD, the traditional date of the occupation of the Pannonian basin. Most of these mirror the change from an earlier fishing and hunting society to new and more advanced forms of production; they are connected with animal husbandry, agriculture, crafts and social life. The later Turkish occupation was by no means as productive of loanwords. The Slavonic languages had a particularly strong influence on Hungarian during the first few centuries after the occupation of Hungary. Most of the vocabulary concerning the Christian faith was transmitted via Slavonic, as were many words connected with a settled existence, including agricultural terms, crafts, and domestic life. Latin has had a lasting effect on Hungarian; not only was it the language of the church, but it was also the official language of state until the middle of the nineteenth century. The extent of this influence can be seen, for example, on the future participle, which is formed by adding *-ó/-ő* to the now extinct future forms in *-and/-end*, i.e., *áll* 'stand' *áll-and-ó* 'that shall stand', 'permanent'; similarity to the Latin gerundive has resulted in the use of such forms as *fizet-endő* 'to be paid' < *fizet* 'pay'. Several Latin words, e.g., *sors* 'fate', and Latinized forms are common. Much more significant, however, has been the influence of Latin on the whole of Hungarian linguistic study and thought; many of the supposed difficulties of the language can be traced to the attempt to relate it to Indo-European concepts and ideas which are ill-suited to it. German has also had a lengthy influence on Hungarian; the earliest loans in the period from the twelfth to the fifteenth century are concerned mainly with town life and aristocratic society, while those from later centuries show a preponderance of military and commercial terms. Apart from these main influences, there are borrowings from Greek, French, Italian and Rumanian.

It is noteworthy that Hungarian is the least conservative of the Finno-Ugrian languages. Moreover, the traffic in loanwords is by no means one-sided – the commonest Hungarian loan in English is undoubtedly 'coach', from the place-name *Kocs*, adj. *kocsi*.

Towards the end of the eighteenth century a linguistic reform was initiated in Hungary, partly directed on nationalistic grounds against undesirable foreign words and partly to enable the language to accommodate the flood of new concepts then current. The movement continued for almost a century and completely altered the face of the language. Old words, or imagined ancient roots, were revived and the opportunities offered by derivation were fully exploited to create new compounds. The results can be seen everywhere in the modern language. It is also possible to follow some of the thought-processes of the early advocates of reform, as in *anyag* 'material' < *anya* 'mother', cf. Latin *mater ~ materies*. The Academy of Sciences has since its foundation kept a careful and generally judicious watch on developments such as this. From time to time there have been attempts to 'purify' the language; the influx of modern technical terms in recent years has overwhelmed such vain attempts effectively.

Until the present century, Hungary was a predominantly agricultural country. In 1906 some 19 per cent of the population were engaged in industry, but now there are more employed in industry than in agriculture. Methods were normally adopted from the west, fostered initially by the indigenous population and Christian missionaries. Fishing and hunting were of less importance. Many areas were found to be suited to viticulture, and the cultivation of the vine was developed especially in the volcanic region north of the Balaton and in the Tokaj area.

Animal husbandry also has a long history, particularly on the plains, where methods appear to have undergone a change during the long Turkish occupation of the region. Enormous herds of horses, cattle, sheep and pigs roamed freely, tended by herdsmen and their assistants who spent most of their time with the animals, receiving periodical supplies of food from the owners. There were strict social grades among the herdsmen, as indeed there were throughout the peasant society of Hungary. The romantic picture of the hard-drinking, dancing horseherd and the gypsy minstrel, fostered by light opera of the last century, is based on a relatively modern tradition. With the gradual increase of agriculture and the more efficient irrigation and flood-control on the plain, this mode of life is fast disappearing.

The pattern of settlement in Hungary has been determined by many factors, both environmental and historical. The contrast between Transdanubia and the plain has already been mentioned. There is no universal pattern; older villages often display a completely irregular plan, while some of those settled in the eighteenth century have a chessboard pattern. There are also ribbon settlements, particularly in narrow valleys, where the houses are built sideways to the village street, the front of the house facing a yard in which numerous outbuildings and sheds are to be found. Beyond these lie gardens, and then open arable land. As the villages vary, so do architectural styles, from the wooden houses of the Székely area, with their high-pitched roofs, to the brick or clay buildings of the great plain. Here the general type is a long, single-storied building with a veranda; inside there are at least two rooms, separated by a kitchen. In the older houses, chimneys were not always in evidence; the smoke from the stove was allowed to escape either through the door or into a loft, from which it found its way eventually into the air. The beehive stove with seats around it was a feature of some districts. Externally and internally decoration tends to be simple; white is the colour preferred. The wall of the veranda, however, may be embellished with gay floral or geometrical designs which vary from place to place. There is considerable variation in the furnishings of the houses. One of the most striking features is the pile of mattresses, pillows and bedclothes stacked high on the bed; another common characteristic is the large wooden chest, often carved and highly decorated.

Dress also varies from district to district. Of the men's garments the long sheepskin cloak or *suba*, particularly associated with the herdsmen on the great plain, is notable. During the winter it is worn with the fur inside, but when summer comes it is reversed; the outside is often highly decorated with coloured embroidery or appliqué. Another traditional garment is the white cloth coat or *szűr*, worn draped over the shoulders. This may be plain and practical or embroidered with colourful local motifs and worn only on special occasions. At one time pleated white linen trousers that gave the appearance of a skirt were also in fashion. This type of garb, however, is rarely seen now; factory products have long been available and have virtually ousted the earlier and more colourful garments.

The same is true of women's dress. There were many varieties of blouse and skirt – or as often as not, skirts, for particularly in the later years of the last century there was in some districts a fashion for narrow waists emphasized by an abundance of short skirts worn on top of each other. Here as elsewhere, where longer and fewer garments were the rule, the apron that covered them might be ornamented with geometrical or floral designs. Women's headdress varied according to status and age; a glance would reveal whether the wearer was unmarried, engaged, married or widowed.

Popular art also reflects a profusion of trends. There are the small, delicately-wrought articles in bone and wood made by herdsmen to their own design, and the highly complicated and riotously colourful embroideries favoured by the women in certain areas. Flowers, particularly the rose, tulip and carnation, are frequently found, either carved or embroidered. There are also many varieties of bird and numerous purely geometrical designs. The choice of design and colour is based on local tradition. In the Matyó district of northern Hungary, for example, large floral designs in a profusion of colours are the rule; in other districts it is possible to find geometrical patterns worked only in red and black. Household articles, notably earthenware jars and bowls, are similarly colourful and varied.

There is a lengthy tradition of folk poetry in Hungary, where interest in its products has been stimulated since the early nineteenth century. There are no traces of early epic, but fragments of secular lyric have survived from before the Turkish occupation, and suggest that there was a lively oral tradition. Of the earlier poems, the so-called 'flower-songs' are notable; these are love songs in which the lovers – either male or female – were called 'flower', or in more recent times were given the names of specific flowers. There are also bird songs of the same type.

The vast corpus of Hungarian folk song, associated particularly with the names of Bartók and Kodály, is now in course of publication. It would be difficult, if not impossible, to find in it specific national characteristics. Much of it is notably unsentimental and contains very concrete pictures. Often the first line of a poem will have no visible connection with the remainder of the text. The whole is generally brief and pithily expressed. It bears, in fact, all the traces of a long settled history and mingling with other peoples as well as the existence alongside the oral tradition of an increasingly effective literary activity. In rhythm and melody there are many varieties. Much research has been devoted to the pentatonic melodies found in Hungary, and links between them and Cheremis have been postulated. Since both these languages were strongly influenced by Turkic, it seems likely that the melodies also should be regarded as possessing Turkic rather than Finno-Ugrian characteristics.

The Hungarians have few instruments to accompany their songs – indeed their tradition is more vocal than instrumental. The zither, which is relatively easy to make, is the most popular instrument, and bagpipes have long been known in the country.

The long Christian tradition in Hungary has not completely eradicated traces of an earlier shamanistic religion. In some instances there is evidence of a mixture of the two, as for example in the three kings of the epiphany, who wear tall 'dunce's hats' with streamers and carry drums with a representation of the sun, moon and stars on them. These can be traced back to the shaman's dress and drum. There are also primitive, probably magical, elements in the *regösénekek*, songs now connected with the winter solstice, with their weird refrain.

The Hungarians have the longest literary tradition of all the Finno-Ugrian peoples. They brought with them into their present habitat a runic script of a Turkic type, but this was replaced with the arrival of Christian missionaries by Latin script. The vicissitudes of history have spared very few relics of early Hungarian. The first connected text is a funeral oration of about 1200 AD, while the earliest known verse is a *planctus* of almost a century later; this latter displays such remarkable virtuosity that one can only regret the lack of further examples of the culture of this period.

Hungarian literature can be conveniently divided into two general periods. The first extends to the end of the eighteenth century and is concerned with the European movements of the times. Latin was the predominant literary language until the Reformation, as in the rest of continental Europe. Codexes in Hungarian have survived from the middle of the fifteenth century; though printing made an early appearance there (in 1473), it was not until the Reformation that there was an upsurge in literary activity. The first grammar to concern itself with Hungarian problems was published by János Sylvester in 1539 (*Grammatica Hungaro-Latina*). The long lyric tradition in Hungarian is most effectively represented at this time by the soldier-poet Bálint Balassi (1554–94), whose verse displays a combination of technical brilliance and passionate emotion. The religious disputes of this and the succeeding century gave rise to some fine rhetorical prose.

The eighteenth century was one of isolated experiment in verse and prose, leading to the opening of the second, modern period of literature which began with the rise of nationalism and attempts to reform the language. From this time onwards literary activity was closely associated with national aspirations; in a country where political opposition was discouraged, literature fulfilled this rôle. The powerful surge of romanticism and demands for reform found expression in the works of such lyric poets as Petőfi before erupting into the revolution of 1848. At the turn of the century, the demands of relatively new urban society were met by the significantly-named journal *Nyugat* 'West' which notably kept a watching brief on developments in Western European literature, but allowed room for experiments in Hungarian writing. Connected with this was the most controversial and most distinctive of all modern Hungarian poets, Endre Ady (1877–1919), whose fierce and tortured symbolism strained the language to the utmost. Between the two world wars, when the fate of Hungariandom and increasing social and economic problems dogged the nation, literary figures, such as the novelist Zsigmond Móricz, the essayist László Németh, and a stream of lyric poets concerned themselves with these questions. Modern Hungarian literature provides a large panorama; like most eastern European literatures, by its very nature it tends to be inward-looking and for this reason alone it has found some difficulty in penetrating a wider audience. There is the further problem of translation. The lyric verse which is undoubtedly the chief glory of the literature makes full use not only of the remarkable flexibility of the language, but also of rhythmic and metrical possibilities which can rarely be interpreted effectively.

Hungarian music, on the other hand, has found no barriers to its widespread acceptance. The names of Liszt, Bartók and Kodály and their contribution to the musical world are universally known and appreciated. Moreover, the stream of conductors and interpreters of music brought up in the Hungarian tradition provides testimony to the effectiveness of musical education in the country.

Of the other arts, it is in film that Hungarian activity has been most appreciated. In the realm of medicine and the sciences Hungary has been more than lavish in her contribution to the world.

The Ob-Ugrians

GENERAL OBSERVATIONS

Ob-Ugrian is the collective name for the languages and peoples known as Vogul (Man'si) and Ostyak (Chanti). Both live in the

Map 3. The Ob-Ugrians and Samoyeds

I Nenets
▲ Enets
↗ Nganasans
△ Selkups
∽ Voguls
} Ostyaks

area mainly covered by the Chanti-Man'si National Region, whose extent is some 550,000 square kilometres, with a population of 125,000. The capital is Chanti-Man'siysk. This part of Western Siberia is a great plain some 100–150 metres above sea level, with a narrow strip close to the eastern slopes of the Urals which reaches an average height of 700–800 metres. Almost the whole of the National Region falls into the taiga zone, but to the north there is scrub country with scanty forests, an area which leads into the tundra proper. A third of the region is covered by forests, mainly of evergreens, though deciduous beech-woods account for about a fifth of them. Many rivers flow through the forests, and these are surrounded by extensive marshlands. The climate is unfavourable, characterized by long, cold winters and brief, relatively warm summers. The average temperature rises from − 20° to − 22°C in January to 15° to 17°C in July. Both spring and autumn are cold; night frosts are not uncommon in June. The average growth period for plants is 120 days, which makes this an unfavourable area for agriculture.

The Voguls and Ostyaks are settled along the banks of the rivers, and it is by the names of these that their settlements are generally known. The Voguls dwell in their national area between the Urals and the Lower Ob, along the River Sosva and its tributary the Sigva; they are also to be found along the Konda, which flows into the Irtysh, and the Lozva, Vagilsk and Pelimka, all tributaries of the Tavda. The Ostyaks inhabit an even larger region. They are found along the lower and middle Ob and its tributaries, the Kazim, Irtysh, Konda, Yugan, Tremyugan, Vah and Vasyugan.

According to the census figures for 1970 there were some 7,700 Voguls, of whom 59.2 per cent spoke Vogul; while some 77 per cent of a total of 21,000 Ostyaks spoke this language. A glance at the map shows that these few thousand folk must live in small and widely scattered settlements in a vast area. This in turn implies that both languages are divided into several dialects, often differing so greatly from one another that contact between their speakers is impossible.

The geographical distribution of the Voguls gives a clue to their dialect regions. Most of them speak the northern dialect (located chiefly along the Sosva and upper Lozva), which itself has several subdivisions, notably those of the Sosva, Sigva and Upper Lozva. This northern dialect forms the basis of the literary language, since it is the most widely spoken. The western dialect region again consists of a variety of dialects, some now moribund, in the Lower Lozva, Pelimka and Vagilsk river valleys. The eastern dialect region is to be found along the Konda valley, while the fourth dialect, the southern, must now be regarded as dead. At the beginning of the century it was still spoken along the Tavda, but the inhabitants of the Vogul villages here have been absorbed into the Tatar and Russian population and have given up their original language. The differences between this Tavda dialect and those of the north were so vast that communication was impossible in the Vogul tongue. As we shall see, there were also great differences in their way of life and general culture, a situation that is repeated among the eastern and northern groups.

There are three main dialect regions of Ostyak. The northern region includes those dialects spoken along the Ob from its mouth to Sherkali, i.e., the dialects of Obdorsk, Berjozov, Kazim, and Sherkali. The southern region extends from Sherkali to the mouth of the Irtysh, but also includes those dialects spoken along the tributaries of the latter river, the Nizam, Irtysh, Demyanka and Konda dialects. The eastern dialect region extends east of the mouth of the Irtysh along the middle Ob and its tributaries, and includes the dialects of Salim, Surgut (Tremyugan, Yugan) and Vah-Vasyugan. These dialects vary so considerably from each other that it has not been possible to develop from any one a unified literary language. After lengthy experiments, in 1957–58 textbooks were devised for schools in the Ostyak region; these take the Kazim, Vah and Surgut dialects as their basis, and are used in the schools where these dialects are spoken. There were so few speakers of the southern dialects that no books were considered necessary for this area. There are therefore three Ostyak literary languages in use today, or four if the works in the Sherkali dialect, introduced in 1940, are included.

The name used by the Voguls for their own people is *Man'si*; the Ostyaks call themselves *Chanti*. The first of these names is connected with the *Magy-* element in *Magyar*, while *Chanti* may be compared with Hungarian *had* 'host, army', which originally had the meaning of 'nationality'. The names Vogul and Ostyak, used generally in Russian and foreign sources, are unknown to them. *Vogul* is probably identical with the name of one of the tributaries of the Ob, the Vogulka (in Vogul *võl'-jã*, 'River Vol' and in Ostyak *woγal'-joγan* 'River *Woγal'*). The word *võl'* appears in other river names, and its general meaning is 'a straight channel between two bends in a river'.

The origin of *Ostyak* can likewise be found in that language. It is customary to name the various Ostyak groups after the river alongside which they live, e.g. *waγ-jaχ* 'Vah folk', *χunte-jaχ* 'Konda folk'. Thus the folk who live along the banks of the Ob are known as *as-jaχ*, *as* being the Ostyak name for this river. This name was given by the Russians to the Ostyaks in general. It acquired a slightly different form in Russian, where the 'nationality' suffix is *-jak*, e.g., *poljak* 'Polish', and a secondary *-t-* appeared between the two elements of the compound.

The Ob-Ugrians live in a wooded, marshy region where for more than six months of the year an average of two metres of snow covers the ground. The climate is cold and continental. In summer the rivers flood the low left banks for several kilometres, and even the right banks may occasionally be inundated. This bleak land, rich as it may be in fish, game and natural beauty, is not inhabited solely by the Ob-Ugrians. In the Tavda and Irtysh regions of the south, they are mingled with Siberian Turkic peoples (Tatars) and Russians, who are slowly absorbing them. In the north, on the lower reaches of the Ob, and in the east they have Samoyed neighbours, the Nenets and Selkups. Here too there are many joint settlements, and particularly along the Ob there is evidence of bilingualism and Samoyed absorption. On the west they have contacts with the Zyryans.

The influence of these neighbours is reflected in the loanwords from their languages. In both Ostyak and Vogul Russian loanwords are found in the greatest numbers. Most of these, apart from some older borrowings, reflect social transformation, new economic forms and names for concepts and objects connected with modern life. Tatar loanwords are found chiefly in the southern dialects of both languages. These are concerned mainly with agriculture and stockbreeding. Similar words, usually names for domestic equipment of a more advanced type, have been adopted from Zyryan. Words concerned with reindeer breeding and certain objects of clothing have entered the northern dialects of both languages from Nenets, while Selkup has left its mark on the eastern dialects of Ostyak, particularly in the Vah-Vasyugan area.

Anthropologically the Voguls and Ostyaks are unlike the other modern Finno-Ugrians, and are perhaps nearest to the Samoyeds. They show mongoloid characteristics, with depigmentation of eyes and hair; they have snub noses, broadening noticeably towards the nostrils, mesocephalic heads, comparatively small faces and short stature. They are classed by anthropologists as Europo-Sibirid or Uralic. This type came into existence through an amalgamation of Europid and Mongoloid elements, and developed later, according to Debets, with an admixture of Americanoid and

Sayan-Mongoloid strains. It is noteworthy that this Uralic type, general among the Ob-Ugrians, was an important component of the early Hungarians, as Pál Lipták's researches have shown.

HISTORY AND SOCIAL LIFE

The name 'Ob-Ugrian' is not merely a geographical appellation; there is also a close historical connection between the Voguls and Ostyaks. We have already seen how the Ugrians split into two main groups, and how the northern Ugrians then became mingled with a foreign hunting people of Western Siberian origin. It was this development, which occurred in the middle of the first millennium BC, that gave rise to the present ethnic composition of the Ob-Ugrians. Although this ethnic influence was important, it cannot be associated with the formation of the Vogul and Ostyak languages, which were separated relatively late in their history. The close relationship of these languages, the customs, way of life, folk traditions and superstitions of the two peoples all show that their material and intellectual life followed the same pattern. The first records to mention them do not distinguish between them.

The history of the Ob-Ugrians is known only from the eleventh century onwards; before that time very little is known of their fate. Towards the end of the Ugrian period they were living in the wooded areas of the Kama river and to the south of it; this remained their home for a long time. It is possible that the ancestors of the Ob-Ugrians are the *Amadoci* of Hellanicus, the Greek author of a description of Scythia in the fifth century BC. This name appears in later works, notably in those of Ptolemy. Their home was stated to be at the confluence of the Kama and Volga rivers. The name itself is of Iranian origin and means 'raw meat eater'. This is an Ob-Ugrian custom, and both folk tradition and historical sources refer to it. Information concerning the Amadoci passed from the Iranians to the Greeks, doubtless through the commercial connections that existed between them at an early period.

The Russian chronicles of the eleventh century refer to the *Jugors*, and this is without doubt their name for the Ob-Ugrians. Describing the events of the year 1096, the Kievan chronicle cites an account of these folk from an inhabitant of Novgorod named

Rogovich, who sent his servant to the Pechora and thence to 'Jugra':

> The Jugras [Jugors] have a dumb language [i.e. incomprehensible to strangers]; to the north their neighbours are the Samoyeds ... The Jugors said to my servant, 'We have made a strange discovery, of which nothing was heard before, and which came to light only three years ago. Towards the sea there is a range of mountains whose height reaches the heavens, and in these mountains much shouting and talking can be heard; the folk strike at the mountain as if they wish to bore through it. A small opening is cut into the mountain, and through this they talk, but their language cannot be understood; gesticulating with their hands, they point at iron, as if that is what they are demanding, and if anyone gives them a knife or an axe, they give furs in return. The road to these mountains is impassable because of ravines, snow and forests, so we cannot always reach them.

This Russian *Jugor, Jugra* refers to the ancestors of the modern Voguls and Ostyaks, and is frequently found in later sources. Arab writers from the eleventh to the fifteenth century tell of a northern country called *Jura*, but their information is second or third hand and it must be treated with caution.[1]

1 Muhammad i Aufi, writing in the thirteenth century, states that the country of the Jura can be reached by dog-sleigh from Bulgaria on the Volga. This is an important reference to the use of dogs by northern peoples. He also says of the Jura folk: 'They bind cattle (? reindeer) bones under their feet, and take two pointed sticks in their hands, sticking them into the snow behind them, and thus slide along the surface of the snow ...' This is the first description of the ski used by the Ob-Ugrians. Later he describes how the Volga-Bulgars trade clothing, salt and other goods with the inhabitants for fine sable furs.

This description tallies with the fourteenth-century Ibn Battuta's account of the country of darkness. Many associate this with Jugra, but for us this is a secondary consideration. He is, however, worth quoting, both on the use of dogs in harness and on the so-called 'silent barter' typical of trade between merchants from the south and northern peoples:

'The road there [i.e., to the country of darkness] can be undertaken only by small wagons [sleighs] drawn by large dogs. For in that wilderness so great is the ice that neither men's feet nor horses' hooves can stand firmly upon it; the dogs, however, have claws with which they can cling on to the ice. The only folk who dare to cross this wilderness are rich merchants who have a hundred or more wagons [sleighs], loaded with food, drink and firewood, for there are no trees, stones or settlements there. In this country the guides are the dogs, which have often made the journey. They cost about 1,000 dinars apiece. The wagon is harnessed to the guide-dog's neck,

The names *Jugra*, *Jugria* and *Jugoria* can all be found in West European histories and geographies between the fifteenth and eighteenth centuries, where they are used to describe the land inhabited by the Voguls and Ostyaks. In Russian sources the name Vogul appears in the fourteenth century and Ostyak in the sixteenth century, and these gradually oust the words *jugor* and *Jugra* – a sign that the Ob-Ugrians, hitherto considered to be one people, had come to be recognized as two separate groups in foreign eyes. Although the older term virtually ceases to exist during the eighteenth century, it appears in geographical names to the present day: e.g., *Jugorskie gor'* (the Ural Mountains), *Jugorskij bereg* (Jugrian coast, on the southern shore of the Kara Sea) and *Jugorskij Shar* (Jugrian Straits, between the island of Vaygach and the mainland). The word has been adopted by the Zyryans from Russian, where in the form *jegra* it has been used sporadically for the Voguls, but occasionally also for the Ostyaks.[1]

It is difficult to locate Jugria. According to the Kievan chronicle, Rogovich's servant travelled in the region of the River Pechora and therefore cannot have been far from the Kama area. His

---

and three others are attached to it. He is the leader, and the others will follow him. If he stops, so do the others. This dog is never struck by his owner, nor provoked by shouts. When it is time to eat, the dogs are fed before the men, otherwise the guide-dog becomes angry, then runs away and leaves his master to certain destruction. After a journey of forty days in this extensive wilderness, travellers encamp on the bounds of the country of darkness. There they all leave their wares and return to their camp. The following day they go back to look at their goods, when they find placed opposite to them sable, grey squirrel and ermine furs. If the merchant is satisfied with the wares he finds set down by his own, he takes them away; if not, he leaves them there, and others are added to them. Sometimes, however, the inhabitants of the country of darkness take away their own goods and leave the merchants' wares in place. This is how they barter. The folk who travel there do not know whethei those who sell to them and buy from they are djinns or human beings, and they never see anyone.' (J. Markwart, *Ungarische Jahrbücher* IV, 288–90.)

Marco Polo gives a similar description (IV, 20–1) of a fur-hunting people in the Irtysh region of the country of the Tatar khan Konchi, and an account of the country of darkness to the north of this. He does not mention Jugria, but it may be postulated that he is talking of the Jugors then living in Siberia.

1 The name *Jugra* is customarily connected with the words *Ungar*, *hongrois*, *ungri*, the names given by foreign sources to the Magyars, which in the last instance are based on a Turkic tribal name *on(o)gur*. According to the Hungarian scholar Zsirai, Russian *Jugra* is derived from an earlier *Ugra*; this in turn arises from the same Turkic **ongur* and applied to the Ob-Ugrians: the Slav **ongr-*, **ungr-* forms from the same root were applied to the Hungarians. This is a pleasing explanation and a possible one, but there are difficulties which prevent its wholehearted acceptance.

account makes it clear that Jugria could have been close to the Pechora and south of the Samoyeds – in other words along the Kama. The mountains in his story can probably be equated with the Urals. But there is no word of the servant having crossed them, indeed the reverse seems to be true. So the land of the Jugors at this time probably lay on the European side of the Urals, between these mountains and the Kama. The eastern frontier of this region may possibly have stretched into Siberia.

Between the twelfth and the fifteenth centuries the Russians and Zyryans gradually pushed eastwards, and the area of Jugria was also extended farther east. The Chuvash people, who lived to the south of Zyryans, forced these latter farther north and east as they extended their bounds, whereupon the Zyryans began to penetrate the Ugrian areas and appropriate their land. This was undoubtedly one of the reasons why the ancestors of the Ob-Ugrians crossed into the thinly populated parts of Western Siberia and began to settle there. This movement was later encouraged by the attempts of the rulers of Novgorod and the Russians to conquer Jugria and Siberia. Campaigns were launched by Novgorod in the twelfth century to conquer Jugria, and from 1265 onwards Jugria appears in the lists of *volosts* or 'counties' belonging to it. Naturally the Jugrians tried to rid themselves of the unpleasant burden of taxation, and this is the reason for the frequent military campaigns of the princes of Novgorod which often led to bitter conflicts. The history of these campaigns also indicates the eastward migration of the people of Jugria; in 1365 the Novgorod army had to cross the Urals and advance to the River Ob to extort taxes from them. Thus by the second half of the fourteenth century the area of Jugria had extended across the Urals to the Ob.

When Novgorod became part of the centralized Russian Empire in 1487, the new Russian capital, Moscow became the centre for cultural and economic links between the Russians and the peoples of Siberia. During the fifteenth and sixteenth centuries new settlements were founded west of the Urals (Izhevsk, Ust-Tsilma and Pustozersk, now Naryan-Mar), and these became important trading stations for the Samoyeds and Ob-Ugrians. During the fifteenth century three campaigns, launched by Ivan III, strengthened the links between the Russian Empire and the territories beyond the Urals. The second of these penetrated along the Pelimka and Tavda valleys to the Irtysh and from there along the Ob to the territory of the Jugors. So by the end of the fifteenth century the centre of the Jugrian region was in Siberia. Final conquest of this region took place in 1499–1500 at the time of the third expedition. In a letter from Ivan III to Matthias Corvinus, dated 29 July 1488, the Russian Tsar uses the title 'Great Prince of the Jugors', the first to use this style.

Although the centre of Jugria was now in Siberia, this does not imply a complete break with Europe. On the western slopes of the Urals, south-west of the present Vogul area, there are numerous place and river names which can be interpreted through common Vogul words. They all indicate that the Voguls and Ostyaks still lived in considerable numbers in their old European habitat after Jugria had become centred in Siberia. Accounts of the seventeenth and eighteenth centuries also mention the Vogul inhabitants of the area between the Kama and Chusovaya rivers; in 1860 there were sixty-nine of them living in the district of Cherdin on the European side of the Urals. But the fate of these fragmented groups, even if they maintained contact with their brethren in Siberia, was sealed. They became submerged in the Russian population about them, and only a few dozen place and river names record their presence there.

The majority of the Voguls and Ostyaks were living in Siberia at the turn of the sixteenth century, when Herberstein's map shows *Iuhra* beside the Ob, with the remark 'Inde ungarorum origo' ('thence the Hungarians originate').[1] By now the Russians were familiar with the route through the Pechora region to the Ob, and by the end of the century with that continuing to the Yenisei.

---

1 Part of Herberstein's description of Jugria is worth citing: 'This is that same Juharia whence the Hungarians went forth and conquered the land of Pannonia, or Hungary; they also occupied several countries of Europe under their leader Attila. The people of Moscow are therefore very proud to this day that their subjects once swarmed over the larger part of Europe ... Some say that even today the Juhars speak the same language as the Hungarians, but I do not know whether this is so. For though I have made careful enquiries, I have not found anyone from this land with whom my servant, who speaks Hungarian well, could talk.' (Siegmund Herberstein, *Moscouiter Wunderbare Historien*, Basle, 1567, XCIII.) This somewhat naive account is one of the first records of the linguistic connection between Hungarian and Ob-Ugrian. According to Herberstein the Juhars paid regular fur taxes to the Tsar at the beginning of the sixteenth century.

The conquest of Siberia was not yet complete; it was, to quote Marx, the campaigns of Yermak (1581–85) that 'laid the foundations of Asiatic Russia'.

The conquest of Siberia, however, was not merely a display of military might. The campaigns played an important part in opening up the country and putting it on the map. Topographical data were collected, as were details of population, language and customs, in order to build up communications and trading settlements. So the campaigns were partly of an expeditionary nature, and it is due to them that knowledge of Siberia as far as the Pacific Ocean was widespread by the middle of the seventeenth century. The only strong state in Siberia at this time was the Tatar Khanate, which put up strong resistance to the Russians. This had been created in the fourteenth century out of the wreckage of the Golden Horde, and was situated on the middle reaches of the Irtysh. Its influence was extended northwards, so that by 1500 the southern Voguls and Ostyaks were paying tribute to the Tatars. Internal strife a century later resulted in a victory for Khan Küchüm, and in this both Ugrian peoples played some part. At this time his territory extended as far as the mouth of the Irtysh. Russian troops soon put an end to Tatar domination, as they destroyed Küchüm's empire and released the inhabitants of Western Siberia from this oppressive rule.

To the Russians, 'Jugria' doubtless referred to the western part of the area settled by the Ob-Ugrians; thus it was the Voguls who were chiefly concerned here, since their habitat, to judge from the present pattern of settlement, was west of the Ostyaks. The term *Vogul* first appears in 1396, and *Ostyak* about 1500. The late appearance of the latter name does not prove that the separation of the two peoples occurred only during the intervening period. Doubtless Proto-Vogul and Proto-Ostyak were in existence at the time of the first references to Jugria, but their similarity, in addition to the identical mode of life followed by their speakers, made it impossible for foreigners to detect any distinction between them. Only when the Russians acquired a better knowledge of the Siberian peoples was this distinction observed.[1] Thus the circumstances of the separation of the two languages are unknown, and the history of the two peoples is closely interwoven. Ethnically

1 See p. 217 below.

the most important moment in their common history was when they became mingled with some Palaeo-Siberian element originating in Western Siberia. This occurred as the Ugrian period was ending; then it is possible to trace the time when they became known to the western world through the Russians. We may also deduce that when Jugria extended into Siberia it became divided during the fourteenth to sixteenth centuries. The northern area came under Russian domination and the southern under Tatar rule. The results of this division can be seen in both language and culture. Its effects were increased by the collapse of Tatar domination and the settlement of Russians, chiefly in the southern part of Jugria. So the southernmost Vogul and Ostyak groups were subjected to the greatest foreign influence, both Tatar and Russian, a situation which is reflected in the southern dialects of both languages.

Although the two peoples have been distinguished from the sixteenth century onwards, their history has remained similar, rooted as it is in that of Western Siberia as a whole. By the year 1600 and for some time afterwards, the Russians had established new fortified settlements in the region, partly to ensure their domination and partly for trading purposes. Surgut, Pelim, Berjozov and Obdorsk (now Salehard) were originally small military settlements, but they soon developed into administrative and trading centres, where taxes were collected and goods sold to the Voguls and Ostyaks. The administration of this vast area was no simple task. While local disputes were settled by the parties concerned, the Russian administrators confined their activity mainly to collecting taxes and, to a lesser extent, to converting the population to Christianity. This latter activity was admittedly in the hands of the church, but the authority of the state was often called in to ensure its success. The size of the territory alone made this task difficult, and results were achieved only by adroit organization.

The Voguls and Ostyaks lived in tribal groups. Russian officials gave the leaders of these groups the title of 'Prince' and exercised their power through them. These 'princes' represented their people and their affairs, and from the seventeenth century onwards their names occur frequently in official tax documents and lists. Each regional authority was divided into several tax districts which, in the case of the northern peoples, were identical with the tribal groups. In the Surgut area, for example, the Ostyaks were divided into five regions and twenty-one tax-districts or tribal groups. These latter were the smallest administrative units. The princes were illiterate, but the tax lists were prepared from the information they supplied; they also had to vouch for them by drawing beneath each list the *tamga* of the tribal group. This *tamga* was a totemistic sign which from primeval times had been associated with the tribe and was its property; it was closely connected with its name, for it was in effect a depiction of the totem ancestor of the tribe. Most frequently it was a stylized or even abstract drawing of some animal, bird or plant. Many of them may be seen in tax-registers beneath such sentences as: 'This tax list of the Yugan district has been certified correct by Prince Vas'ka Lokchakov in his own and his people's name with the sign of the black grouse.'

Some scholars have seen signs of feudalism in Ob-Ugrian society, but their tribal organization and way of life do not support this view.

Taxes were high and 'gifts' to the Russian administrators frequent. When the Vogul and Ostyak tribal groups saw how the administrative officials were growing rich on the valuable furs they supplied, they rebelled against the Russians. In 1592 there was a Vogul revolt led by 'Prince' Ablegirim, while in 1607 Anna, princess of the Konda, and Vasiliy, prince of Obdorsk, organized an Ostyak uprising and occupied the fort of Berjozov. This heralded a period of general unrest in Western Siberia, involving the Ostyaks of Surgut, the Tatars of the Irtysh, the Voguls and finally the Tatars of Tyumen and Tura; the revolt was crushed in 1609 and its leaders executed.

There were other facets of Russian exploitation also. From the seventeenth century onwards both Russian and Zyryan traders took advantage of the credulity of the Ob-Ugrians, buying their furs at rock-bottom prices and selling to them shoddy goods, salt, flour and (last but not least) spirits, which had hitherto been unknown to them. It was a favourite trick of the merchants to make their customers drunk, so that they would mortgage the following year's furs for the goods they received. Some of the population thus became completely subservient to the traders; in some areas the fishermen lost the entire catch of whole stretches of rivers to these unscrupulous folk. Through such practices, the Russian and Zyryan merchants slowly took over the best fishing and hunting grounds, while the Vogul and Ostyak population sank to the level of serfs.

Further risings took place during the nineteenth century, notably that of 1841, when some of the Ostyaks of Obdorsk joined the insurrection led by the Nenets Vavljo Nenang (otherwise known as Vauli Piettomin). The rebels attempted to besiege Obdorsk, but met with no success. In addition to the greedy traders of Russian and Zyryan origin, there were numbers of Russian émigrés who settled among the Ob-Ugrians. These occupied themselves with hunting and fishing and in the southern parts of the area with agriculture, and together with the exiles lived in relative harmony with the Voguls and Ostyaks. It was partly through these settlers that the Ob-Ugrians became acquainted with more advanced methods of production, including stockbreeding and agriculture in some places.

The Ob-Ugrians retained their patriarchal tribal society until the present century, and its traces can still be found among them. They are divided into two fraternities, one known in Vogul as *mōś* (Ostyak *mońt'*) and the other as *por*. Both practised exogamy: it was forbidden to marry within the fraternity. This may be a relic of an old matriarchal society in which the fraternity was composed entirely of blood-relatives descended from one common ancestor. Among the Voguls of the Ob and Sosva this custom is still observed, but elsewhere it has been superseded by a ban on marriage within the tribal group and the significance of the fraternity has diminished. Both fraternities consisted of several tribes, of which there was a surprisingly large number in recent times. Earlier in history there were far fewer such tribes; natural increase so swelled their numbers that they were compelled to divide. Thus the tribe was also a group of blood-relatives, but smaller than the fraternity. It only remains to add that the ban on marriage within the tribe is no longer strictly observed by the younger generation.

Each tribe, as has been seen, has its own particular name. The oldest of these take the names of totem animals, such as the beaver, bear and moose, from whom they believed themselves to have been descended. Later, when patriarchal society was at its zenith, the names were those of heroes. The *tamga*, or tribal sign, was the property of the tribe and used as its common signature. At one time these were drawn on their jurts and even tattooed on their bodies. As the tribal system disintegrated, these signs became personal or family property.

Writing of the Iroquois, Morgan notes that every tribe had its own personal names, which were its private property. This custom can be observed among the Voguls and Ostyaks, among whom a child at the age of fifteen received his final name from an earlier, deceased member of the tribe whose spirit then entered him. The spirits of the dead, like the living, belonged to tribes and might be reincarnated in the newly-born members of their own tribe; hence the system of inherited personal names. Associated with this belief was the tribal burial-ground in which it was forbidden to bury strangers.

The cult of animal worship was closely connected with the tribal system. The image representing the ancestor of the tribe was placed in a separate holy shrine where the tribe gathered to offer sacrifice. It was forbidden for other tribes to enter it, so that its site was usually in some out-of-the-way spot, difficult of access and unknown to the uninitiated. The ancestor protected the tribe and helped it in misfortune. Sacrifices were offered to obtain its favours, and to ensure success in hunting and fishing. Only members of the tribe were allowed to take part in the sacrificial ceremonies, which meant that wives and brothers-in-law, who were of foreign origin and very frequently of another fraternity, were excluded. One of the main ceremonies was the slaughter of the sacrificial beast, though very little of this ever reached the image. Usually its mouth was smeared with the blood and fat of the animal (often a reindeer) and the rest was consumed by the participants. These sacrifices were often associated with yearly (or less frequent) tribal festivals, when the life of the totem-ancestor was commemorated with heroic lays and songs, or dramatic scenes and dances of magic and totemistic significance were performed. The tribe thus formed a closed society, based on blood-relationship, and its members supported it through thick and thin. One of the manifestations of this was the necessity for the whole tribe to revenge the murder of any one of its members.

Each tribe had its leader, whose say in its affairs was decisive.

The disintegration of this ancient society probably began quite early in the history of the Ob-Ugrians, but it was a slow process. With the development of new means of livelihood and the opportunities offered by trade in the nineteenth century, money and goods began to play an increasing rôle in their lives and a more capitalistic society developed. Not only foreign traders, but Voguls and Ostyaks themselves began to grow rich at the expense of their poorer brethren as they acquired reindeer herds or better means of production, such as better nets and boats.

Nevertheless, Ob-Ugrian society retained its patriarchal characteristics until the beginning of the present century. Women had a subordinate place; in marriage the bride had no choice, for her parents discussed with the bridegroom her *kalim* or buying-price, which was normally paid in reindeer, domestic utensils, furs and clothing, and varied according to place and status. Castrén, the Finnish scholar, records that in the middle of the nineteenth century a rich Ostyak bride commanded a price of 50–100 reindeer in the Obdorsk region, while a poor father would accept 20–25 for his daughter to be taken off his hands. Polygamy was not forbidden, but from the last century onwards it has been rare for one man to have the means to buy and keep more than one wife. Traces of matriarchy lingered on in their wedding customs, including the so-called 'matrilocal' marriage-custom whereby the bridegroom worked for his future father-in-law for three or four years instead of paying the price for his bride. After this he might marry and move away, though not infrequently the young husband would continue to live in the same jurt with his wife's parents.

The main features of Ob-Ugrian religious life have already been mentioned: ancestor-worship and worship of the dead in general were its characteristic traits. A few further details will complete the sketch. The totem animal personifying the ancestor of the tribe might not be killed by its members. If they did so, a propitiatory ceremony was demanded, and the flesh of the dead animal might not be eaten. Apart from the spirits of the ancestors and the dead, natural phenomena and objects were treated with reverence. These included helpful and evil spirits of the water and the forest, as well as the highest god, Numi-Torem.

There were various categories of shaman, magician and sooth-sayer. The shaman was the priest of the tribe, whose presence was necessary at sacrificial ceremonies, the healing of sickness and the prevention of troubles. The existence of a separate order of shamans may well have come to an end long ago; their duties were performed later by old men of authority or by various inter-preters of dreams and soothsayers.

A special feature of their religious life was the cult of the bear. This cult certainly existed elsewhere, but among the Voguls and Ostyaks it appeared in a concentrated form unknown elsewhere. Its characteristics are best reflected in the ceremonies of the bear festivals which are commonly held in winter after a bear hunt. Various ceremonies are held before the hunt to ensure its success, but the main festival occurs afterwards, with plays and rituals that last for several days. First the bear is 'unbuttoned' and its 'cloak' is removed – in other words, it is skinned; then it is 'put into a cradle' – stuffed, placed on a sleigh and taken home to the accom-paniment of music and song. There the stuffed skin is set up on a platform and 'clothed' with broadcloth, skins and silks; it is then adorned and 'feasted'. After eating and drinking, the hunters propitiate the bear, apologizing for their deed and shifting re-sponsibility for it to the Russians who made the rifle. After this the bear is 'entertained' with bear songs and dances in its honour. Then follows further feasting, and satirical bear dramas are per-formed by masked men.

The bear festival continues for several days; although it is clear from several motifs that it originated as a propitiatory sacrifice, it has now lost its religious significance and has become a popular festival of eating, drinking, dancing, singing and plays. It is cele-brated yearly by the Ostyaks and Voguls.

Attempts to convert these people to Christianity during the seventeenth and eighteenth centuries led to frequent clashes be-tween them and the Russian missionaries, whose efforts were sup-ported by soldiers. Their resistance soon collapsed and they were forcibly compelled to accept Orthodoxy. This conversion was external; they continued their shamanistic practices and paid lip-service and ecclesiastical taxes to the God of the Russians. The monk Grigoriy Novitskiy, who took part in the crusade to convert the Ob-Ugrians at the beginning of the eighteenth century, records that the Konda Voguls were willing to accept baptism on three conditions: first, they wanted their idols to be baptized and placed alongside the icons in churches; secondly, they did not wish to be forbidden to eat horseflesh; and thirdly, they desired to remain polygamous and themselves to be permitted to baptize their wives. These demands show their reaction to the new faith and the limited effectiveness of the missionaries.

MATERIAL CULTURE

Considerable changes took place in the life of the Ob-Ugrians as they came into contact with other peoples. Only the most isolated groups in the north and east retained the hunting and fishing tradition intact as the basis of their livelihood. In the south, under Russian and Tatar influence, they turned to agriculture and stock-breeding, while those who lived on the borders of the tundra and the forests in the vicinity of the Nenets began like them to keep reindeer. Despite these variations, hunting and fishing retained their places as the most characteristic activities of the Voguls and Ostyaks. The importance of these two modes of life is not uniform throughout the region. Along the Ob and its tributaries, the Kazim, Sosva, Vah, Vasyugan, Agan and Yugan, fishing is predominant and hunting takes a secondary place. Those who live near the sources of the tributaries, however, are concerned chiefly with hunting, and fishing is merely an occasional occupation.

In the summer fishing season, the Ob-Ugrians move with their families to the Ob, where they establish their quarters until the river freezes. They then return to their winter dwellings with their catch; this is more than sufficient for the needs of the whole family and most of it is sold. Fishing is carried on throughout the year, in both summer and winter quarters. Various types of trap, net and pot are used, as well as harpoons and fish hooks.

In hunting they have two aims. They hunt wildfowl and game (particularly moose and wild reindeer) for food, and other animals for their fur, which provides them with their main income. The fur markets are always eager to obtain supplies of squirrel, marten, weasel, rabbit, fox, otter and other skins, and the skilled hunter can obtain a good income from them. In earlier times the sable was the most sought and most expensive fur, with the result that Vogul and Ostyak hunters almost succeeded in exterminating this animal in the pine forests of Western Siberia. The hunting season normally lasts from the end of September, when the first snow falls, till December, when the hunters return to their winter quarters. In the past they would dress the skins and set out in mid-January to market, where they paid their taxes, sold their furs and bought a year's requirements from the merchants. The second hunting season began after their return home, and lasted from February till April, when the snow began to melt and the hunters could move to their summer quarters by the river; here they spent their time fishing and hunting water fowl until the following autumn hunting season.

Today they hunt with rifles, but their weapons were once bows and arrows. Guns began to be used in the eighteenth century, but took a long time to achieve popularity and to replace their more primitive, home-made weapons; indeed bow and arrow were still in general use in the first quarter of the present century. The bow was made of two kinds of wood, the inside of Siberian pine, and the outside of beech; these were glued together and tightly bound with strips of birch bark boiled soft. This bow was about two metres long, and demanded great strength and agility. Numerous types of arrow were in use. For squirrel and other furred animals, club-tipped arrows were used, to prevent damage to the valuable skins. Pointed arrows, tipped with bone or iron, were used for big game or otters, while forked arrows were intended for duck and water fowl. There were flat-bladed, iron-tipped arrows for hunting reindeer; these were aimed at the hooves to cut the tendons, and when the animal fell it was killed with a knife thrust. The most interesting of the numerous other types was the whistling arrow; this had a hollow club-tip with two holes and in flight sounded like an attacking kite. When they heard it, flocks of waterfowl in flight would drop into or under the water in panic, and there the hunter had a relatively easy task to catch them. Spears were also used for killing larger animals, such as deer, moose and bears, but the usual method has always been to use traps, daggers and nets for these. Very many types of trap, sometimes with arrows, have been constructed to catch sable, squirrel, wolverine, ermine and other furred animals. The Voguls and Ostyaks are experts in this branch of knowledge. Nets are employed to catch flocks of birds.

Among the northern Ob-Ugrians reindeer breeding has been known since the fourteenth century. In some areas, notably towards the mouth of the Ob and its northern tributaries, it has become the basis of their economy. From the evidence of the vocabulary, it appears that reindeer breeding in its entirety has been taken from the Nenets, together with their way of life and even clothing. These groups are usually bilingual, and some of them, mainly Ostyaks, have been absorbed completely into the Samoyed tradition. Their herds are not so large as those of the Nenets. In spring these nomads penetrate as far as the shores of the Arctic Sea. Other Voguls and Ostyaks also breed reindeer: the Ostyaks of the Kazim, Vah and Agan districts and most of the Voguls use them in harness to pull sleighs.

Apart from reindeer, the dog is used to haul sleighs, chiefly among the Voguls of the Konda and the Ob-Ostyaks. Their use of the dog, however, is much more primitive than is found among the peoples of Eastern Siberia. Other animals are of even less importance. Horses, sheep and fowl can be found around the dwellings of the Ob-Ugrians in a few places. Cattle are even rarer.

Their knowledge of agriculture is primitive, although the Ostyaks of the Irtysh and the Tavda Voguls became acquainted with it centuries ago, mainly through the Tatars. The southern Ob-Ugrians used the hoe, and produced mainly oats and barley, which were harvested by simply pulling the stalks out by hand. Obviously these methods were not productive.

Their living-quarters are determined by their mode of life. The nomadic reindeer breeders live in Nenets-type tents, which are portable and can be erected and taken down swiftly and easily. Hunters and fishermen, who live a semi-settled existence, live either in lone jurts or scattered groups of them, two to ten in number and widely spaced. These settlements are called *paul* in Vogul and *puyol* in Ostyak (cf. Hungarian *falu* 'village'). Their life is one of seasonal changes. In winter they live in simple, permanent huts 2–3 metres high, 5–9 metres long and 4–5 metres wide. The eastern Ostyaks build similar huts, but dig them into the ground and cover them with earth to provide better protection against the elements. Nowadays these are constructed only half a metre below the surface of the earth, but in the seventeenth century and perhaps even later they were much deeper; access was by means of the smoke hole in the roof. This type of building is found also among the Palaeo-Asiatic peoples of Eastern Siberia.

Characteristic of the Vogul and Ostyak settlements is the shed built on piles beside their houses; here they store their provisions, clothes, implements and the results of their hunting and fishing expeditions. The piles are from one to two metres high and ensure protection from floods and from the depredations of wild beasts. In summer, when they go on hunting or fishing expeditions, they build for themselves temporary shelters of wooden poles covered with birch bark wherever they find a suitable spot. The permanent winter quarters have nothing inside except a few benches covered with skins to serve as beds and in one corner a stove made of clay. The nomads' tents and the summer jurts are furnished even more sparsely; they contain only an open hearth in the middle. Domestic equipment, such as plates, ladles, cups and drinking vessels, they usually make for themselves out of birch bark or wood, but earthenware crockery, spoons and other utensils can be bought and are widely used. Their food is cooked in large iron or copper cooking-pots which are likewise obtained from traders.

The reindeer breeders among the Ob-Ugrians dress like the Nenets; the rest, however, still cling to their folk costume, though factory-made cloth has ousted this to some extent. The severity of the Siberian winter ensures the continued popularity of the fur coat. In winter they wear outer clothing of reindeer, rabbit, squirrel or fox skins, fully open in front and straight-backed, reaching to the ankle. In summer there are variations; in the north they wear old short fur coats, while to the east and south cloaks of rough broadcloth are the fashion. They make their short boots of reindeer or moose hide. Their underwear is of flax and nettles, although modern factory-made cotton goods are now common. At one time not only coats, cloaks, gloves and boots but also shirts were beautifully decorated with rich and colourful embroidery, generally in blue and red. Much of their linen was woven at home, but domestic weaving has declined rapidly during the present century. Their clothes were further decorated by colourful glass beads, which were sewn to shirts, headdresses and boots, and also used to make long necklaces, worn like ties over the shirt. While embroidered shirts were passing out of fashion at the beginning of this century, beads remained very much in favour.

Until recent times their diet was monotonous, consisting chiefly of meat and fish. Waterfowl, wild reindeer and moose counted as delicacies. Certain parts of these latter animals, brains, eyes, liver, kidneys, ears, cheeks and the soft antlers of the young deer, were eaten raw. They also drank the warm blood of an animal immediately after it had been slaughtered. The remaining meat was cooked or preserved. Their method of preservation is interesting: the flesh is cut into long strips and dried on high trestles. They like their fish either raw or cooked, frozen or dried in the same way as their meat. The inner parts of the fish are cooked in large pots to produce fish-fat, which is an important part of their diet. This is consumed raw, but also eaten mixed with crushed berries, from which they also bake a kind of cake. For their long hunting expeditions they always take fish-fat mixed with flaked dried fish.

Some variety in this diet is provided by the various edible berries, such as bilberries, and pine kernels. Bread is a relatively recent addition, though it has long been known among them. Vegetables were unknown until the Soviet authorities began to introduce them into their diet in an attempt to get rid of the many serious diseases, including tapeworm, that resulted from their traditional eating habits.

Although the aeroplane has now made access to this region easy, local transport is still carried on by traditional means. Various types of boat, all home-made, are in use; there are simple dugouts of birch for one or two persons, long light boats of pine, and sailing boats to carry loads of 7–8 tons on longer journeys; these latter are often used as summer quarters.

In winter the reindeer breeding Ob-Ugrians use sleighs of a Nenets type, while those who live further south travel on horse-drawn Russian sledges. Most of them, however, possessing neither reindeer nor horses, use short, broad skis for lengthy journeys. Their hunting equipment and their eventual quarry are carried on sledges drawn by dogs; these may also be used to pull passenger sledges. The dog-sleigh is now rare, but has been known for centuries, as may be deduced from medieval Arabic sources.

FOLK ART AND POETRY

The general educational standards of the Ob-Ugrians were low. They had no schools, and literacy was confined to a few individuals who lived in Russian surroundings and gradually became russified. Statistics produced in 1897 indicated that only four Voguls had reached more than an elementary stage of education. Civilization was slow to reach the area.

Despite this drawback, folk art flourished. Vessels made of birch bark display a high degree of artistry; their ornamentation consists either of stylized animal and plant designs or of geometrical patterns. The same is true of the decoration used for clothing, whether with beads, appliqué work or embroidery. The importance of the stylized animal and plant motifs can be gauged by the names given to the separate designs: horseshoe, fox trail, swallow, partridge, bear's paw, rabbit ear, pike tooth, beaver and fly agaric.

The folk poetry of the Ob-Ugrians is remarkable in both form and content; it is distinctive and of very great artistic merit. This unwritten treasury, handed down orally from generation to generation, is the richest legacy of the Voguls and Ostyaks. From their folk songs we can gain a picture of land and people, their views of the natural phenomena around them, their everyday life, the heroic deeds of their ancestors, their wars and adventures – in brief, all the features of Ob-Ugrian society. These songs can be divided into several types; there are mythical cosmogonic legends and songs, heroic songs, bear songs and bear dramas and spells to conjure up the gods, as well as narrative poems. The prose tales of both peoples appear to be of much more recent origin and contain many foreign elements.

The form of their songs is of particular interest. They have a regular metre, the basis of which is stress. One stressed syllable may be followed by not more than three unstressed syllables; the number varies, but one is the normal standard. Each line of verse contains either four or six such 'feet'. In the verse collections already published there often occur apparent half-lines containing only two stresses; these have given rise to the suggestion that there is no rhythmical regularity in Ob-Ugrian verse. The reason, however, is that these verses were normally taken down at dictation; when they are sung, the text is filled out with extra syllables to maintain the rhythm. The basic text of an Ostyak poem has been printed thus:

> *wētijem | tujpe | tujeŋ | kur*
> *χōrijen | taχaś | kat jam | ńir*
> *ma | tūmetsem*

> On to my five-toed foot
> Two good boots of reindeer-hide
> I pull.

The first two of these lines contain the four regular stresses, but the third appears to be irregular. In singing, however, this is doubled thus:

> *mā tam | tūmti | jet | mem*

(or possibly *mā | tam | tūmti | jetmem*).
The extra syllables consist of *tam* 'that, there' and line-filling particles (*-ti-, -jet*).

One of the main characteristics of Ob-Ugrian folk poetry is parallelism. Certain words, often adjectives, are replaced by synonyms in the repetition of a line:

Scarcely had the region of my sleeping *throat* found sleep,
Scarcely had the region of my sleeping *tongue* found sleep . . .
(When) I was dreaming a *neck*-cracking, *deep-rooted* dream there,
(When) I was dreaming a *back*-cracking, *far-seated* dream there.

Another unusual feature is the so-called *figura etymologica*, the use of two derivatives of the same word to express one concept. In one song, the silver-hooped, silver-ribbed cradle becomes the 'silver-hooped hooped cradle, the silver-ribbed ribbed cradle'. The source of a stream becomes the 'source of a sourced stream' and 'the man sings' becomes 'the singing man sings'.

The effect of these songs is heightened by the repetition of traditional epithets and similes. Thus the autumn often appears as 'the thinly-snowed autumn of the visible dog-track; the thinly-snowed autumn of the visible human footprint.' Thick frost becomes 'frost as thick as an animal's hide'; the river 'winds like

the entrails of a goose' or is 'as thin as a knife-blade' and has the
frequent epithets 'nutritious, rich in fish'. The larder is 'full of
nourishment from the Ob, full of nourishment from the lake'.
The high fortress is 'high as the fleeting cloud, the running cloud',
or 'high as the neck of the gods'. The thought of growing fat
after a good meal is picturesquely expressed: 'I had grown so fat
that my five-buttoned buttoned coat would scarcely meet' (In
this instance it is a bear speaking). The old man Tēk, suspecting
that the god Ajäs wishes to destroy him, says 'Old god Ajäs!
what flesh, what bone have I for you to chop to pieces?', in
other words, 'Why do you wish to kill me at sword-point?'
The action of a man beginning to speak is thus described: 'the
hero, my brother-in-law, thus opens suddenly his ten-toothed
toothed mouth . . .' Noise is depicted in this simile: 'As fingers
crack, as the frozen pine cracks, such was the noise'; and swift
flight: 'Fly like the swiftly falling raindrop, like the swiftly-flying
wisp of a breeze.'

Apart from these characteristics of metre and style, the texts
are extremely valuable for their frequent use of old grammatical
forms and vocabulary long since out of use. There are many
reasons for supposing that Vogul and Ostyak verse, epic and lyric,
is very old. Its performance, however, is unfortunately becoming a
thing of the past. Scholars of the last and present centuries have
collected and preserved the best of this poetry; the earlier scholars
did not pay great attention to the melodies which accompanied it,
a loss which has been partially redeemed by the activity of Artturi
Kannisto in this field. The verse was most frequently sung by
'professional' singers and accompanied by instruments unknown
elsewhere in Western Siberia. The first of these is a long five-
stringed lyre shaped like a fish or boat (Ostyak *nares-juχ* 'singing
wood', Vogul *sankweltep*), and the second is a swan-necked instrument of nine or thirteen strings (Ostyak *torop-juχ* 'crane-wood',
Vogul *tär-šip* 'crane-neck'). These instruments are from the
south, in the final instance from Asia Minor, and probably reached
the Ob-Ugrians through the Iranians during the centuries before
the birth of Christ. Music is not merely an accompaniment for the
songs; it plays an important part in the dances which are
performed at various festivals, notably the bear festivals and
dramas.

NEW DEVELOPMENTS

After the October Revolution and the campaigns which ensued, a new period of Ostyak and Vogul history began. The Ostyak-Vogul (Chanti-Man'si) National Area was created in 1931, with its capital at Chanti-Man'siysk, a few miles from Samarovskoje. The first kolkhoz was founded by ten Ostyak and Russian families in 1929, and collectivization was completed in 1939. In these, traditional activities such as hunting, fishing and reindeer breeding are developed alongside new ones (animal husbandry, animal breeding for furs, and agriculture). The kolkhozes still depend upon fishing for some 50 per cent of their income, and some of them are devoted entirely to this activity. In these fishing methods have been modernized by the use of motorboats and very large nets, and the fish processed by mechanical methods. The earlier fishing implements, however, have not yet lost their importance.

Hunting has also been improved by the introduction of modern weapons and new animals such as the skunk and mink. Attempts have also been made in the last few decades to increase the number of sables in the Siberian forests. Silver fox farming has provided a useful source of new income. There are some fifty-eight kolkhozes in the National Region, mainly in the Berjozov area, where reindeer are bred. All are equipped with veterinary services to improve the breed and to prevent the various plagues that frequently attacked the animals. Agriculture has been extended northwards, while horses and cattle have been increased in the area. The arrival of the kolhoz system has led to the building of larger permanent settlements and the gradual extinction of the old scattered villages; there is no need for summer and winter quarters with the introduction of new methods and redistribution of labour. Semi-nomadic life is fast disappearing. Further developments include fish-canning factories and sawmills in the capital and other places. Communications have been improved and the standard of education raised – Chanti-Man'siysk, for example, possesses a library, museum, cultural centre, cinema and fourteen schools. To meet the needs of the outlying areas there are two other cultural centres, one by the Kazim and the other by the Sosva. These include boarding schools, libraries, regional study centres, veterinary and medical services and baths in one complex.

Tradition, however, dies hard in this region. The kolkhozes have found it difficult to combat the traditional division of work between man and woman, for the latter, as a lesser and often despised member of society, was allowed to perform only certain types of work. Old beliefs and superstitions still persist. In the Surgut district it is still possible to see Ostyak women who veil their faces, while in the Berjozov area houses have been known to burn to the ground in the absence of men, although the women could have prevented this. Ancient custom forbids women to climb on house roofs for any purpose whatsoever.

Various improvements can be seen. The houses are better built and furnished; no longer are they divided into male and female quarters. The population have begun to realize the benefits of washing themselves and their clothing which now, in summer at least, tends to follow Russian fashion. Their diet, as we have seen, has been improved.

Education has had to overcome stiff resistance; in the thirties for example, it was rumoured that the newly-built schools were the abode of evil spirits. Moreover, the lack of a literary language, scarcity of native teachers and absence of textbooks were grave obstacles to progress. The first Ostyak primer appeared in 1930 and the first Vogul primer in 1932; both used the Latin alphabet. This caused considerable difficulties, since Russian was also taught in schools. The Cyrillic alphabet was therefore introduced in 1939–40. The first Ostyak school was opened in 1924, and by 1952 there were seventy-two boarding schools offering free education for some 3,000 Ostyak and Vogul children. Secondary and higher education have also been developed, together with specialized training institutions such as agricultural colleges, medical and midwifery establishments and teacher-training colleges.

Apart from textbooks in the literary languages, translations have been made of Russian classics, political and cultural works. Since 1933 newspapers have been published in the Ob-Ugrian languages. With these developments, native authors have come to the fore. A collection of Vogul and Ostyak verse was published in 1940, and several short stories and memoirs have appeared in both languages. The first Russian-Vogul dictionary is the work of a Vogul scholar, J. A. Rombandjejeva, a member of the Leningrad Linguistic Institute. These developments augur well for the future of two peoples who were the subject of gloomy prophecies a century ago.

The Permians

The Zyryans (Komi)

The Zyryans or Komi, as they call themselves, live in the north-eastern area of Russia in Europe. Most of them are in the Komi Autonomous Soviet Socialist Republic, but the so-called Permjaks who form their southernmost group live in the Komi-Permjak National Region. They are settled along the Vychegda and its tributaries, and the Mezen valley; they also inhabit the Pechora valley. All these rivers flow northwards. The Komi-Permjaks are isolated from the main body of Zyryans and live in the region almost bounded by the Upper Kama and its tributaries. Isolated groups are to be found in Western Siberia and the Kola Peninsula, while a further fragmented group of unusual linguistic interest is settled in the Yazva valley. The Yazva rises in the Urals and flows westward into the Kama.

According to the census of 1970 there were 475,000 Zyryans, of whom 86·7 per cent spoke the Zyryan language. This figure shows a considerable increase on those for 1926 (364,000) and 1939 (408,000).

Linguistically the Zyryans are divided into three separate groups. Since no detailed statistics have been issued since 1926, only their relative sizes can be indicated. The largest is the Komi-Zyryan group, numbering 322,000 in 1970. Most of these live in the Komi ASSR, but some ten per cent live outside its boundaries, some in Western Siberia near the mouth of the Ob, others along the River Tagil and near Tyumen, while others are to be found in the Kola Peninsula and the Nenets National Region. The second group is formed by the Komi-Permjaks, of whom there were 153,000 in 1970. Most of these live in the National Region bearing their name, but some 20,000 live elsewhere (partly in Siberia). The third group consists of some 4,000 Zyryans living along the Yazva. It is now customary to regard Komi-Zyryan and Komi-Permjak as separate languages rather than dialects, and this is reflected in the existence of two literary languages. The small group of Yazva Zyryans has no literary language and is generally included with the Permjaks. Despite these differences, there is no reason linguistically to distinguish between two quite different languages; it is more correct to regard Komi-Zyryan, Komi-Permjak and Yazva as three main dialects of one and the same language.[1] Variations between them are fewer than those existing between Russian and Ukrainian, Plattdeutsch and Bavarian, or Northern and Eastern Ostyak.

In 1959 the population of the Komi ASSR was some 800,000. The Zyryans accounted for about a third of this number; the rest, apart from a few Nenets, were Russians. The area is 410,000 square kilometres; its capital, Syktyvkar, with a population of 60,000, is at the confluence of the Sysola and Vychegda rivers. Most of the area is flat; only in the Urals which form its eastern boundary are there any sizeable mountains, the highest of which is the peak of Narodnaya, 1,894 metres. The north-east is in the tundra zone; south of this is an intermediate area of mixed forest and tundra, while the rest of the republic is mainly covered with mixed forest. The Komi ASSR is rich not only in wood, but in other natural resources such as coal, mineral oil, iron and manganese ore, non-ferrous metals, salt and other minerals. The forests are threaded by large rivers with their surrounding marshes (12–13 per cent of the area of the republic is marshland). The climate is harsh, but there are considerable variations between the north and the south. In the far north the mean annual temperature is −2·6°C, while in the capital it is +0·1°C. In the north the growing season for plants is only two and a half months, while in the south it extends to four months. Annual rainfall is 500 mm., and this occurs mainly in the warmer seasons.

The Permjaks inhabit their National Region, an area of 22,000 square kilometres bordering the south-east boundary of the Komi ASSR; the population numbers 220,000, and its capital is Kudymkar. Situated close to the Urals the Permjak National Region consists of undulating countryside and flat areas. Its climate is similar to that of the southern Komi ASSR, except that the average rainfall is somewhat higher. 80 per cent of the area is wooded, mainly with coniferous trees. There is an extensive river system connected with the Kama, which facilitates the transport of wood. Rich in fish and game-birds, this region is a hunter's and angler's paradise.

---

[1] The Yazva dialect is the most distinctive of the three.

The name *Komi*, used by all three groups, is related to Votyak *kumy* 'human being', Vogul *χum* 'man' and Hungarian *hím* 'male'. This is in accord with the usual Finno-Ugrian and Samoyed practice. The origin of the name Zyryan has never been satisfactorily explained. Certainly it was through the Russians that it came into general use in Western Europe. Russian *Zyryan(in)* contains the element *-jan(in)* which is used to form national names. Perhaps the Russian word is based on Ob-Ugrian *saran* or Votyak *sara-kum*, these being the names given in the respective languages to the Zyryans.

Even more problematic is the name Permian, the collective term for both Zyryan and Votyak; it also appears with the typical Russian *-jak* suffix in the name of the Komi-Permjak National Region. No explanation has yet been accepted, though attempts have been made to connect it with the name *Bjarma*, which occurs in Scandinavian sagas to designate the Baltic-Finnic peoples living on the White Sea coast. Not only is this connection uncertain, but the origin of the word *Bjarma* is also unknown.

Since there are few characteristics which distinguish the three Zyryan groups already mentioned – they share a common name, language and culture – they will be treated in the present account as one people.

Dialectal divisions into Komi-Zyryan, Komi-Permjak and Yazva Zyryan are capable of still further subdivision. Komi-Zyryan includes the dialects of Lower Vychegda, Sysola, Syktyvkar, Upper Sysola, Upper Vychegda, Udora, Izhma, Vim, Pechora and Luzaletka. Komi-Permjak has two main divisions: north (Kosa-Kama) and south (Kudymkar-In'va). Yazva-Zyryan, spoken only in fifty-four villages, has no significant variations. These dialects may be divided into different types according to the history of the Proto-Zyryan *l*. Non-initial *-l-* is retained in certain dialects, while in others it becomes *-v-* and in certain others disappears entirely. The following four types of dialect may be distinguished:

1. The *l* type, in which *l* remains unaltered, e.g. *lol* 'soul'. This type is characteristic of the Zyryan spoken in the Sysola, Luza and Pechora areas, some of the Permjak dialects and Yazva.

2. The *l*~*v* type. Final -*l* and medial -*l*-+consonant > *v*, while medial -*l*-+vowel remains unchanged (e.g. *lov* 'soul', *lov-lyś* 'from a soul' but *lol-yś* 'out of a soul'). This is found mainly along the Vychegda, and is called the Vychegda type. The dialects of Udora, Syktyvkar and Vim also have this feature.

3. The *l*~*Ø* type. Final -*l* and medial -*l*-+consonant disappear, with resulting lengthening of the preceding vowel, but medial -*l*-+vowel remains unchanged, e.g. *lō* 'soul', *lō-lyś*, *lol-yś*. This type, also known as the Izhma type, extends from the northern area of this name to the Lower Pechora and the Upper Vim.

4. The *v* type, in which every early *l* has been replaced by *v*, e.g. *vov* 'soul', *vov-vyś*, *vov-yś*.

These four types show a remarkably even distribution; the first is spoken by 33 per cent, type 2 by 25 per cent, type 3 by 18 per cent and type 4 by 24 per cent. The literary languages both use type 2.

Agriculture is the basis of the economy among the southern Zyryans. Methods have much in common with those of the neighbouring Russians and were doubtless adopted from them. Up to the nineteenth century forests were cleared and burnt; then the three-course rotation system came into general use in these areas. The main crops are barley, oats and rye. Although the Zyryans north of the Vychegda also cultivate the land, hunting is of much greater importance. They use modern equipment, but traps and nets of earlier kinds are also to be found among them. Fishing plays a great rôle in the lives of the Zyryans both in the republic and in the Komi-Permjak region. Animal breeding is less common; only among the Zyryans of the Izhma area has the breeding of reindeer developed, and this they have learnt from their northern neighbours, the Nenets, whose methods they have improved.

Domestic crafts have not developed greatly; they are limited virtually to weaving, spinning and hand-thrown pottery.

There is nothing to distinguish the Komi-Zyryan and Permjak villages from those of the Russians. They are built chiefly on river-banks, and consist of log houses divided normally into three rooms. Two-storey houses are not uncommon. Their clothing varies little from the Russian peasant style. Women's dress has retained some of the older characteristics, such as the tunic-like cut of their blouses. One of the unusual features of the men's clothes is the *laz*, a sleeveless hunting-jacket made of broadcloth or linen edged with soft leather; it is cut square and has a hole for the head in the centre; worn over outer clothing, it gives added protection to the chest and back as far as the waist. It is also worn when heavy loads are carried. Their coloured woollen stockings with geometrical designs and their home-made boots are also distinctive.

Strong Russian influence is noticeable in their folk art. Their folklore contains themes and motifs which are very close to the Russian tales, although several of their legends display an older and more original tradition. Wood carving has a long native history, and in the southern Zyryan area a distinctive type of ecclesiastical statuary has been evolved. This differs sharply from the usual Orthodox style, and preserves old pre-Christian elements. It is interesting to note that A. N. Voronyikin, the builder of the Kazan church in Leningrad, was descended on the maternal side from these Permjak wood-carvers. Christianity reached the Zyryans in the fourteenth and fifteenth centuries, yet they retained traces of their earlier beliefs until modern times. The various woodland, water and domestic spirits that recur in their folklore can also be found, at least in part, amongst their neighbours. One feature of Zyryan mythology is the belief in a protecting spirit or *ort*. Each human has his own *ort*, which acts exactly as he does. In earlier ages there were magicians and soothsayers (*tun*) amongst them, no doubt the successors of the ancient shamans. It is also recorded that sacrifices were once offered to placate the spirits and gain their favour. Their original beliefs, however, are difficult to reconstruct from the scanty evidence available.

Little is known of the earliest history of the Zyryans. Linguistic evidence suggests that Proto-Zyryan broke away from Permian around the eighth century AD, but there are no historical records of this period. The name *Bjarma* which appears in the Scandinavian sagas in all probability refers to the Baltic Finns, so that the names 'Perm' and 'Pechera' of the Kievan chronicle are probably the first records of their existence. Thus the Zyryan people came into existence at a time which has left no historical material; other branches of scholarship enable us to reconstruct the outline of their progress.

During the Permian period the ancestors of the Votyaks and Zyryans lived in the Vyatka and Lower Kama region. Here they had as their neighbours Iranians and later, from the sixth century onwards, the Volga Bulgars. The loanwords from the latter source are more frequent in Votyak than in Zyryan, from which it is assumed that the Zyryans lived in the north of the region, and that the two Permian peoples separated not long after this contact with the Volga Bulgars. The Zyryans, not unnaturally, moved northwards. Archaeological discoveries demonstrate certain differences between the Kama and Vyatka cultures of the eighth and ninth centuries; this is a clue to the separation of the two peoples. The distinctive ethnic characteristics of the Zyryans were developed in two regions. One source was in the north, along the Mezen-Vashka and Vychegda-Vim valleys, and the other in the south east, the Upper Kama area. The cultures of these two areas developed more or less independently during the first thousand years AD, and this is doubtless one reason why the modern Zyryans do not show a common anthropological aspect. Among those of the north and north-west the so-called White Sea type (Northern Europid) is predominant, while the south-eastern Zyryans, and in particular the Permjaks display traces of the Uralic type already mentioned in connection with the Ob-Ugrians.

The links between these two groups grew stronger during the tenth century and reached their climax in the following period when there was large scale migration from the north-east towards the Kama. This was caused at first by the inroads of the Slav settlers, and later by the desire to escape the ever increasing taxes demanded by Moscow. The Zyryans of the Sysola area form a bridge between the two groups, and their intermediate rôle can be observed in the linguistic and cultural peculiarities of this region as well as in their anthropological structure.

During the period from the eleventh to the thirteenth century, considerable social changes took place. The tribal system disintegrated, and new communities were established under the leadership of dominating groups intent on exploiting their power. The result was the beginning of a feudal structure, and the majority of Zyryans, like the Russians of the northern forests, became un-privileged peasants. At this period they lived chiefly from hunting and fishing; in addition they practised rudimentary agriculture and stockbreeding as they cleared parts of the forests. Trade connections already existed with Novgorod, and when they came under the rule of Moscow in the sixteenth century their economic and cultural life underwent considerable development.

The conversion of the Zyryans to Christianity is chiefly connected with the name of Bishop (later Saint) Stephen of Perm, who lived at the end of the fourteenth century. He decided that the use of force was less effective than persuasion, and having learnt Zyryan at an early age he encouraged his missionaries to use this language. The introduction of the liturgy in Zyryan was a constructive step in the development of literacy, as was the creation of the so-called Old Permian alphabet connected with the name of St Stephen. This alphabet, also known as *abur* from its first two letters, was devised from Greek and Cyrillic characters suitably modified, and is to be found in early documents, glosses and inscriptions. The importance of these texts in Finno-Ugrian linguistic and cultural history is very great, since of all the languages in the group only Zyryan and Hungarian possess connected texts from this period. Nevertheless, the Old Permian alphabet was confined to ecclesiastical use and was known to a relatively small section of the population; it did not provide the foundation for a Zyryan literary language.

As the Church extended its activities, it acquired large estates in the Zyryan region, many of whose inhabitants became serfs on them. The Permjaks on the Kama suffered a similar fate when the Stroganov family was given this area by Ivan the Terrible in the middle of the sixteenth century.

With the opening-up of Siberia in this and the next century, the Zyryan region grew in importance, since it lay on the direct route there. It was also an escape route from the ever-growing burdens of feudal oppression, and some Zyryans left their homes to settle along the Urals or in Siberia. In these circumstances local trade and industry were slow to develop. Only after 1700 did local markets begin to evolve; with these some families acquired considerable wealth and estates, and peasant risings were not infrequent. The Zyryan traders built up a network of connections with the Russians, Nenets and smaller peoples of Siberia and gained a reputation for their exploitation. Minerals discovered in this century led to the establishment of small industries worked by Zyryans and Russians together. The land problem, however, grew more serious, and the reform of 1866, which gave the peasants one quarter to half a hectare each, could not satisfy the demand. In general these small holdings were gradually swallowed up once again into large estates.

Meanwhile industry, based on metals and oil, forged ahead, as did trade; the latter was greatly assisted by the development of water transport. Both agricultural and industrial workers took part in the 1905 revolution, while that of 1917 resulted in lengthy battles and campaigns in the area. Not until 1921 was the Zyryan Autonomous Territory formed; this became the Autonomous Republic in 1936.

New developments include the mining and industrial centres of Uhta and Vorkuta, and the building from 1937 to 1942 of the railway to the latter town. Even today forestry and the timber industry account for 23 per cent of the total production of the Republic. Agriculture has been modernized with the introduction of collective farming and machinery, and the area under cultivation has been increased to four times its extent in 1913. Stockbreeding has also been encouraged, and cattle, sheep and goats as well as reindeer are to be found in vastly increased numbers.

The educational field has also seen important developments. Before the First World War some 25 per cent of the population was literate, and in the few schools then existing tuition was in Russian. By 1952 there were 6,000–8,000 children studying at both elementary and secondary level; 186 hostels were provided for children studying away from home. Syktyvkar, the capital now possesses all the cultural institutions of a modern city, including a teachers' training college with four faculties and a branch of the Academy.

Zyryan literature is a modern development. Newspapers first appeared in the language in 1918; there are now twenty-six, together with a literary journal and one concerned with social and political problems. In 1940 one hundred and thirty books were published in Komi-Zyryan. The beginnings of literary activity are connected with the name of I. A. Kuratov (1837–75), an outstanding poet and translator whose works were little known in his lifetime but have now received belated recognition. G. S. Lytkin (1835–1906), author and scholar, was also active in the development of the literary language. New writers in all genres have come forward since the revolution, notably V. I. Lytkin who has an international reputation as a Finno-Ugrian scholar. Since 1939 there has existed a Zyryan section of the Association of Soviet Authors.

The Komi-Permjak National Region was created in 1925. Conditions here were much more backward; 99 per cent of the women and 89 per cent of the male population were illiterate. To-day textbooks, literary and political works are published in the language. The capital, Kudymkar, has its own permanent theatre, and considerable progress has been made in the development of Permjak art, particularly through the activity of P. I. Subbot'in-Permjak (1886–1923), who was both artist and scholar.

The Votyaks (Udmurts)

The Votyaks live to the south of the Zyryans in the region bounded by the Vyatka and the Lower Kama, with some scattered groups living west of the Vyatka and south and east of the Kama.

According to the statistics of 1970 they number 704,000, 89 per cent of whom use Votyak as their native language. The majority of them live in the Udmurt Autonomous Soviet Republic which was created on 28 December 1934. This has an area of 42,000 square kilometres, and its capital is Izhevsk, on the River Izh. The total population is 1,420,000, so that the Votyaks account for about half; the rest are mainly Russians, though some Cheremis and Tatars are also to be found. It lies to the north of the Tatar ASSR and to the north-west of the Bashkir ASSR. Its central location means that its railways and industries are more developed than those of the Komi ASSR. The countryside is undulating, gradually descending towards flat lands in the south-west. Its rivers are linked with the Volga; of these the Kama, which affords communications with both the Urals and the mainstream of the Volga, is economically the most important. The climate can hardly be termed warm; the average temperature in January is − 16°C, and in July + 19°C, with a growing season of about 160 days. Forty-four per cent of the area is covered by forests, in which bears, foxes, wolves, wolverines, ermine, martens and squirrels are found. Only the hare, weasel and polecat are native. The region is also rich in birds and fish.

The name Udmurt is a compound, of which the second element *murt* means 'human being'; the first is of doubtful origin, but appears to be connected with the Cheremis *odo* 'Udmurt, Votyak'. The name *Votyak* has been transmitted by Russian to the western world; in early Russian sources these people were known as *oti, otin, otjak*, which last form with the addition of an initial *v-* gives their present name. It is likely that the *ud-* and *ot-* initial syllables of the two names are of common origin, while the second syllable *-yak* is the Russian suffix already seen in such national names as *Ostyak*, and *Permjak*.

The Votyak language is closely related to Zyryan. About 80 per cent of the vocabulary of the two languages has a common origin; the majority of the grammatical and syntactical elements are inherited from Permian. Despite these similarities, the two peoples cannot understand each other's language. Considerable differences have evolved in the forms of the words, e.g., Votyak *žuk* ~ Zyryan *rok* 'porridge'. Votyak *uj* ~ Zyryan *voj* 'night', Votyak *myny-* ~ Zyryan *mun-* 'go'. Similar divergences may be noted in grammatical elements of common origin; possession is indicated in Votyak by the suffix *-len*, and in Zyryan by *-len*, while the plural possessive suffixes show even greater disparity:

	Votyak	*Zyryan*
'our'	*-my*	*-nym*
'your'	*-dy*	*-nyd*
'their'	*-zy*	*-nys*

In addition to the common Permian loanwords from Iranian, Votyak possesses a considerable number of Bulgar-Turkic and Tatar words unknown in Zyryan.

Anthropologically the Votyaks betray their contacts with southern (Turkic and Tatar) races. Unlike the Zyryans, they are predominantly mesocephalic, with dark hair and eyes.

Since the Votyaks live for the most part in a closely-knit community, their language is relatively uniform. Its dialects are not far removed from the common norm, and both literary and spoken language can be easily understood throughout the region. These dialects are the Glazov and Sarapul in the north, Urzhum, Malmizh and Yelabuga to the south, and Ufa and Perm to the east. The Besermans, who live in the north of the republic, form an interesting group; although they now speak Votyak, they are probably a mixture of older Volga-Bulgar, Tatar and Votyak elements.

The Votyaks have long been acquainted with agriculture, and their methods have shown little variation from those of the Cheremis, Mordvins and Russians near by. Up to the nineteenth century, clearings were made in the forests, and then triple-course rotation was introduced. This alone was insufficient to supply their needs, so that forestry, hunting, bee-keeping and charcoal-burning were all practised. All these occupations demanded a settled population; thus for centuries there have been no traces of nomadic life among the Votyaks, as can be seen from their villages. They live in wooden houses of the Russian type, built along broad streets – though this is a nineteenth century innovation; until this time their buildings were more scattered and irregularly sited. Certain older features are, however, still preserved; they surround their plots of land with their houses and various farm-buildings in a U shape, and some of the latter show traces of an earlier type of building. The storehouse or *kenos* in the yard was perhaps originally a dwelling-house which was later adapted for this purpose, and the *kvala*, a building without windows or ceiling, once the abode of the tribal and family gods, came to be used as a summer-kitchen.

The folk dress of the Votyaks is notably different from that of the Russians. The women's dresses are especially rich in colour and ornament, and there are two distinct types. In the north it has preserved older fashion and resembles that of the Meadow Cheremis; in the south there are traces of later Tatar influence. The most important article of dress is the *derem*, a richly embroidered blouse decorated with metal pendants and chains, often worn under a similarly decorated cloak. They also wear high-crowned headdresses decorated with coins and other pieces of metal. The men, on the other hand, follow Russian peasant fashion. It is in the women's dress that Votyak folk art is best seen; geometrical decorative elements are used, while animal and plant motifs are rarely found. Their most usual musical instrument is the guzla (Votyak *kreʐ̌*), but this is by no means confined to the Votyaks.

From the linguistic and ethnographical viewpoint, Votyak folk poetry is particularly interesting in that it preserves relics of pagan beliefs, old customs and superstitions.

The Votyaks retained many interesting characteristics in their social structure until the beginning of the present century. Tribal traditions lingered on in the settlement of large families together to work on the same farm, with their houses built side by side. As the family grew, so did the number of houses. Each tribe (*böl'ak*) formed a separate unit of 10 to 15 related families, holding the land in common and claiming descent from a common ancestor. Marriage within the tribe was not permitted. Some such tribes united to form a larger unit (*vyʐ̌i*), which generally occupied the whole of a village. This unit was strictly endogamous. It also differed from the *böl'ak* in that it was chiefly a religious community, and not a strong social and economic organization. It was ruled by a council of elders (*keñeš*) whose powers were virtually unrestricted. Within this tribal organization there were considerable social distinctions; in practice the *keñeš* consisted of the richer members of the tribe who did not scruple to oppress the poorer Votyaks.

From the eighteenth century onwards the Votyaks were officially members of the Orthodox Church, but many of their older religious practices were retained. One of these was the cult of the dead, seen in their burial customs and respect for the dead or their spirits. There were considerable variations among tribes and even families. The *kvala*, already mentioned, belonged to the tribe or family. Built in the farmyard, it contained the box or birch bark vessel in which were placed the sacred objects representing the ancestor and protector of the family. The large *vyʐ̌i* also had a separate common *kvala* respected by the whole tribe. Sacrifices were normally offered here, or in a sacred enclosure, the *lud*, not far from the village. This was usually the place where animals were sacrificed to placate evil spirits, and in the ceremonies held here an important rôle was played by the *tuno*, a priestly figure whose functions resembled those of the shaman.

After the eighth century, when they separated from the ancestors of the Zyryans, the Votyaks had a chequered history. During the next two centuries they still continued the pursuits of the Permian period: agriculture and stockbreeding were of less importance than hunting. Their ethnical and linguistic progress was strongly influenced by the Volga-Bulgars and the establishment of Magna Bulgaria. They then lived to the west of their present habitat and absorbed many of the characteristics of their more developed overlords, for they remained under Bulgar domination until the twelfth century. When the Mongol invasions of the thirteenth century put an end to Magna Bulgaria, the majority of the Votyaks fled to the Vyatka-Kama region and settled there.

At the end of the fifteenth century the Vyatka region was incorporated into the principate of Moscow, but the Kama Votyaks were dependants of the Tatar khans of Kazan until 1552, when Ivan IV destroyed their authority. All the Votyaks then became part of the Russian Empire. This event was followed by progressive Russian settlement of the Votyak area, particularly when the mines and industrial settlements were developed at the end of the eighteenth century. These became cultural and commercial centres and had considerable influence on the general development of the Votyaks, who nevertheless found much cause for discontent in high taxation, forced conversion and inhuman labour demands. It is not surprising that they took part in various insurrections, notably that of Pugachev in 1773–5.

In the nineteenth century the Votyaks were involved in a notorious murder case, that of an old man killed in the village of Stary Multan. No murderer could be discovered, and the Votyak inhabitants of the village were charged with ritual murder of the man as a human sacrifice to their pagan gods. The trial lasted from 1892 to 1896, and only after the intervention of various Russian authors and scholars, including V. G. Korolenko, were they acquitted.

The Russian land reform did little to alleviate the situation of the poorer peasants, who found the increased tax burden intolerable. On the other hand, the isolation of the region was lessened with the development of shipping on the Kama and Vyatka and the coming of the railways. In the closing years of the last century there were thirty factories in the area, but the workers were mainly Russian.

After the revolution, the Votyak Autonomous Territory was created (1920); this changed its name in 1932 to the Udmurt Autonomous Region, and on 28 December 1934 it became a republic. Under the Soviet régime agriculture and engineering were both developed. Izhevsk, with 300,000 inhabitants, has become the largest industrial centre, with factories for the production of machine-tools, locomotives and motor cycles. Elsewhere radio, chemical and oil industries, as well as the manufacture of consumer goods and food, are represented. The result of industrialization was that in 1955 production was ninety-five times as great as it had been in 1913, and accounted for 85 per cent of the total production of the Republic. Agriculture has been mechanized and collectivized, and the general educational standards improved. Illiteracy, which was high at the beginning of the century, has ceased to exist. There are some 1,500 schools in the republic, and numerous specialist institutions including the Udmurt Scientific Institute in Izhevsk, which concerns itself particularly with the language, literature and history of the Votyaks.

Votyak literature was barely in existence before the Soviet period, but began to flourish between the two world wars. Poets, novelists and dramatists laid the foundations of an active literary tradition, and research into folklore and art was encouraged. In 1955 seventy newspapers were published in the Udmurt ASSR, and of these thirty were in the Votyak language. Art and music have also been actively promoted.

The Volga Finno-Ugrians

The Cheremis (Mari)

The Cheremis or Mari form the northern branch of the Volga Finno-Ugrians. They number 599,000, of whom 95.1 per cent speak and use the Cheremis language. They live in two widely separated groups; the majority are to be found in the Mari Autonomous Soviet Socialist Republic on the left bank of the Volga between the rivers Vetluga and Vyatka, also on the right

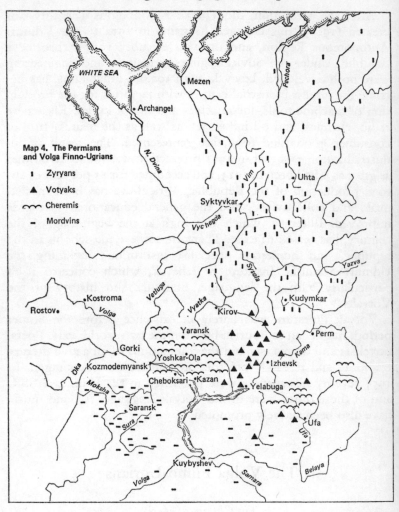

Map 4. The Permians
and Volga Finno-Ugrians

1 Zyryans
▲ Votyaks
〰 Cheremis
– Mordvins

bank of the Volga in the Sura valley region. The other group lives in the Bashkir ASSR along the Belaya and Ufa valleys, while there are smaller isolated settlements in the Tatar and Udmurt Republics also.

The name *Mari*, meaning 'human, man', is of uncertain origin. It has no Finno-Ugrian cognates, but has been linked with an Indo-European root of similar meaning, appearing in Sanskrit as *marya* and in Middle Iranian as *mērak*. If this connection is genuine, *Mari* is an ancient loanword; its form, however, suggests that it is of relatively recent origin, and the circumstances of any borrowing from Indo-European have so far received no satisfactory explanation.

Their name to the outside world, Cheremis, has been transmitted by Russian sources, and indeed appears in medieval chronicles, but it is not of Slavonic origin. It is presumed to have been adopted from some other people who had been in contact with the Mari long before the Russians. Their history suggests that the Volga-Bulgars may be the source of the name, and some support is given to this theory by the modern Chuvash name for them: *śarmys*. The origin of this word is also doubtful; it may be derived from Chuvash *śar* 'army'. It is certainly ancient, since in the form *ẕarmis* it occurs in a Khazar source of the tenth century, where it is the name of a people living on the Volga; Arab sources also record a name *tsarmis*.

Anthropologically the Cheremis differ considerably from their nearest relatives, the Mordvins. Although the predominant Finno-Ugrian type in the west, the Eastern Europid, is to be found among them, the majority of them betray strong Mongoloid strains. They tend to be short, flat-nosed and smooth-skinned. This is the result of long connections with Turkic and Tatar peoples, who have also left their mark on language, culture and way of life. The Cheremis language has borrowed hundreds of Chuvash words and even a few grammatical features.

The chief dialectal divisions follow the geographical distribution of the Cheremis. The so-called Meadow or Forest Cheremis, who form the majority of this people, live on the left bank of the Volga in the Mari ASSR; their dialect differs from that of the Hill Cheremis, who live on the right bank, chiefly in phonological and lexical elements. These differences have necessitated the creation of two separate literary languages. The Cheremis of Bashkiria speak the so-called Eastern dialect, which is different again from both Meadow and Hill Cheremis, chiefly because of its Tatar and Bashkir loanwords. Since its grammatical structure is in the main like that of Meadow Cheremis, it has no separate literary language. Moreover Meadow Cheremis is understood and used in the eastern region, so that the name 'Meadow-

Eastern' is sometimes applied to this dialect. Within these three main groups there are relatively insignificant local variations; the relative density of the population has been a great levelling factor here.

More than half of the Cheremis region is covered by forests, and deciduous trees are considerably more frequent than in the Komi and Udmurt Republics. There are many rivers, which form part of the Volga river system. The climate is cold, but less severe than that of the Udmurt ASSR to the north; it varies from − 13 °C in January to + 19°C in July. The growing season lasts for over five months, from the end of April to the beginning of October, and is favourable for agriculture, which has long been the main occupation of the Hill and Eastern Cheremis. According to statistics for 1897, 98 per cent of them were engaged in it. Their practices followed those of the Votyaks.

In the wooded, marshy districts of the left bank of the Volga, where there was less opportunity to cultivate the soil, hunting and fishing were the main pursuits. Stockbreeding played little part in the economy until recent times, but bee-keeping had a long tradition. In early times honeycombs were collected from swarms settled in hollow trees; in the last century domestic bee-keeping was developed. The Cheremis also followed various trades; there were coopers and charcoal-burners among them, and some of the Hill Cheremis became skilled gold and silversmiths whose talents were used mainly to make ornaments for women's clothing.

Like the Votyaks and Mordvins, they shed all traces of nomadic existence long ago. By the nineteenth century they were living in timber houses of the Russian type in more or less regularly planned villages. Like the Votyaks, the Cheremis still possess a primitive type of building, the single-roomed *kudo* used as a summer kitchen. Like the Votyak *kvala*, this was once used as a house (it is related etymologically to the Hungarian *ház* 'house'), and was also the repository for the family gods. From the Finno-Ugrian period onwards, the meaning of *kudo* may well have been 'dwelling quarters, home'. It is a simple, rectangular building without windows or ceiling; the floor is of puddled earth, with an open hearth in the centre surrounded by stones, the smoke escaping through a hole in the roof. Its furnishings consist of benches, shelves, a simple table and stumps of wood for seats. This is where sacrifices and other religious ceremonies were performed. For this reason the *kudo* was often divided into two parts; later the smaller section served as a store or larder.

Their dress – and particularly that of the women – has preserved its folk-characteristics. The Finno-Ugrians of the Volga and Kama regions, the Cheremis, Mordvins and Votyaks, all have similar tastes in clothing, which in some details correspond with that of the neighbouring Chuvash, Tatar and Bashkir peoples. The women wear a highly embroidered and decorated knee-length gown (*tuwyr*) and, a relic of nomadic times, trousers. To this they add a high-coned headdress with a birch bark or leather foundation covered with coloured embroidered cloth and decorated with metal ornaments – a variation of the Votyak type. This fashion may well be of southern (Scythian-Sarmatian) origin. Indeed, the Finno-Ugrians of this area display many southern and particularly Turkic elements in their clothing, reflecting the lengthy connection between them. The men have been quicker to adopt Russian town fashions. In older times their clothing was usually made of white homespun linen, and the colour has remained a favourite with them.

Cheremis folk tradition can be observed in poetry and music also. There is a rich store of traditions, and of particular interest are their lyric songs expressing joy and sorrow in a simple and intimate form. It is common knowledge that scholars have found many startling similarities between Hungarian and Cheremis folk melodies. These create the impression that these two peoples have best preserved the musical heritage of the Finno-Ugrians. The problem, however, is much more complicated; it must not be forgotten that of all the Finno-Ugrians the Cheremis and Hungarians were most affected in language and culture by Turkic influence which has left an indelible mark upon them. The music of the Finno-Ugrians is not characteristically pentatonic, while this is a feature of the common melodies found in Cheremis and Hungarian; the links here are to be traced rather to Turkic and Central Asiatic roots than to anything Finno-Ugrian.

Cheremis society, which was in constant and lengthy contact with foreign peoples, developed more swiftly than did that of the northern Finno-Ugrians. One result is that the tribal system has left hardly any traces, although at the end of the last century some scholars found that the inhabitants of neighbouring villages believed themselves to be descended from a common ancestor. Common tribal sacrifices are recalled by the word *kümyž*, now a dish made of earthenware or wood, but once the name of the great wooden bowl in which food was placed to be eaten at tribal ceremonies and sacrifices. The word was also used to denote the crowd of guests, i.e. the members of the tribe, who ate from this bowl.

Traces of ancestor worship may be seen in the mourning customs of the Cheremis. At one time animals were sacrificed in honour of the dead. Perhaps the domestic god kept in the *kudo* may have been the ancestor of the tribe, although there is no proof of this.

Officially and nominally the Cheremis are Orthodox in religion, but many traits of their earlier faith have been preserved. Not only did they hold the dead in respect, but they believed in various good and evil spirits of human form; they personified natural objects and phenomena, to which belonged the highest god *Jumo*,[1] representing the heavens and climate together. They also personified the sun, moon and stars, the wind, clouds, earth, water and forests. Sacrifices were offered to the spirits they revered – even at the end of the nineteenth century sixty-four sacrificial groves are mentioned in one account. There were various kinds of sacrificial ground. The best known was the *keremet*, a fenced-off sacrificial grove where sacrifices were offered to the evil spirits. Women were forbidden to enter it, but might take part in ceremonies held in the grove called *jumon oto* 'the grove of the god'. Cheremis religious beliefs contained a mixture of animistic, Christian and Moslem elements; they were maintained by a priestly order and numerous soothsayers, magicians and visionaries.

In the second half of the last century a peculiar sect known as *kuyu sorta* 'the great candle' made rapid progress among the Cheremis. It took its name from the unusually large candles burnt at their meetings. The members were forbidden to worship the lower orders of spirits, but continued to respect the higher gods and spirits. From Christianity they adopted strict asceticism, which

1 *Jumo* is a cognate of the Finnish *Jumala* 'God'.

was shown in their attitude to clothing, food and pleasure (tobacco, spirits and even tea were forbidden). By the beginning of the present century this sect had acquired a very large following.

The independent history of the Cheremis people begins with their separation from the Mordvins in the sixth and seventh centuries. This date is established by linguistic research; after the seventh century there is evidence of strong Volga Bulgar influence which affects the Cheremis separately from the Mordvins. It is likely that even before this the ancestors of the two peoples were living apart, though not far removed geographically. Proof of this is found in Jordanes' *Getica*, written in the sixth century; in this he lists the northern peoples conquered by the Gothic King Hermanarich in the fourth century. Of these three demand our attention: *Merens*, *Mordens* and *Inniscaris*. *Mordens* is evidently the name of the Mordvins; *Inniscaris* has been regarded as the first appearance of the Cheremis, but this is extremely difficult to prove. It is nevertheless significant that Jordanes mentions the *Inniscaris* alongside the *Mordens*, and the reference may indeed be to the Cheremis. Even more important is the name *Merens*, which is to be associated with the *Meri* or *Merja*, a now defunct Finno-Ugrian people of the Volga region. Jordanes' account at least makes it clear that distinctions were already made between the various Finno-Ugrians of the Volga. This in turn suggests that the links between them were now so scanty that foreign observers felt it necessary to distinguish between them.

At this period the Cheremis were living to the west of their present habitat, on both banks of the Volga near the mouth of the Oka. Their contacts with the Volga Bulgars began at the beginning of the eighth century, when these latter fled northwards to the Volga-Kama region before the Khazars. At this time the Cheremis also came under Khazar domination. From the end of the ninth century until the Mongol invasions of the thirteenth century they lived in the Volga Bulgarian Empire. It was during this period that their language, culture and society were strongly influenced by their Chuvash-speaking Turkic neighbours, whose effects are to be seen in the stock of loanwords concerning agriculture, animal breeding, domestic crafts and building methods.

From the thirteenth century till 1552 the Cheremis were ruled by the Tatar khans of Kazan. This too was a period of considerable foreign influence, testified by some 650 Tatar loanwords. Thus Turkic influence played a dominant part for centuries in Cheremis life; it is no surprise to discover that of all the Finno-Ugrians, the Cheremis have had the most intensive Turkic connections, nor did these cease with the end of their political power; they continued to live alongside Chuvash and Tatar peoples, with strong mutual interaction as the result.

Connections with the Russians also began early. The Kievan chronicle records that the Cheremis were paying taxes to the Russians in the eleventh century; this, however, can only refer to a western group since, as we have seen, this was the period of ever-increasing Turkic influence among them. From the fourteenth century onwards they were drawn increasingly into Russian connections, notably with the important centre of Nizhni Novgorod and the Vyatka principate. The Cheremis began to provide soldiers for various campaigns and wars.

Under the Tatar khans the tribal system disintegrated rapidly. The Cheremis leaders paid dues to the Tatar khans and provided troops when required; in 1455 they supplied some 30,000 soldiers to fight for the Tatars against Ivan III. In the fifteenth and sixteenth centuries Cheremis soldiers were taking part in Russian campaigns against the Tatars, which suggests that by this time the power of the latter was growing weaker. In 1546 the Hill Cheremis transferred their allegiance to the Russians, offering their services to Ivan IV in his wars against the Tatars. They took part in the decisive capture of Kazan in 1552, when the Meadow Cheremis also came under Russian domination.

The Russians built new fortresses and towns in the region, such as Yaransk, Urzhum and Tsarevokoksaysk, the present Yoshkar-Ola. These all played an important rôle in the economic and cultural development of the Cheremis area. During the sixteenth and seventeenth centuries the lands of the Cheremis rulers were divided among Russian boyars, monasteries and churches, and the forests became royal property. Only Orthodox believers might possess peasant lands, and this compelled many to accept Christianity. Taxes mounted and many insurrections resulted. The Cheremis joined the Russians in the rising of Stenka Razin (1667–71), and in 1670 an army of 15,000 of them drove their masters from a vast area in the Volga-Vetluga region, seizing it for themselves. The rising was savagely suppressed. The following centuries saw no alleviation of the situation, nor was it improved when the eighteenth century numbers of Cheremis were resettled in what is now Bashkiria by order of Catherine II. There they joined many who had fled to that region to escape the burden of taxes and forced conversion. These were the elements that formed the eastern Cheremis group, with its separate linguistic and cultural development.

After this the Cheremis were in a state of almost continuous rebellion throughout the nineteenth century. Despite this, a few factories were built in the region, and these employed local as well as Russian labour.

It is no surprise that the Cheremis played their part in the revolution of 1917. The Mari Autonomous Region was created in 1920, and on 5 December 1936 it was proclaimed an Autonomous Soviet Socialist Republic. In 1959 there were 647,000 inhabitants, and the capital, Yoshkar-Ola had a population of 88,000.

Industries were rapidly developed, notably heavy engineering, paper and wood mills and food-processing. Although 56 per cent of the area is forest and only 30 per cent is arable land, rye and oats are grown in large quantities on the mechanized and collectivized farms. Animal breeding and fishing, together with bee-keeping, also provide an important source of income. Communications have been improved; almost half the goods are transported by water, while railways provide links with Kazan and more distant parts of the USSR.

At the end of the last century only ten per cent of the Cheremis were literate, despite the efforts of the missionary schools in the area. In 1952 there were almost 800 schools; tuition in Cheremis was also provided.

The earliest texts in the language date from the eighteenth century and consist chiefly of liturgical works and prayers. In the following century the gospels and catechisms were published in Cheremis. These were generally translated by folk who knew little of the language, and read awkwardly. Illiteracy was a great hindrance to their propagation. In the present century calendars were made by some of the more educated Cheremis, and in these may be seen the germ of the present literary language, or languages, for until recently there was no uniformity; newspapers and periodicals after the First World War were published in various dialects. In Kazan they appeared in Meadow Cheremis, in Vyatka in the Urzhum dialect and in Birsk in the Eastern dialect. After the creation of the Autonomous Region, books and other printed material appeared in the two main dialects of the area, thus giving rise to two literary languages. After long discussion, in 1953 it was agreed that one literary language alone should be developed; this was to be based on Meadow and Eastern Cheremis, which was understood by some 80 per cent of the population. To unify the orthography new rules of spelling have been introduced; these will draw the existing Hill and Meadow Cheremis dialects closer to each other.

Cheremis literature has thus existed for only a few decades, but it has already produced two writers, the poet Mikaj (M. S. Gerasimov, 1885–1944) and the novelist M. Sketan (J. P. Majorov, 1898–1937), whose works have come to be regarded as classics.

The musical life of the republic has drawn on the rich store of folk music available. This was fostered at first by choral works, but now there is a Mari State Philharmonic Society which is the custodian of Cheremis tradition.

Cheremis scholarship is centred on the Academic Institute in Yoshkar-Ola, founded in 1931. The work of V. M. Vasilev (b. 1883) in linguistics is well known abroad; he has written a dialect dictionary and published works on the beliefs and customs of the people, as well as playing a major rôle in the creation of a literary language. There are many younger scholars in the Finno-Ugrian field, while other Cheremis academics have received wide recognition outside the republic; among these V. P. Mosolov (1888–1951) became vice-president of the Soviet Agricultural Academy.

The Mordvins

The Mordvins, who in 1970 numbered 1,263,000, form the third largest Finno-Ugrian people. At the same time they are the largest and most widely scattered Finno-Ugrian people in the Soviet Union. The Mordvin Autonomous Soviet Socialist Republic has a population of a million in an area of 26,000 square kilometres

(1970), but of these only 37.4 per cent were Mordvins in 1939; 57 per cent were Russians and the rest Tatars. Thus over half the Mordvins live elsewhere – in the Tatar and Bashkir ASSRs, in the Penza, Gorki, Ulyanovsk and Kuybyshev areas of the USSR and in Siberia. Only 78 per cent of them use the Mordvin language.

The live in widely scattered groups between the Oka and Belaya rivers; the two largest groups are found in the Moksha and Sura valleys, and in the Sura-Volga area. In ethnic, anthropological and linguistic characteristics alike they are divided into two separate groups: the western or Moksha, and the eastern or Erzä groups. The boundary between them is the River Insar, a tributary of the Alatyr.

The differences between the Moksha and Erzä dialects are considerable, affecting phonology, stress, vocabulary and syntax. Since speakers of one dialect have great difficulty in comprehending the other, two literary languages are in use. The Erzä Mordvins outnumber the Mokshas.

The name *Mordvin* or *Mordva* is normally assumed to have appeared first in the works of Jordanes in the sixth century. The form of it here was *Mordens*, where *-ns* is a Gothic suffix. Later Constantinus Porphyrogennetus mentions *Mordia* in his *De administrando imperio* stating that, 'this country lies ten days' journey from the land of the Petchenegs'. The same name appears in the Russian chronicles as *Mordva*, where *-v-* is a secondary development in Russian. The origin of the word is in doubt; one supposition is that it is connected with Votyak *murt* ∼ Zyryan *mort* 'human, man', but the corresponding forms of the Permian words in Mordvin have front, and not back, vowels, e.g., *mirde* 'man, husband', from an original **mertä*. Moreover the Mordvins themselves do not use this term; they employ either *Erzä* or *Moksha*, and both of these names remain of doubtful origin.

None of the other Finno-Ugrian peoples in Russia live so far south as the Mordvins. They inhabit a region bordering on the steppes, and their rivers are part of the Volga river-system. Forests are rarer here, although they still account for 25 per cent of the area of the Mordvin ASSR and consist mainly of oak, beech and poplar. Since this region falls in the black earth zone, it is excellent for agriculture and animal husbandry. The Mordvins have developed these far beyond their more northerly Finno-Ugrian neighbours, and have enjoyed a settled existence for almost a thousand years. Some of them managed to acquire large landholdings, but the majority were small peasants; at the beginning of the present century almost a third of their holdings had no draught animals available. Triple-course agriculture was extended in this region during the seventeenth century, while it reached the more northerly peoples only two centuries later. Apart from rye, barley and oats, wheat, buckwheat, peas, beans, cabbage, flax, hemp and hops were cultivated. In the wooded areas bee-keeping was practised, and until the seventeenth century hunting and fishing were relatively important in their economy.

As the peasants became poorer, those who lost their land or possessed only very small holdings were compelled to turn to domestic crafts to eke out their livelihood. At the end of the nineteenth century there were hosts of Mordvin craftsmen – weavers, leather-workers, tanners and felt-makers – who were generally at the mercy of the big dealers and traders.

The appearance of the Mordvin villages testifies to a long established settled life. There are small differences in the building styles of the various regions, but for the most part they follow either Russian or Tatar models. Their houses are of timber, divided into two or three rooms, and often thatched with straw. The plot of land is surrounded with a wattle fence, and the front of the house opens not directly on to the street, but into the front part of the courtyard. The siting of the house, indeed, depends upon climatic conditions, so that the side facing the street may have no windows whatsoever. The farm buildings are erected in various parts of the courtyard.

The costume of the Mordvins varies according to groups. The Moksha women, for example, wear trousers and long white pleated dresses to the knee; these are often embroidered in red. The Erzä women do not wear trousers, but have ankle-length dresses without pleats. The Moksha women normally wear long linen headscarves, embroidered at both ends, while the Erzäs prefer embroidered linen caps ending in ornamented kerchiefs to cover their neck and shoulders. Ornamental clips and necklaces play a great part in their dress. The Erzä women are characterized by the *pulagaj* or apron worn at the back: this is studded with pearls and other decorations, and fringed with tassels, and is worn attached to the belt. At one time they wore sandals of bark, but these are no longer found. For many years these folk costumes have been worn only at festivals; now they are seen chiefly among the Mokshas.

Before the revolution, Mordvin society differed hardly at all from that of the Russians in the south. Tribal organization disappeared very early and left practically no traces. At the end of the last century, however, there were still some large family groups among the Mokshas farming in common; these consisted of some twenty-five to forty members. The head of the family was elected by the members, and held this office till his death. In these communities private property was unknown; all earnings were handed in to be used in common. In many places these communities developed from the practice of the newly married sons building themselves houses in the farmyard, but continuing to work the family land in common.

Earlier scholars observed many archaic traits in their marriage-customs. There was, for example, the strange custom of betrothing a marriageable girl to a young boy; in these cases the actual marriage took place only when the 'husband' came of age. This practice is recalled in Mordvin folk poetry; there are many interesting songs in which the woman sings of her 'husband' who is still a child.

Very few traces of their early religious beliefs have survived. From the scanty reports on these, they appear to have been like those of the Permians and Cheremis. Nothing has remained of ancestor-worship. Although their folklore has not retained any concept of the highest god (like the Cheremis *Jumo* and Votyak *Inmar*), lesser local deities were worshipped and sacrifices offered in their sacred places. Horse-sacrifices, widely known among the Volga Finno-Ugrians and Turkic peoples, appear to have been known among the Mordvins also; there are even suggestions that human sacrifices were offered. In one remote Erzä village, far from Russian influence, it was apparently a custom to place a widow upon a tree trunk in the sacrificial place, then bind her to it hand and foot, and pretend to cut her throat. After this she was carried back to the village in a cart, but throughout the ceremony she had to feign death. There exist no satisfactory accounts of their idols, but relics of former idol worship may be seen in the eighteenth-century practice of decorating a sacred tree with icons and 'entertaining' the saints depicted on them.[1]

The modern divisions of the Mordvins are the result of a lengthy historical process. During the first few centuries of our era they lived in a relatively homogeneous group in the Volga-Oka-Moksha-Sura region. Jordanes, as we have seen, mentions the *Mordens* as subjects of Hermanarich. At the time of Constantinus Porphyrogennetus they were doubtless paying taxes to the Volga Bulgars. From the twelfth century onwards there are more frequent references to them in the Russian chronicles and other sources.

According to the Kievan chronicle Jaroslav Svyatoslavich, Prince of Muroma, fought the Mordvins in 1103 and was defeated. In 1184 the prince of Vladimir attacked them. In the early years of the following century there were frequent skirmishes, and the fortress of Nizhni-Novgorod was erected then as a base for campaigns against them. By this time the Mordvins had split into smaller, regional groups, and the Moksha and Erzä tribes had begun to develop separately. This is confirmed by the account of a campaign of 1228, when the southern (Moksha) prince of the Mordvins, Puresh, was fighting as an ally of the Russians against the northern (Erzä) prince Puras; it was his son who finally achieved victory.

Friar Julian also mentions the Mordvins. He set out from Hungary to search for Hungarians who had remained in Magna Hungaria, and on his return he crossed their territory in 1236. Julian depicts them as merciless pagans who think nothing of a man who has not slain many of his fellows. When they go out, they have the dead men's heads carried before them, and the more skulls on view, the more the warrior is respected. From these

---

1 The replacement of pagan idols by Christian icons is nothing unusual. Among many of the Finno-Ugrian peoples a mixture of pagan and Christian worship was to be found, and sacrificial offerings were made to the 'Russian gods'. An account of 1901 describes how an Ostyak woman fell ill and lit a candle before an icon she had in the corner of the room. The 'icon' however was none other than a portrait of Pushkin, sold by a wily trader to the unsuspecting family as a miracle-working icon of the prophet Elijah.

skulls, drinking vessels are made and used. The man who has not killed a human being may not marry.

In 1239 the Tatars occupied the Mordvin lands and used them in their campaigns in the west. According to Rubruquis (Ruysbroeck), the thirteenth-century Flemish Franciscan, a troop of Mokshas ('Moxel') reached Germany in 1253. After the disintegration of the Golden Horde, the Mordvins came under the domination of the Tatar khans of Kazan.

In the northern area of Mordvin settlements, Russians made their appearance in the fourteenth century, and there were many conflicts between them and the Tatars before the final victory of Ivan IV in 1552, after which all the Mordvins became part of the Russian Empire. To defend the south-east of this empire, two defensive lines were built across their lands in the sixteenth and seventeenth centuries; they were to keep out the nomads and prevent their depredations in the area. The fortresses along these lines later became commercial and industrial centres, like Saransk, the present capital of the Mordvin ASSR, which was founded in 1641. Instead of the Mordvin and Tatar princes, it was now the Russian boyars who oppressed the people, for these and the monasteries took over much of the land. At first taxes were unchanged, but they soon began to rise.

The dispersion of the Mordvins, which had already begun before the Russian victory over the Tatars, continued apace; they fled south and east to avoid oppression and taxation. The severity with which insurrections were suppressed was a further reason for moving away, and the missionary activity of the Russian church also played its part. Ivan IV founded two monasteries in the Erzä territory, while in 1654–55 the Bishop of Ryazan instituted a campaign of forced conversion in the Tambov district. The sacred places, groves and trees were destroyed and many Mordvins baptized compulsorily. They gained their revenge by killing the bishop. Then tactics were changed; the converts were rewarded with gifts of money, freedom from military service and remission of taxes, while the recalcitrants were forced to pay increased taxes or to leave their villages. The result was that all the Mordvins accepted Christianity in the eighteenth century.

Meanwhile social and economic problems caused further unrest. Growth of commercial contacts between the Mordvins and Russian centres such as Nizhni-Novgorod and Saratov did not serve the interests of the peasants, who frequently rebelled against the growing power of their overlords. Their opposition eventually led to the creation in the nineteenth century of a reforming sect, like the Cheremis *kuyu sorta*, which attempted to remedy the ills of the people. Founded by the Mordvin Kuzma Alexeyev who proclaimed himself a prophet, it replaced Christ with the ancient native deities. The movement did not have great success, particularly since the old pagan practices were scarcely remembered, and their revival was artificial.

The Russian land reform had its customary effect. The best lands went to the larger owners and widened the gap between rich and poor peasants. As a result of the land famine, 40 per cent of the male labour force was compelled to undertake casual work, and a new migration began towards Kazakhstan and Siberia. At the beginning of the nineteenth century the Mordvins had been living in six administrative regions; by the end they were scattered in eleven. The building of the Moscow-Kazan railway and its branches at the end of the century strengthened the links with Moscow.

After the Russian revolution, in which the Mordvins played a part, the question of an autonomous region was raised. The existence of various national groups in the area made a solution difficult, and an autonomous area was created only in 1928; it was declared a Region in 1930 and a Republic in 1934, since which time industry and agriculture have been developed considerably. Before the Revolution this was a backward area, with only 7,500 workers in industry. Between 1896 and 1910 over 200,000 were compelled to seek work elsewhere. New industries were introduced and the old ones, chiefly concerned with wood and paper, further developed, so that industrial production in 1940 was ten times greater than it had been in 1913. Similar achievements have been recorded in agriculture, which has now been completely mechanized; the wheat harvest of 1953 was six times as great as that of 1913. Some 51 per cent of the total area is under cultivation.

In education great strides have been made. Before 1917 only 3.7 per cent of the male population were literate, and only 0.04 per cent of the women could write their names. In 1952 the

Republic contained 1,341 schools. Saransk, the capital, a town of 70,000 inhabitants, is the centre of Mordvin education; both press and radio use three languages – Erzä, Moksha and Russian.

Literary activity began in the last century with the publication by the Kazan Missionary Society of gospels and primers. The development of literature in the two languages of Mordvin has been a lengthy process. Poetry and drama appeared first, with the novel following in the thirties of this century. The Mordvin oral tradition has also been revived, and Mordvin scholars have begun to investigate folklore, hitherto the province of foreign researchers. The university and the Mordvin Academic Institute at Saransk have been in the forefront of these activities. Other arts have also begun to develop, notably painting, sculpture and opera.

Extinct Finno-Ugrian Peoples of the Volga Region

The vicissitudes of the area settled by the Mordvins and Cheremis led to the disappearance of certain Finno-Ugrian peoples in the Volga region. Their traces can be found in old historical sources. The *Merens* of Jordanes, for example, are the Merja or Meri people (or perhaps more correctly, tribe) mentioned by the Russian chronicles as neighbours of the Mordvins and Cheremis.

The chronicle of Nestor, however, mentions not only the Merja, but the Muroma. The passage reads: 'Beside the White Lake there live the Vesi [Vepsians], beside the Rostov Lake [Lake Nyero in the former province of Yaroslavl] live the Merja, and by the Kleshchino Lake [Lake Pleshcheyevo in the former Vladimir province] also the Merja. But by the River Oka, where it flows into the Volga, there live the Muroma, a people of a different language, also the Cheremis, with a language of their own, and the Mordva, with their own language.' Little is known of the Merja, whose habitat is located exactly by the Russian chronicler. The lakes he mentions are to be found about sixty kilometres south and south-west of the Volga near the town of Rostov. How large the area was is unknown, but they have left their name in numerous geographical appellations, in the river-names Merja, Merska and Merskaya, and in place-names such as Meryakova, Merinovo, Mereleva, Merli and Merlina. According to this chronicle they took part in a campaign against the Varangians, and in 882 they took part in the battles waged by Prince Oleg of Kiev in the Dnieper region. Their name also occurs in the list of participants in the first campaign against Constantinople in 907. Their language appears to have resembled Cheremis. Not only did they live immediately to their west, but their name is considered to be a variant of *Mari*. Some of the names of the former Merja territory can be explained through Cheremis, and this again speaks of a close connection. The termination *änger* 'stream', common in Cheremis place-names, is also found in the Merja region.

The linguistic affinity of the Muroma is much more problematical. They lived to the south-east of the Merja, between the Lower Oka and the Klyazma, immediately west of the Mordvins. Both the Muroma and the Merja were engaged in agriculture and animal breeding, but they also hunted and fished. Craftsmen were to be found among them, such as blacksmiths, potters, weavers and workers in leather, wood and bone. They traded with both Slavs and the Volga Bulgars. From the archaeological discoveries in this area it is clear that there were wealthy leaders in their patriarchal society; in graveyards from the ninth to the eleventh century rich ornaments and other articles have been found. Slave girls and splendidly caparisoned horses were buried with them. The women's clothes discovered in these graves are also decorated with metal ornaments.

Both the Merja and Muroma peoples became assimilated to the Russians in the tenth century.

Two other tribes must also be mentioned here, the Terjuhans and the Karatays. These have not become extinct, but have renounced their Finno-Ugrian language. Originally they were branches of the Mordvins and spoke this language.

There are some 16,000 Terjuhans in the Gorki district of the USSR. They became Russian speakers at the end of the eighteenth century, but their customs and dress still preserve traces of their origin. They had earlier belonged to the Erzä group of Mordvins.

The Karatays inhabit three villages in the Tatar ASSR. They also spoke Mordvin in the seventeenth century, but now use Tatar, though with phonological peculiarities that betray their origin. Apart from these, only the women's dress and a few Mordvin words recall their past.

The Baltic Finns

The Finns

The Finns constitute the largest group of Baltic Finns. Their homeland is in the eastern part of Scandinavia, and has an area of 337,000 square kilometres; of this total, 32,000 square kilometres are lakes, hence the poetic name 'the land of a thousand lakes'. The number of these lakes has been estimated at over 55,000.

Finland is also famous for its dense forests, which cover about 70 per cent of the land. Consisting of birch and pine, they represent the most important source of the national income. Industry is well developed, and is by no means confined to wood and paper products. Agricultural land is relatively scarce, and accounts for only some ten per cent of the total area. Rye, oats, barley and potatoes are the most important crops. Cattle breeding is well developed and the export of butter and dairy products plays a considerable rôle in the economic life of the country.

All forms of communication have made rapid progress. There are good rail and road networks and internal air services. The Finnish mercantile marine includes some 770,000 net tons of seagoing ships, and plays an important part in foreign trade.

, The population of Finland numbered 4,695,000 in 1970, and of these nine per cent spoke Swedish as their native tongue. This language is officially recognized as one of the two state languages; in practice it is confined to certain areas. Finnish speakers are also found outside Finland; there are some 93,000 in the USSR, about 200,000 in North America, and smaller groups in Sweden and Australia. The total number of Finns is therefore in the region of 4¾ million.

The name Finn is first found in the *Fenni* of Tacitus's *Germania* of the first century AD, but here it applies to the Lapps. In the following century Ptolemy mentions two groups, one in the northern part of Scandinavia and the other beside the Vistula. The first of these may be identified as Lapps, the second as Baltic Finns. This double use of the word continues for a long time; not until the seventeenth century does it come to be used only in connection

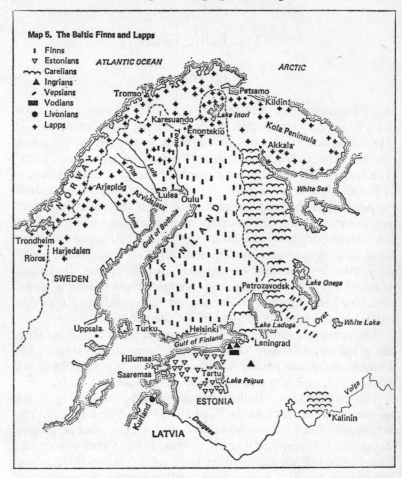

Map 5. The Baltic Finns and Lapps

| Finns
∇ Estonians
⌢⌢ Carelians
▲ Ingrians
⸙ Vepsians
▦ Vodians
● Livonians
+ Lapps

with the Finns in Finland. The name is probably Germanic in origin; *finn-, fenn-* 'walker, wanderer' was the name given by the Scandinavians to the nomadic Lapps.

The Finns themselves have never used this word to refer either to the Lapps or to themselves. They are *Suomalainen*, derived from *Suomi* 'Finland, the Finnish language'. The origin of this name has occasioned much discussion through the ages, but no unanimity has resulted. One theory has been revived with appropriate phonological and semantic support – that there is a connection between Finn. *suomi* and Lapp *čuobmâ* 'fish skin'; the implication is that the Finns were so named after their ancient waterproof clothing, presumably made of this material. Another explanation is that it is a loanword from Swedish, derived from Old Swedish **some* 'band, group'.

In any event the name was used to describe only the people who occupied the south-west part of Finland and their land (*Peri-Suomi*, from 1848 *Varsinais-Suomi* 'Finland proper'). Even around 1500 it still had this implication. In the introduction to his translation of the New Testament, Agricola distinguishes between *suomalainen* (Suomi-Finns), *hämäläinen* (Häme-Finns) and *karjalainen* (Carelian-Finns) and their languages, but notes that the whole country is called *Some* (= Suomi), for it is the 'mother' of the other provinces. In modern Estonia there are several old place names which include *Soome* (an older form of Suomi) and it may therefore be presumed that the Suomi tribe brought this name with it from the common Finnic homeland in the Baltic, and later transmitted it to all the Finnish people.

Apart from the Baltic, Germanic and Slavonic loanwords inherited from the common Finnic period, the modern language possesses many more recent loans from Swedish and Russian. The first texts date from the thirteenth century, and consist of fragments in Swedish and Latin documents. The first connected texts do not appear until the first half of the sixteenth century.

There are relatively wide dialectal divergences in Finnish, showing differences in phonology, morphology, syntax and vocabulary. Five dialect groups are distinguished in the modern language:

1 *The South-West group*, spoken by the descendants of the Varsinais-Suomi province mentioned earlier. Their speech is quite different from that in the other dialect groups, and in many respects resembles Estonian.

2 *The Häme group*, spoken in a larger area to the north-east of the previous dialects, in the province of Häme and part of Satakunta.

3 *Northern dialect-group*, spoken in Pohjanmaa province on the shore of the Gulf of Bothnia and throughout the northern half of Finland. It is divided into three dialects: those of south, central and north Pohjanmaa.

4 *The Savo group*, found in the eastern part of Finland, north-east of the Häme group and east of south and central Pohjanmaa.
5 *The South-East group*, in a comparatively small area of the south-east border country.

Apart from this division of dialects, Finnish may be generally divided into two main types, Western and Eastern. The boundary between them is not always sharply defined. The Eastern type includes the Savo and south-east groups, but many of its features are also to be found in the northern area. The western type consists of those dialects which are free from, or only slightly affected by, the influence of the Savo and South-East groups. The differences are shown in the following table, which also includes the standard literary form for comparison:

Literary	Western	Eastern	
padan	*paran, palan*	*paan*	'pot' (acc.)
lehden	*lehren, lehlen*	*lehen, lehjen*	'leaf' (acc.)
metsä	*mettä*	*mehtä*	'forest'
kaura	*kaura*	*kakra*	'oats'
maa	*maa*	*moa, mua*	'land'
pää	*pää*	*peä, piä*	'head'
juoda	*juoda*	*juua, juuvva*	'to drink'
juo	*juo, jua*	*juop (i)*	'he drinks'
te	*te, tei, tee, tet*	*työ*	'you' (pl.)
lasi	*klasi*	*lasi*	'glass'
teen	*teen, tehen*	*tien*	'I put'
ottakaa	*ottaka (a),*	*ottoa (ten)*	'take!' (pl.)
	ottakkai	*ottoo (ten)*	
		ottakkoa	

There are also differences in vocabulary:

Western	Eastern	
suvi	*kesä*	'summer'
puhua	*haastaa*	'to talk'
ehtoo	*ilta*	'evening'
sonni, mulli	*härkä*	'bull'
karitsa	*vuona*	'lamb'
liina	*huivi*	'kerchief'

The Finnish dialects have come into existence through the development of the old tribal dialects and their mixture.

An examination of the development of modern Finnish and its dialects must start with the Common Finnic period. This came to an end with the disintegration of the Baltic Finns at about the time of Christ. In the ensuing centuries certain tribes changed their habitat, moving from their home south of the Gulf of Finland to its northern shores and penetrating the interior of modern Finland.[1] Various theories have been advanced concerning their movements, and the development and settlement of Finland.

One of the many problems concerns the division of the tribes in the Common Finnic period, and which of these may be regarded as the ancestors of the modern Finns. E. N. Setälä, the well-known Finnish scholar at the turn of the present century, held the view that the tribal divisions of the Common Finnic people and the subsequent separate dialectal development of their language gave rise to the present national divisions. According to his theory, there were eight Common Finnic tribes whose geographical distribution he also attempted to reconstruct. Furthest to the south lived the ancestors of the present Livonians and Vepsians, the former to the west, the latter to the east. North-west of the Livonians there were the Estonians, while the Carelians lived north-east of the Vepsians. North of the Estonians came the Vodians, then the (Varsinais-)Suomi, Häme and Kainuu tribes. The following sketch shows their distribution:

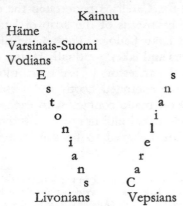

<pre>
                  Kainuu
      Häme
      Varsinais-Suomi
      Vodians
         E   s
         s   n
         t   a
         o   i
           n   l
           i   e
           a   r
           n   a
           s   C
      Livonians   Vepsians
</pre>

---

1 Finno-Ugrian peoples may possibly have inhabited this area in the neolithic age. Archaeologists who have discovered traces of the Sperrings-culture (3000 BC) in Southern Finland believe that an early Finno-Ugrian migration may have brought

In Setälä's opinion the present Finns are descended from a mixture of the three northernmost peoples, the Kainuu, Häme and Suomi, and this process took place in the territory of modern Finland.

It is, however, questionable whether it is necessary to trace the ancestry of the Kainuu back to Common Finnic. The Kainulainen once lived on the coasts of South-West, West and Northern Finland, but it is doubtful whether they were among the tribes who settled there. Ottar of Heligoland, Alfred the Great's Norwegian vassal, mentions Cwenland (= Kainuu) as a northern neighbour of Norway, whose inhabitants are frequently involved in skirmishes with the Norwegians. Egill Skallagrímsson, the Icelandic scald of the tenth century, mentions them together with the Häme, Suomi and Carelians. After this they become increasingly difficult to trace; their name lives on in oral tradition and place names. Their origin is dubious and many scholars now believe that they were not among the Finnic peoples who occupied the country, but were a mixture of other tribal groups.

The rest of Setälä's theory of the settlement of Finland by the Suomi and Häme tribes has been accepted as part of tradition. They crossed the Gulf of Finland from their homeland on the south side, and gradually settled on the south-west coast. Archaeological discoveries support the theory of gradual settlement during the early centuries AD.

At the same time the Carelians penetrated the eastern area of Finland, reaching it by means of the strip of land between the Gulf of Finland and Lake Ladoga. They made their way northwards along the rivers and lakes, gradually taking more land into their possession. As the ancestors of the Finns moved north and east, so the Carelians penetrated north and west, and the two groups of settlers soon made contact with each other. From a mixture of these, new tribal and linguistic divisions arose. The Savo, for example, are believed to be a mixture of Häme and

---

them there. Some scholars (Ailio, Moora) see in the neolithic culture which extends from the Gulf of Bothnia to Lake Ladoga evidence for the existence there of the direct ancestors of the Finns; others (Äyräpää) regard the early inhabitants of Southern Finland as Finno-Ugrian tribes who merged with the Common Finnic peoples who crossed the Baltic in the early centuries AD. These undoubtedly contributed to the development of the Finns, but cannot be regarded as direct ancestors. Linguistic evidence supports this second view.

Carelians. The dialect of South Pohjanmaa is the result of a fusion between South-West Suomi and Häme, while Central Pohjanmaa displays not only western elements but traces of the Savo dialect of the Eastern type. From this constant movement and mixture of the population and its subsequent effect on their dialects, the Finnish language came to be established in the eleventh and twelfth centuries.

Other views have been advanced on the Finnic tribes and the development of the Baltic Finnic languages. Lauri Kettunen, for example, believes that there were only four original Finnic tribes: Livonians, Estonians, Häme and Vepsians. The Vodians, in his view, arose from a mixture of Estonian and Häme stock, and the Carelians developed from a mixture of Vepsians and Western Finns who settled in the eighth to tenth centuries by Lake Ladoga. The Savo he regards as Carelians partly mixed with Häme. Thus the original Finnish tribe comprised the Häme, who crossed the sea to Finland, then inhabited by Lapps and Scandinavians. In the first centuries of their occupation, only the Häme lived in South-West Finland, but later Estonian settlers crossed the Gulf of Finland, and the Finns of today are a mixture of the two.

More recently the Estonian linguist P. Ariste has put forward an interesting explanation of the formation of the Baltic Finnic languages. He notes the considerable linguistic and ethnic differences between the northern and southern Estonians, and points out that there are strong links between the South-West dialects of Finnish and Northern Estonian. He argues that modern Estonians and their language are descended from two Common Finnic tribes (the so-called northern and southern Proto-Estonians). He does not agree with Setälä and Kettunen that the Häme were one of the original Common Finnic tribes; in his view they were descendants of groups of northern Proto-Estonians living on the coast mingled with other Finnic tribes who had already migrated to the northern coast of the Gulf of Finland. Other Proto-Estonian tribes subsequently joined the Häme from the western parts of modern Estonia, and these formed the basis of the Suomi people. It was a mixture of Häme Suomi and the originally separate Carelian peoples that developed into the modern Finnish people and their language. Vodian he regards as a branch of the North-

East dialect of Estonian mingled with strong Finnish or Ingrian influences. So Ariste traces the origin of the modern Baltic Finnic languages and peoples to five tribes: Northern 'Estonians', Southern 'Estonians', Carelians, Livonians and Vepsians.

Ariste's theory is interesting because it does not depend upon a mechanical identification of the modern Finnic peoples with their appropriate Common Finnic tribes. He breaks away from the idea of 'one language – one tribe', and bases his arguments first and foremost on linguistic evidence which he supports with archaeological discoveries.

The settlement of Finland was a lengthy process. The various groups and tribes filtered into their new habitat for some seven or eight centuries after Christ. As they advanced, so the Lapps who were living in the central and eastern areas moved further north, while the Scandinavian inhabitants of the western and south-western coastal strip became merged with the newcomers. These Finns cultivated the land and extended the area under cultivation by clearing forests; they also learnt from the Vikings their method of trading by sea and began a doubtless profitable commercial activity. The domination of the Finnish tribes did not result in political authority. They had no central state organization; the tribes lived side by side in a land with virtually unlimited space for expansion, and they grew apace in numbers and economic power. They soon drew the attention of the Swedes, who launched a series of campaigns against them, partly on the pretext of converting them to Christianity. The first of these crusades took place in the middle of the twelfth century under Erik IX, but the conquest of Finland was not completed until 1249, when a powerful Swedish army occupied south-west and central Finland, establishing fortresses and garrisons there.

Swedish domination lasted until 1809. During this time the Finns became united into one people, a process which was assisted both by the adoption of Christianity and by Swedish cultural influence. The creation of the diocese of Turku strengthened the power of the Roman Catholic church, but Christianity spread very slowly among the pagan Finns; with the Reformation, however, the situation changed, and today the majority of Finns (some 96 per cent) are Lutherans.

With the Swedes came the feudal system and a large part of the agricultural land fell into the hands of the Swedish nobility; at the end of the seventeenth century three fifths of the country was in their possession, and the Finns were the victims of considerable oppression. They made various attempts to improve their lot, notably in the rising of 1596. Their situation was not improved by the incidence of numerous foreign campaigns involving the Swedes and Russians or Swedes and Poles; these kept the eastern borderlands in a constant state of war, whose burdens fell heavily on the Finnish population. Not only did the economic life of the country suffer, but they were also called upon to provide soldiers. In the Thirty Years' War they provided about a third of the army of Gustavus Adolphus – the so-called hakkapelita, from their battle-cry *hakkaa päälle*! 'Strike him on the head!'.

In the seventeenth century the Swedes began to make improvements in Finland. They built towns which became commercial centres, established schools and in 1640 founded the University of Åbo (Turku); not unnaturally these cultural institutions served primarily the Swedish population – the university in its first year had thirty-six Swedish and only eight Finnish students.

In the eighteenth century Finland again became a theatre of war for many long years, when Charles XII of Sweden was finally defeated by Peter the Great of Russia, and at the Peace of Uusikaupunki (1721) renounced his claims to Estonia and the south-east of Finland. The Swedes attempted to redress their losses in 1741, but after a very brief campaign they were forced to cede new areas of eastern Finland to the Russians. Finally in 1809, after the Two Years' War the whole of Finland became part of Russia at the Peace of Hamina. It was governed by a Finnish senate and a governor appointed by the Tsar – the only official who, under the constitution, need not be of Finnish nationality.

In 1819 Alexander I transferred the seat of government of the Grand Duchy from Turku to Helsinki. Meanwhile a rapidly-growing Fennophile movement was making efforts to promote Finnish culture and language to counterbalance Swedish influence. At first the Russian administration made no attempt to hinder its efforts, but later a strong programme of Russification was introduced. Nevertheless, in the second half of the last century Finnish was recognized as an official language, and became used in schools; in the seventies Finland had its own currency. These concessions were withdrawn towards the end of the century in a further attempt at Russification. After the revolution of 1905, a new constitution was approved and voting-rights granted to all citizens over the age of twenty-four.

In 1917 the Finnish diet proclaimed the independence of the country, and for a brief time a revolutionary government was in power. After General Mannerheim and his White troops had defeated this, the Republic of Finland was created in 1919. War broke out between Finland and the USSR in 1939; when peace was made in 1940 Finland ceded West Carelia and Petsamo to the Russians. After the conclusion of the Second World War, the Treaty of Paris (1947) confirmed the new frontiers, but the naval base of Porkkala was not recovered until 1956.

Like the dialects, popular culture in Finland can be divided into two types, with considerable differences between western and eastern. These are the result of the way in which the country was settled. Two separate cultural areas came into existence, one in the south-west and the other on the Carelian border. Although the differences gradually disappeared with the settlement of the lands between them, ethnic and linguistic characteristics have not disappeared completely, and the existence of Swedish influence in the west and Russian in the east has helped to keep them alive.

These differences can be seen, for example, in dress and diet. In the west there are many Scandinavian traits in the folk costume, but these diminish towards the east. While dairy products, fish and potatoes are part of the general diet, certain articles betray an eastern or western origin. The hard, thin rye bread known as *näkkileipä*, which lasts for months, is of western origin; in Savo and the eastern areas of Finland soft bread is preferred.

The old form of building, with the so-called *savupirtti* 'smoke-room', has long disappeared from western Finland, but it could still be seen in the east in the present century. It was a simple structure of wood, usually divided into living room, store room and an entrance lobby between them; its name came from the fact that the smoke from the stove escaped through a hole in the ceiling and not through a chimney. In western Finland this type of house has been transformed by making the enlarged storeroom into a living room and the original living room into a sitting room. The furnishings of the East Finnish house were simple, while in the west, especially after the eighteenth century, beautifully carved and coloured cupboards, chests and clocks came into fashion, showing the effects of baroque and rococo. The rocking chair, which originated in the west, has become popular throughout the country. The use of wood in building is still in fashion, but modern styles predominate; archaic methods have been retained only in farm buildings and in the necessary sauna.

This last is an important feature of Finnish life. In modern blocks of flats there are cement-floored, electrically heated saunas, while in the country the old type of wooden building without a chimney is found; in these water is thrown over heated stones to provide the steam.

The geography of Finland, with its forests and scattered lakes, naturally makes for scattered settlements. The so-called church-village acts as a central administrative point to which the distant farms are linked.

In agriculture, there was a striking difference between the implements used in the east and the modern methods of the west. Even at the beginning of the present century, reaping in the east was done with a sickle, threshing with a flail, and ploughing with a wooden forked plough, and the inhabitants were loath to give up their methods. The character of agriculture in the richer lands of the south and south-west has always been far more advanced. The scanty land was not always able to grow enough corn, nor could produce from the forests make up this deficiency. The Finnish peasants, particularly in the central and eastern areas where the need was greatest, were compelled to clear the forests and bring new land under the plough. This was done by clearing and burning, and continued to the beginning of the nineteenth century. After the tree trunks had been burnt, the land was still full of stones and stumps, and very little of it could be cultivated at first with the plough. They therefore used a primitive pronged wooden hoe to sow the seed in the ash-strewn soil. It was exceptionally hard labour, for this type of land would produce crops only twice at the most, and a new patch would then have to be cleared.

Stock-breeding was known in the Common Finnic period, but it did not play a great part in the economy of Finland for a long time. In more recent centuries, cattle raising has made great strides and with the introduction of modern methods it is one of the most advanced examples in the world. Milk, butter and dairy products are an important source of income, and seventy-five per cent of the total agricultural production of the country comes from cattle and dairy farming; there are now some two million cattle in Finland.

For many centuries tar was one of the most important products, especially from the sixteenth to the eighteenth century. Northern Finland was the main area of this activity, and most of the world's requirements were met by Finland at this period. It was transported by lake and river to the coastal ports. When steam replaced sail during the last century the industry dwindled, and in its place the large-scale development of wood products has been encouraged, with the result that Finland now supplies some six per cent of the western world with its needs. Timber and wood products account for about three-quarters of Finnish exports.

Since communication by water was important in the country, boat-building developed quickly. There were many types, suitable for inland or sea transport. One of the characteristic vessels was the so-called 'church boat' in which folk from scattered hamlets and farms would travel to the central village on Sundays to attend church; these boats might reach twenty metres in length and be manned by fifteen pairs of oars.

Fishing naturally plays a part in Finnish life, but it is not one of the major branches of the economy. Nets, weirs and pots are used by both sea and river fishermen, whose annual haul amounts to some 65,000 tons. Hunting has been of considerably less significance.

As for domestic crafts, weaving, spinning and wood-carving have a long tradition. The distinctive and colourful tapestries known as *ryijy* are among the most notable products of folk art. These began to appear in Western Finland in the middle ages. In the east, folk embroidery reached a high standard.

Modern Finland has rapidly cast off its earlier traditions and adopted the most up-to-date techniques. The standard of life has risen fast with industrialization, as has the general level of education. The result has been a lessening of differences between town and country life.

Some idea of the riches of Finnish folk poetry has reached the outside world with the publication of *Kalevala* and to a lesser extent of *Kanteletar*. The first mention of this poetry and the pagan beliefs of the Finns occurs in the work of the translator and bishop Agricola. In the verse preface to his translation of the psalter (1551) he records the names of Väinämöinen and Ilmarinen, who appear in *Kalevala*; he mentions Väinämöinen's 'forging of songs' and lists the pagan deities of the Finns. Here he shows that he knew not only Finnish mythology, but also the prosody of Finnish folk verse.

Agricola naturally regarded these matters with the eye of the missionary. Scholarly investigation began in the eighteenth century. One of the first results was Henricus Florinus's *Wanhain Suomalaisten Tawalliset ja Suloiset Sananlaskut* (1702), a collection of proverbs of the ancient Finns. The first real impetus to study was given by H. G. Porthan's *De Poesi Fennica* (1766–78), an investigation of folk poetry in several volumes. Others became interested in its problems, notably Ganander (the author of the Finnish-Swedish-Latin dictionary), who published *Mythologia Fennica* (1789) and *Suomalaiset Arwotuxet* (Finnish Riddles, 1783). At the beginning of the nineteenth century Sakari Topelius and C. A. Gottlund drew attention to the riches of Finnish folk poetry. The crowning achievement, however, was that of Elias Lönnrot (1802–84), who began to collect folk songs while a university student. Later he spent twenty-one years as a doctor in Kajaani, Northern Finland, and continued his collection. He travelled on foot for thousands of miles, particularly in the eastern area and the Carelian border country.

The results of his first journey to collect runes (1828) were published in four booklets between 1829 and 1831; to these he gave the name *Kantele*, after the stringed instrument used to accompany the songs. As he continued his work, he concluded that some of the songs and their variants might well be the fragments of a folk epic. After many experiments he was able to work these fragments into a unified epic, and in 1835 he published the first version of *Kalevala* (generally known as the Old Kalevala, *Vanha-Kalevala*); *Kalev(a)* is the ancestor of the heroes of the epic, and *Kalevala* the land or people of Kaleva. This contains thirty-two runes (cantos) and about 12,000 lines, but it is not the final form of the epic. New variants, episodes and lyrical sections helped to give the work a more complete and more satisfactory form; the result was the final version or New Kalevala of 22,795 lines, published in 1849. This is not to be regarded as Lönnrot's own individual creation. He selected the best versions of the songs he had noted, edited and arranged them to form a unified epic. While he was engaged on this work he published two volumes of lyrical folk verse (*Kanteletar*, 1840–41).

Lönnrot's efforts helped to preserve Finnish folk poetry and its treasures at a time when the traditional folk culture was in rapid decline. Yet even then there was a general liking for singing, particularly at festivals when the old songs would be sung, often by specially invited well-known singers whose programmes were the highlight of the entertainment. The chief singer and his associate would sit opposite or close to each other, link hands and sway their bodies to the rhythm of the verse or nod their heads to it. The chief singer would begin each verse alone, the companion joining in when it was repeated. The usual accompanying instrument was the kantele.

Kalevala, thanks to Lönnrot, has become one of the best-known epics in the world; it has been translated into all the major languages and has had a great effect on Finnish literature and art.

The Finnish Literary Society, founded in 1831, organized the work of collecting folk poetry (and, incidentally, published *Kalevala* and *Kanteletar*). Its archives now contain some 1,250,000 records of old and new songs, tales, proverbs and other material of interest to folklorists, and is one of the richest collections in the world. The series of old Finnish folk poems and variants (*Suomen Kansan Vanhat Runot*) was begun in 1908 and by 1945 had reached thirty-three large volumes.

One of the major problems of Finnish folk poetry concerns the provenance and date of the runes of *Kalevala*. These have provoked considerable discussion. Lönnrot believed Carelia to be the birthplace of Finnish folk poetry, but later scholars inclined to the view that it began in Western Finland and later spread to the east. Now once again the idea of the eastern or Carelian origin of *Kalevala* has been mooted. The conflicting views show how complicated the whole question is, and they have not yet been resolved. One fact is, however, certain: the majority of the runes were noted in Russian and Finnish Carelia, while no epic poems have been discovered in Western Finland. Kaarle Krohn believed the epic to date from medieval times; other scholars note that there are relics of tribal society in the runes, and they may therefore come from earlier times.

For a long time *Kalevala* was the only Finnish literary work known outside the country, though Finnish literature has roots dating back to Agricola, whose numerous works formed the basis of the literary language. He spent his childhood in the Häme dialect area, and took his knowledge of it to Viipuri where he began his studies. Here he became acquainted with the eastern dialect and later still, on his removal to Turku, he was influenced by the mixed south-western and Häme dialect which was spoken there. He based his works on the spoken dialect of Turku but used elements from other regions to make them comprehensible to all Finnish speakers. Since Swedish and Latin were the cultural languages at the time, his works were not widely circulated, and his influence was mainly seen in ecclesiastical language. There were relatively few writers of Finnish literary works until the beginning of the nineteenth century.

Nevertheless, several modern literary and oral tendencies can be traced back to the orthography of Agricola. In his age the western dialects frequently used intervocalic *ð* ('-th-' as in 'mother') and *θ* ('th' as in 'faith'), e.g. *käðet* 'hands', *meθθä* 'wood'. Agricola used *-dh-* (*kädhet*) for the former and *-tz-* for the latter (*metza*). But *ð* > *r* or *l* in western dialects, and had already disappeared from the eastern group in Agricola's time (*käret*, *kälet ~ käet*, *käjet*). Through his use of *-d-*, the spelling pronunciation *kädet* came into fashion and was standardized *θθ* > *tt* in western dialects, but Agricola's *tz* began to be pronounced as *ts* after German and Swedish; later this spelling gave rise to the literary form *metsä*.

The rise of nationalism in the first half of the last century caused great advances in the Finnish language. The great names connected with this movement are those of H. G. Porthan, A. I. Arwidsson and J. V. Snellmann, the majority of whose works appeared in Swedish, as did those of the great national poet Runeberg (1804–77). The appearance of *Kalevala* gave impetus to literature in Finnish, and the novelist Aleksis Kivi (1834–72) may be regarded as the first classic writer of Finnish prose. Towards the end of the century the restless voices of the 'Young Finland' movement began to be heard, particularly in the works of Minna Canth (1844–97), whose dramas and stories show the influence of Ibsen and the Russian classics.

The present century has seen such rapid diversification in Finnish literature that it is impossible to record the many writers who have made a name for themselves. An exception must be made in the case of Frans Eemil Sillanpää (b. 1888), a Nobel prize-winner.

The academic and artistic achievements of modern Finland are equally impressive, as the names of the composer Sibelius (1865–1957) and the architects Eliel Saarinen (1873–1950) and Alvar Aalto (b. 1898) bear witness.

The Estonians

The Estonians, together with the Finns and the Hungarians, constitute the most developed Finno-Ugrian peoples in modern Europe. The Estonian Soviet Socialist Republic has a population of 1,300,000, of whom about eighty per cent are of Estonian nationality. In 1959 the total number of Estonians in the Soviet Union was 969,000; there are also quite large enclaves in Sweden and North America.

The names *eesti*, *eestlane* 'Estonian' and *Eesti(maa)* 'Estonia' have been in use among the Estonians only since the nineteenth century. Earlier they used *maamees* (*maa* 'land' + *mees* 'man, human') and *maarahvas* (*rahvas* 'people') to describe themselves. The name *Aestii* first appears in Tacitus's *Germania*, and is frequently found in foreign sources. This word and its variants (*aist*, *eist*, etc.) were probably used originally to designate Baltic Slavonic peoples such as the Latvians, Lithuanians and Old Prussians, and only later did they acquire their present connotation. The origin of the word is doubtless Germanic.

The Estonians are divided ethnographically and linguistically into two large groups: the northern and southern Estonians. There is a single southern dialect, but two northern ones, the northern dialect proper and the north-eastern. The two northern dialects do not differ greatly from each other, but are much closer to Finnish than to the southern dialect. Most of the Estonians are Lutherans, but there is a small Orthodox group, the Setu, who have been almost unaffected by German and Swedish influence, and are also ethnically distinct.

The literary language is based on the northern dialect and uses the Latin alphabet. There are fragments dating from 1219, and connected texts from 1524 onwards. The language contains not only Baltic, Germanic and Slavonic loanwords from the Common Finnic period, but also large numbers of more recent German, Russian and Latvian loanwords.

Mention has already been made (pp. 181–4) of the development of Estonian. The dispersion of the Common Finnic peoples resulted in many movements and mixtures of the tribes. Not all of them left the Baltic coast. The ancestors of the Estonians (possibly a northern and a southern tribe) remained more or less in their old habitat. It was from this fusion of two tribes that the Estonian people and language developed if the evidence of the two main dialects and their differences is to be accepted. In addition there were probably certain Baltic fragments which were assimilated.

The flat, marshy land to the south of the Gulf of Finland, with its relatively mild climate, was suited to the development of agriculture and stockbreeding at an early period in history. Both archaeological and linguistic evidence suggests that the Estonian tribes generally engaged in agriculture. They also carried on a vigorous foreign trade, like the neighbouring Baltic peoples. From the tenth to the twelfth century animal breeding grew in importance, and certain domestic crafts, such as pottery and ironware, became independent occupations. At this time the independent Estonians began to entrust the direction of their affairs to a tribal 'aristocracy' which replaced government by elders.

In the eleventh century the south-eastern part of Estonia became subject to the principality of Kiev. During the following two centuries the whole of the country was penetrated thoroughly by the Teutonic knights, and there were fierce battles between the pagan Estonians and the foreign invaders. Many thousands of Estonians died in battle, including their legendary hero Lembi. In vain did Novgorod and Pskov come to their aid; in 1219 the Danes entered the fray on the side of the Teutonic knights and the country, pressed hard from both north and south, fell to them in 1227. The conquerors divided the land between them, but in 1347 the Danes, wearied by continual rebellions, sold their northern area to the Teutonic knights. The land came into the possession either of the church or of members of the order, and the Estonians suffered ever-increasing oppression until in the fifteenth century they lost the right of free movement.

During this period several towns and fortresses were erected (Tartu, Pärnu, Tallinn – *Taan-linn* 'Danish town', which betrays its origin). The inhabitants of these towns consisted chiefly of German soldiers, tradesmen and craftsmen. The ports were active, not only as centres for the export of Estonian grain, but also as transit ports for trade between Russia and Western Europe. This situation militated against the creation of close economic and cultural links between the Estonian lands themselves, and retarded progress towards the establishment of an Estonian state.

The power of the Teutonic knights and the church was overthrown in the Livonian War (1558–83). After a short period of Russian domination, the Estonian territories were divided; the southern area became part of Poland, the northern was annexed by Sweden, while the island of Saaremaa was held by the Danes. Further skirmishes between Poles and Swedes left poverty and famine in the land. In 1586 Stephen Bátory, King of Poland, wrote in a letter to the Livonian diet: 'The poor peasants are so oppressed by their lords, who demand exhausting labour and punish them severely, that even the pagans and barbarians throughout the whole world could not have permitted such treatment.' Conflict between the Poles and the Swedes was resolved in 1629 when the latter took over the land previously under Polish domination; later in the century they also occupied Saaremaa. Thus the whole of Estonia came under Swedish rule.

Printing was established in Estonia at the beginning of the seventeenth century, when the first printed works appeared in Estonian. Some secondary schools were founded, and in 1632 a university was created at Tartu (it was closed in 1656, opened again between 1690 and 1710, and finally reopened in 1802). Ecclesiastical literature was established, with two literary languages, one based on the northern dialect of Tallinn and the other on the southern dialect of Tartu.

Swedish domination ended with the Peace of Uusikaupunki in 1721, when Estonia was attached to the Russian Empire. The German landlords still remained in power, and the language of administration remained German. Despite political and cultural pressures, the economic life of Estonia improved during the eighteenth and nineteenth centuries. Personal liberty was given to the serfs in 1816, though this had little effect on their economic burdens. Industry, established in the eighteenth century, gradually developed; some 26,000 workers were employed in 1901. The revolution of 1905 caused widespread unrest in Estonia, as did that of 1917. In 1919 the Republic of Estonia was created, and this lasted until 1940, when the country became part of the Soviet Union, only to be occupied by German troops until 1944.

After this occupation, considerable reorganization and modernization were necessary, and new industries were rapidly developed. Shale-oil production played a leading part in the economy – Estonia accounted for two thirds of the total production of the Soviet Union. In addition to the traditional textile, machine and shipbuilding industries, new chemical and electrical industries have been introduced. Collectivization of agriculture began in 1947; some 48 per cent of the total land is cultivated, while forests account for 25 per cent.

Although the Estonians were long engaged in agriculture, their methods remained primitive until the present century. The three-course system was in use, but clearing and burning were still found in places. In the eastern part of the country the forked plough was employed, as it was in Finland and the neighbouring Russian territories. In the north-west and on the islands a Scandinavian-type wooden plough was used. The main crop was rye, which was still cut with sickles, although the short-handled scythe, introduced from Latvia, made some headway. Two methods of threshing were practised: the majority of farmers used the flail, but in the west they employed a wooden club. These implements were still to be seen in the twenties of the present century.

Animal breeding, now one of the main branches of farming, was of minor importance. In South Estonia there was an interesting transitional form of bee-keeping; the bees were settled in 'hives' hollowed out of tree trunks, and each autumn part of the swarm was destroyed in order to make room for new swarms to settle the following spring. Hunting played little part in the economy, but fishing in both fresh and salt water retained its importance.

The old type of Estonian dwelling was a grain-dryer equipped with a stove (*rehetuba* 'grain-drying room') which was used as a house in the winter. Here the threshed corn was stored and the smaller animals brought inside for the winter. Beside it there was usually an (unheated) store or larder. There was no separate living room; in summer they lived in the larder, in winter in the grain-dryer. Originally the smoke from the stove escaped through the door. Next to the drying-room, which was usually from five to seven metres long, there was an even larger room with a floor of stone or earth (*rehealune*), where the grain was threshed. In winter this served as a cart-shed or stable, and it was equipped with large doors on both sides. Since the *rehetuba* was surrounded with various smaller store-rooms, it was completely dark, or at most got its light indirectly. A similar type of house is found among the northern Latvians, who probably adopted it from the Estonians. Later the *rehetuba* was enlarged and provided with windows, serving as a drawing room, while the larder was heated and turned into a living room. The roof was usually of straw or reed thatch. Naturally the poorer serfs did not live in such luxury; they lived in a *saun* (sauna), a small hovel with an open fire.

There are several varieties of Estonian village. The older type consisted of a line of houses strung out along a river bank or at the foot of a hill. But in South-East Estonia villages were planned with streets. Under German rule the villages disintegrated, and this process continued until the isolated farmstead, resembling the Hungarian *tanya*, took their place in the nineteenth century. By the present century many of the villages had disappeared completely; only in the islands and the Setu district did they still exist in any number.

Folk costume in Estonia has given way to cheaper, simpler factory-made clothing, and is only to be seen rarely at the most important festivals. The old costume is seen chiefly in the islands and in the south; in the north there are many relatively new eighteenth-century elements. Among the Setu there is strong Russian influence. The women's costumes, and especially their blouses, were decorated with embroidery; in the north multicoloured floral designs were favoured, in sharp contrast to the south, where strict geometrical patterns were in use. The men display their art in fine wood-carvings, frequently found in drinking vessels and other domestic articles.

There are many similarities between Finnish, Estonian and Baltic-Finnic folk poetry, traditions and beliefs. Estonia possesses a particularly rich treasury of folk songs, of which over 300,000 (originals and variants) have been collected. Most of these are lyrical, and are performed to the accompaniment of the *kannel* (Finn. *kantele*). There is also a strong vein of epic poetry, some of which tells of Kalevipoeg, the son of Kalevi (Kaleva), and of battles against oppression. The Estonian Academic Society, founded in 1838 at the instigation of Friedrich Fählmann (1798–1850) and his friends, made the collection of folk verse one of its main aims. Fählmann began the systematic collection of such verse, intending to unite the epic lays concerning Kalevipoeg into a folk epic like *Kalevala*. His work was continued by Friedrich R. Kreutzwald (1803–82), whose life and work may be compared with those of Lönnrot in Finland. The appearance of *Kalevala* and the stimulating influence of Lönnrot undoubtedly played a great part in the compilation of *Kalevipoeg*.

Kreutzwald had to contend with many problems. A large number of the epic lays do not concern themselves with Kalevipoeg, and the action is hard to trace. Kreutzwald was compelled to use many prose tales and legends to complete his work, and these he himself turned into verse. Fortunately he was a fine poet with an unrivalled knowledge of folk poetry and language; thus his reconstructions do not stand out in sharp contrast to the genuine original verse. The result of his labours is that *Kalevipoeg* has a much more unified structure than *Kalevala*, but it does not possess the same vitality. The epic, in twenty cantos of 19,047 lines, appeared between 1857 and 1861. It was the greatest event in Estonian literary and cultural life during the nineteenth century, and roused a great interest in folk poetry. The work of collection was carried on under Jakob Hurt (1839–1906), and a total of some 75,000 manuscript pages of songs, melodies, tales, legends, customs and beliefs was noted down.

The Estonian Literary Society was founded in 1872 and acted as a focus for a rapidly growing number of authors. In 1905 a new movement, *Noor Eesti* ('Young Estonia') was started with the aim of developing Estonian culture on European lines; not surprisingly it soon became the centre of impressionism. The result of these literary activities is seen in the vigorous and flourishing literary life of Estonia in the present century.

There are large numbers of historic buildings in the towns of Estonia; these include examples of Romanesque, Gothic, late Renaissance and Baroque. A national style of art was developed in the last century, and Tallinn became a musical centre, with its opera and ballet.

Academic life is centred on the university in Tartu, and has been encouraged by the foundation of the Estonian Academy of Sciences in 1946, with twenty-five scholastic institutions in its charge. These include the much older Emakeele Selts (Native Language Society), whose members have carried out extensive investigations into dialects and oral traditions. Schooling in the country has a lengthy tradition, and literacy is high. Today Estonia is one of the most highly developed republics in the Soviet Union.

The Carelians

The Carelians are the most numerous Baltic Finnic people after the Finns and Estonians. Politically and historically they fall into two groups: the west or Finnish Carelians, and the east or Russian group. Apart from the differences arising from the influences under which they have lived, there are many linguistic, cultural and even religious distinctions between them.

The Carelians played a great part in the creation of the modern Finnish language, and it is not customary to regard the west Carelians as a separate people with their own separate language. The differences between Finnish and Carelian do not make for difficulties in conversation, for example. Nevertheless, for historical reasons it is convenient to discuss the Carelians and their language separately, particularly in the case of the inhabitants of Soviet Carelia.

Since the West Carelians are counted as Finns, there are no exact details of their numbers. In Soviet Carelia there are 167,000 of them, of whom 71.3 per cent speak Carelian. They are found in two large groups. The larger of these is in the Carelian-Finnish Autonomous Soviet Socialist Republic, which has a common frontier with Finland. The area of the republic is 178,000 square kilometres, and there are some 600,000 inhabitants; the capital is Petrozavodsk. The smaller group lives in the Kalinin (formerly Tver) region north of the Upper Volga; their settlement of the region dates from the seventeenth century, when Ingermanland, the north and west shores of Lake Ladoga, were annexed by Sweden as a result of the Peace of Stolbova. Molestation by Swedish officials caused a mass migration to the safer Russian lands.

The linguistic divisions of the Carelians are more complicated than their geographical distribution. Tver Carelian is spoken in the Upper Volga region, Aunus or Olonets to the north-east of Lake Ladoga; the northern or Archangel dialect is used north of a line joining the northernmost points of Lakes Ladoga and Onega. To the east of the Aunus dialect area the Ludian dialect is spoken in a narrow strip of territory; some regard this as a separate language, but in fact it is to be counted as a dialect of Carelian. Ludian developed under strong Vepsian influence. The Carelian dialects of Finland are included with the Savo and South-Eastern groups.

The ancestors of the Carelians, as we have seen, formed a separate tribe during the Common Finnic period.[1] During the first ten centuries AD they gradually settled in the Carelian isthmus and the Ladoga and Onega regions. The settlement of modern Carelia began around 800 AD and ended in the twelfth century according to archaeological evidence. Carelians were to be found as far east as the White Sea and the Northern Dvina. It is probable that the inhabitants of *Bjarma ~ Beorma* in Scandinavian sources of the tenth to twelfth centuries were Carelians. They spoke a language related to Lapp, and called their god *jomali* (cf. Finn. *jumala*, Carelian *jumal(u)*). Strong linguistic evidence supports this theory; in this area there are Carelian geographical names, and Zyryan contains certain Baltic Finnic loanwords.

First mention of them occurs in the Scandinavian sagas. Ivar Vidfamne records at the beginning of the eighth century that he

---

1 Setälä and Ariste hold this view, which is opposed by Lauri Kettunen. He regards the Carelians as a mixture of Suomi and Vepsians.

was shipwrecked in *Kyrjálabotn*, i.e. near Carelia in the Gulf o Finland. Norse sources also know of their existence, and their name appears several times from the ninth century onwards. They first figure in Russian chronicles in the twelfth century; according to these, the 'korels' were at war with the 'jams' (Häme) in 1143. From this period onwards the Carelians are often mentioned in documents, chronicles and other sources.

The Carelians were acquainted with agriculture when they first settled in their northern habitat, and have continued to practise it throughout their history. The southern part of Carelia is more suited to it than the north, where forests and rivers give more scope for hunting, fishing and forestry. There are few differences between their life and that of the eastern Finns. Folk traditions and folk art were retained longer than in western Finland; the majority of the runes constituting *Kalevala* were collected by Lönnrot in Carelia. Such differences as do exist are mainly due to differences in their historical development. From the twelfth century onwards the ancestors of the Finns were drawn into western, Scandinavian cultural activity under the Swedes, while the Carelians were allies of Novgorod from the tenth to the eleventh century. Thus Russian influence began to spread; it was strengthened when the greater part of Carelia became part of Russia after the Peace of Pähkinäsaari in 1323.

In Finland the Swedes first introduced the Roman Catholic faith, with very little success, and then after the Reformation, Lutheranism. In Russian Carelia, however, the Orthodox faith gained ground from the thirteenth century onward and gradually became the accepted religion. Russian customs also spread among the Carelians. Their semi-feudal state was not unlike that of the Russians; their leaders became boyars, and the rest of the inhabitants became serfs on ecclesiastical or private estates.

Since Carelia was a frontier area, it suffered considerably from the devastations of war. Swedish and Russian armies often clashed there, and its borders changed from time to time when peace was concluded. In 1917 Carelia was divided when the Republic of Finland was created; the western areas became part of Finland until 1940. The larger eastern part remained in Russia; after the revolution, a Carelian Autonomous Region was proclaimed, becoming a Republic in 1923. When Western Carelia was added to

it in 1940, it became known as the Carelian-Finnish Soviet
Socialist Republic, and in 1956 it was declared autonomous.

Several dialects of Carelian are spoken in the Republic, as well
as other Finnic languages. The official languages are Russian and
Finnish; the latter is taught in schools. The industry and agriculture of the region have been developed, and with the increase of
educational facilities literacy has become general. A university was
opened in Petrozavodsk in 1940, and a branch of the Soviet
Academy of Sciences directs scholarly research there.

The Ingrians (Inkeri, Izhors)

In recent years the language spoken by the Ingrians or Izhors of
Ingermanland, on the southern shore of the Gulf of Finland, has
been treated as an independent Baltic Finnic language. Formerly
it was regarded as part of either the Finnish or the Carelian language area, since it is close to both. It is the result of a mixture of
early South-West Carelian and later (seventeenth-century) Finnish brought by settlers to the area. The number of Ingrians is
1,100, of whom one-third speak the language.

The Vepsians

Vepsian is closely related to Carelian, which represents a midway
stage between this language and Finnish. In 1959 the Vepsians
numbered 16,000. They are widely scattered in a Russian-
speaking area, and this has caused rapid Russification among
them. Recent data show that nearly half speak Vepsian (in 1895
there were some 25,000 of them).

They live in the triangle formed between the three lakes –
Ladoga, Onega and the White Lake – and are administratively
divided between Leningrad, Vologda and the Sheltozero district
of the Carelian-Finnish ASSR. There are four dialects, arising
from their geographical distribution:

1 The northern dialect, spoken on the south-west shore of
Lake Onega.
2 The central dialect, spoken between the northern dialect
area and the upper reaches of the River Oyat.

3 The southern dialect, to the south of the River Oyat.
4 The eastern dialect, by the White Lake.

The Vepsians who live by Lake Onega are mainly occupied in fishing, while the rest live by agriculture and stockbreeding. Forestry also plays an important part in their economy, as did hunting in former days.

The modern Vepsians are the remnants of an independent and once-powerful tribe of the Common Finnic period. They are usually associated with the folk known to the tenth-century Arab traveller Ibn Fadlan as *visu*, and in the old Russian chronicles as *ves'*. From historical records it may be deduced that they were living in the White Lake area before the tenth century AD, and bartered goods with the Volga Bulgars, exchanging furs and skins for metal objects and arms. During the following two centuries they came under strong Slavonic influence and were slowly assimilated.

During the thirties of the present century efforts were made to introduce a Vepsian literary language, and Vepsian was taught in schools. Grammars, dictionaries and textbooks were written, but these did not evoke any great response, and the experiment was dropped. Many of the Vepsians now live in towns and are employed in various trades. Some scholars have taken great interest in the language and its dialects, notably N. I. Bogdanov. The separate history of the Vepsians, however, appears to be drawing to a close.

The Vodians

The Vodians have almost died out. They inhabit a few villages between the north-east of Estonia and Leningrad. In the forties of this century there were still about five hundred who spoke the language in West Ingermanland, but these were nearly all killed or scattered during the retreat of the German troops in 1943–44. Today it is estimated that only twenty speakers of the language still live in these villages. The Soviet statistics of 1959 made no mention of them – nationalities numbering less than five hundred were not included. Their language was not uniform; virtually each village had its own dialect.

According to P. Ariste, one of the greatest experts in the subject, the Vodian language was originally a dialect of Estonian. A group of speakers of the north-eastern dialect became isolated from the main body and formed the nucleus of the new language. Various emigrations occurred, resulting in strong Finnish and Ingrian influence upon Vodian, and then from the nineteenth century onwards there was equally strong Estonian influence. After the formation of the independent language – estimated at about the eighth century AD – large numbers of Vodians emigrated to Estonia, where they became assimilated. The results of this can be seen in the Kodavere dialect of Estonian (by Lake Peipus). Another group of Vodians was forcibly settled by the Teutonic knights in Kurland in the fifteenth century. These Latvian Vodians were known as Krevins (cf. Latvian *krews* 'Russian'), but by the middle of the last century all of them had been assimilated.

The Livonians

In the eleventh century the Livonians were a strong and numerous people, descended from an independent Common Finnic tribe. At that time they lived north of the River Daugava (Western Dvina or Düna), along the Gulf of Riga in Livonia or Livland. Today, however, their descendants can be found only on the northernmost tip of the Kurland peninsula in Latvia. There they live in twelve fishing villages. At the end of the last century there were about three thousand of them, but their numbers dwindled to half of this between the two world wars, and there are now fewer than five hundred still surviving.

Their power began to decrease in the thirteenth century, when the Teutonic knights overran Livonia; their weakened remnants could not withstand the assimilating power of their Latvian neighbours and they gradually merged with them. The language of the few remaining fishermen also shows strong Latvian influence, yet still retains traces of former Livonian culture.

The Lapps

The Lapps, who number about 31,000, live in the northern parts of Norway, Sweden and Finland, and in the Kola Peninsula. This vast area, altogether some 400,000 square kilometres in extent, consists in the west of rocky wooded mountain country, and in the east of bare stretches of tundra with a few stunted shrubs and low hills. About 18,500 of them live in Finnmark, Tromsö and Nordland, the three northernmost districts of Norway. The Swedish Lapps, about 8,500 altogether, dwell in Jämtland, Härjedalen and along the northern rivers. In Finland there are 2,300 Lapps, living alongside Lake Inari and in the Enontekiö, Utsjoki and Sodankylä districts; in the Soviet Union 1,800 of them live in the Kola Peninsula and the Petsamo area.

The dialects spoken by the scattered Lapp communities are independent of political boundaries; thus the commonly used terms – Norwegian, Swedish, Finnish and Russian Lapp – refer to geographical and not linguistic divisions. There are three groups of dialects, west, south and east, comprising eight dialects in all.

Western (also called Northern) Lapp

1   The northern or Ruija dialect is found in Finnmark and Tromsö (Norway), Karesuando (Sweden), Enontekiö and Utsjoki (Finland); it is also used by the reindeer-breeding nomads of Lake Inari and Sodankylä in Finland. About two thirds of all the Lapps speak this dialect.

2   The Lule dialect, spoken along the River Lule in the Gällivare and Jokkmokk districts of Sweden.

3   The Pite dialect, spoken along the River Pite in the Arjeplog and Arvidsjaur districts of Sweden, also in parts of Nordland in Norway.

Southern Lapp

4   The Ume dialect is found along the upper stretches of the River Ume, south of Arjeplog and Arvidsjaur, and includes the dialect spoken by the Lapps of Lycksele, Mala and Sorsele. It is a transitional type, between the northern and southern groups.

5   Southern Lapp proper extends to the south of the previous area and is spoken in Jämtland and Härjedalen, also in the Röros district of Norway.

Eastern Lapp

6   The Inari dialect takes its name from the lake around which it is found.

7   The Koltta dialect is spoken on the western border of the Kola Peninsula, in the Petsamo region. Some of its speakers crossed into Finland after the Second World War.

8   The Kola dialect is found in the peninsula of this name, more particularly in the areas of Kildin, Akkala and Turjala.

The Ruija dialect (1 above) is also called Norwegian Lapp, dialects 2–5 Swedish, Inari Lapp Finnish, and Koltta and Kola Russian Lapp. The differences between them are so considerable that there is some justification for regarding them as separate Lapp languages and not mere dialects. Some of them are incomprehensible to speakers of other dialects.

Part of the Lapp vocabulary has links with other Finno-Ugrian or Samoyed languages, but most of it can be related only to the Baltic Finnic languages. This includes Baltic and Germanic loanwords which have been transmitted to Lapp through common Finnic or Proto-Finnish. There are large numbers of more recent Finnish loanwords, and numbers of Old Scandinavian, Norwegian, Swedish and Russian borrowings, but almost a third of the Lapp vocabulary consists of words of unknown origin.

The grammatical system of Lapp has much in common with Finnish and the Baltic Finnic languages in general. Most of the agreements found in suffixes, formatives and syntactical elements prove to be loans from an earlier form of the Finnic languages.

Although the similarities between Lapp and the Finnic languages are striking, the anthropological differences between their speakers are equally surprising. The Lapps are short in stature, with short limbs, comparatively long bodies, and small heads. They have broad noses, small, dark eyes and dark hair; facial hair is scanty. They are of an individual anthropological type known as Lappid or Lapponoid, whose development is still the subject of controversy.

This distinction between racial type and language has caused many scholars to take the view that the Lapps acquired their language from some foreign source. This raises two difficult problems: when did the Lapp language develop and under what

Finno-Ugrian influence, and what was the original language of the Lapps? These questions have long occupied the minds of scholars, and have not yet been answered completely satisfactorily. Several theories have been advanced.

According to the Swedish linguist K. B. Wiklund, the Lapps had no connection either ethnically or linguistically with the Finno-Ugrians. Their language, which he terms 'Proto-Lapp', was lost as they became assimilated to Finno-Ugrian stock early in the Common Finnic period. Wiklund also attempted to discover traces of Proto-Lapp in the modern language, and regarded it as an Ice-Age European language.

The Norwegian scholar K. Nielsen believes it impossible to determine whether the Proto-Lapps took over their language during the early Common Finnic period or at an earlier Finno-Ugrian stage. He is certain that they are of eastern origin, and notes the similarity between Lapp and Samoyed methods of reindeer breeding, which leads him to conclude that the Proto-Lapp language is of Samoyed type.

Wiklund's contemporary Setälä believed that the Lapps had adopted their new language much earlier, and that the change was completed during the Finno-Ugrian period. The Lapps lived to the north of the Finno-Ugrians, and their language developed under Finnic-Permian, then Volga Finnic and Common Finnic influence.

A completely different theory was advanced by the Finnish linguist Lagercrantz in 1941. In his view, the Lapps, Ob-Ugrians and Samoyeds are the remnants of an ancient Arctic people who spoke Proto-Uralic. This language was transmitted by them to Europid peoples from further south who were the ancestors of the other Finno-Ugrian peoples. These folk later had considerable influence on the development of the Lapp language.

Paavo Ravila made a special study of the problem in 1935. In certain respects his views are close to Wiklund's: the Lapp language derived its main characteristics from the Common Finnic or a 'Pre-Finnic' period of Finnic, Mordvin and Lapp linguistic unity. Thus the Lapps did not adopt their language all at once from the ancestors of the Finns, but gradually acquired it. With the dispersion of the 'Pre-Finnic' peoples and the migration of the Mordvins, only Proto-Lapp and Common Finnic remained, and the differences between these were simply dialectal. Ravila regards it as possible that the ancestors of the Lapps may originally have spoken a Samoyed language or that of some ancient Arctic people.

Björn Collinder of Uppsala, arguing this theory with Ravila (1944, 1945) and later with Toivonen (1954), concluded that the only sure fact was that the Lapps belonged to the western branch of the Finno-Ugrians. He disputes the morphological agreements used by Ravila to prove the close connection between Lapp and the Finnic languages, and shows that certain phenomena in Lapp distinguish it from Common Finnic but can be traced back to Proto-Uralic times. So Collinder declares that the Lapp language is just as much a branch of Uralic or Finno-Ugrian as Votyak or Mordvin. He argues that there is no linguistic problem concerning Proto-Lapp; at most there remains the question of whether the Lapps (and Samoyeds) are closer ethnically to the Proto-Uralic people than the Finns, Mordvins and Cheremis. In this connection he does not rule out the possibility that these three peoples adopted their language from the ancestors of the Lapps.

In 1949 Toivonen produced new evidence to support the Samoyed origin of the Lapps. In the Lapp vocabulary he found almost one hundred words which have cognates only in Samoyed and the Ugrian languages. Of these sixty are common only to Lapp and Samoyed. Thus he argues that the Proto-Lapps spoke a Samoyed language, then broke away from the main body of Samoyeds; they next came into contact with the Ugrians – which would explain the Lapp-Ugrian concordances – then migrated further west and met other Finno-Ugrian peoples. These contacts became so intensive at the Volga-Finnic period that the Lapps changed their language.

More recently (1955) Erkki Itkonen produced strong linguistic evidence to show that Toivonen's thesis was not sufficient proof that the Proto-Lapp language was of a Samoyed type. In his view, Lapp is the direct continuation of one of the early dialects of Common Finnic, without any traces of 'Proto-Lapp'. He does not attempt to give a date for the unity of the ancestors of the Lapps and Finnic peoples in one linguistic community, but believes it to have existed in the Volga-Finnic period at the latest.

With all these theories in mind, it is not easy to come to a conclusion concerning the origin of the Lapps. Linguistic analysis certainly points to a strong link between Lapp and the Baltic Finnic languages, close enough to suggest that Lapp may be a branch of early Common Finnic. The ethnic characteristics of the Lapps, however, pose problems which cannot be answered by linguistic research. It is possible that the 'Proto-Lapps' spoke another language and began to acquire the tongue of their southern neighbours during the Volga-Finnic period, resulting in a certain degree of linguistic unity early in the Common Finnic period. The original language remains an unsolved mystery.

The Lapps always lived to the north of their Finno-Ugrian relations, and their withdrawal to their present habitat is largely the result of migrations during the Common Finnic period. During the last few centuries before Christ, the linguistic unity between Lapp and Common Finnic came to an end. By this time the Lapps had penetrated into the region of modern Finland and Scandinavia, where hunters were always certain of plentiful prey in the dense forests. They did not adopt the agricultural mode of life of the Common Finnic period, but continued to live as nomads, supporting themselves by hunting and fishing. They had reached Scandinavia probably quite early in the third century BC, as is testified by the earliest loanwords. The Finnic tribes who later slowly penetrated northwards gradually drove the Lapps into the northernmost regions of the area. This was a lengthy process; up to the fourteenth century a large part of Eastern Carelia was inhabited by Lapps, and they were still living in Central Finland from the fifteenth to the eighteenth century.

History records them first in the first century AD. The *Fenni* of Tacitus' *Germania* are normally regarded as Lapps. This is how he described them in 98 AD:

The Fenni are exceedingly wild and nauseating in their poverty. They have no arms, horses or dwellings. They eat grass, their clothes are made of animal-skins, they sleep on the ground and their only means of defence is the arrow which they tip with bone in the absence of iron. Men and women alike live by hunting, for the women accompany their husbands everywhere and demand a share of the prey. Against wild animals and the vagaries of the climate not even the children have any refuge other than a hut thrown together out of branches; to this the young return home, and here the old folk have their dwelling. But they believe that they are happier thus than they would be groaning in ploughed fields, toiling in houses, and tossed between hope and despair with their own or others' property. Caring for neither god nor man, they have achieved that most difficult state of all – they have no desires. (*Germania*, ch. 46.)

This description does not fit the Baltic Finns, who at the time of Tacitus had reached a higher standard of culture.

Ptolemy's geography distinguishes two nations of 'Finns'; one lived by the Vistula (the ancestors of the Baltic Finns), and the other was in the northern regions of Scandinavia. These latter are to be identified as Lapps. The Byzantine writer Procopius, who lived in the sixth century, writes: 'The men and women hunt continually in the extensive forests and the nearby mountainous country. They live exclusively on the flesh of the animals they kill and make clothes of their skins. They have no knowledge of cloth or of sewing, so they join the skins with the sinews of wild animals and thus cover their bodies with them.'

It is from the time of Procopius that the name *Scrithifinoi* or *Scrithi-finni* begins to be found; it recurs in Jordanes and Paulus Diaconus, for example. The first element is probably connected with Old Norse *skrida* 'to go on skis'; thus to foreign observers this was the most remarkable characteristic of the Lapps. The origin of the word *Finn* has already (page 178) been discussed. It is worth noting, however, that the Norwegian name *Finne* still refers to the Lapps.

The first reference to the modern name is found in Saxo Grammaticus (thirteenth century), where *Lappia* is mentioned. This name has long been used by the Finns (*Lappi* 'Lapland' – *lappalainen* 'Lapp'), Swedes and Russians, and is now in general use throughout the world. It is of disputed origin. While it may possibly be of Finnish origin (cf. *lappea*, *lape* 'the side of something'), it seems more likely to have come from Swedish. The Swedes translated into their own language the Lapp word *vuowjoš*, the name of one group of Lapps, and used it for the whole nation. This is a derivation of Lapp *vuowje* 'wedge-shaped insert' (in clothing or tent-coverings); the Swedish word *lapp* is also 'a small piece of skin or cloth'. The explanation appears to come from the wearing of triangular pieces of cloth as amulets, a practice found both among the Lapps and among certain pagan Finnic tribes. Lapp *vuowje* is related to Finnish *vaaja* 'wedge, spike'; the Vodians call themselves *vad'ja*. The word is of Baltic origin (*vōkja*). The use of the word by Lapps and Vodians as a national name suggests very early connections between them.

This name is no longer in use among the Lapps today. They generally use the term *sabme* (*sāmi*). Although attempts have been made to relate this to the name Samoyed, Lapp scholars generally believe that it is derived from *sämä-*, whose Finnish equivalent is *Häme*, the tribal name. The connection between *sabme* and *häme* suggests a link similar to that already noted between *vuowjoš* and Vodian *vad'ja*.

The history of the Lapps is uneventful. By the end of the ninth century the Lapps in the north of Scandinavia were paying taxes to the Norwegians, while those in the area of modern Finland had already been trading and perhaps paying taxes to Common Finnic tribes. These links continued in the following centuries. The Carelians made them pay taxes in the thirteenth century, and others did so later. The eastern Lapps fell within the sphere of influence of Novgorod and later of Moscow, while those in the west became associated with Swedish and Norwegian aspirations. Their conversion to Christianity was for long nominal.

The Lapps living in the more southerly areas and in contact with their Norwegian, Swedish, Finnish and Russian neighbours became assimilated, while those unwilling to give up their traditions were driven northwards. Changes occurred in their society, as some began to grow rich and acquire more European habits, but for a long time the old tribal system held firm.

Early records and oral tradition alike provide evidence of their religious beliefs and shamanism. Many Scandinavian elements and Christian ideas became mingled with these. At one time they had various orders of magicians, whose activities included the use of the shaman's drum.

Reindeer breeding, hunting and fishing are the most important features in the economic life of the Lapps, but not in equal measure throughout the region. The sea-Lapps of the Norwegian fjords and those around Lake Inari are mainly occupied with fishing;

those whose habitat lies inland, in the mountainous areas of Norway, Sweden and the Enontekiö district of Finland, are reindeer breeding nomads who follow their herds and change their home from season to season. Hunting plays a secondary rôle. More recently they have begun to breed cattle and cultivate the land.

Standards of life vary greatly between the groups of Lapps. It almost goes without saying that the reindeer breeding Lapps are richer than the fishermen, for they can gain considerable wealth. Some Lapps possess herds of 2,000–3,000 animals and employ numerous herdsmen to care for them.

At one time attempts were made to draw parallels between Lapp and Samoyed methods of reindeer breeding, and both were thought to be an inheritance from the Uralic period; there are, however, no convincing proofs of this. Both Lapps and Samoyeds have developed reindeer breeding to a high standard, but their methods are different. While the Samoyeds use reindeer for pulling sledges (i.e. in harness), for food and clothing, the Lapps saddle their animals as well and use them either to carry goods or for personal transport. They also milk them and make cheese of the milk. This last practice may be due to the influence of Scandinavian animal breeding customs, but even so the connection between the two methods should not be stressed. Lapp reindeer breeding began to develop in the first centuries AD, when there were several thousand kilometres to separate them from the Samoyeds. The boat-shaped travelling sled, used in the Lapp areas and in Siberia, is commonly regarded as decisive proof of the link, but this is not so, for the Samoyeds normally pull this type of sled themselves, and do not use reindeer like the Lapps. So the sled has survived among the Lapps as a relic of some ancient hunting culture and does not represent the continuation of a Uralic method of reindeer breeding, which is relatively new to the Lapps. Hunting and fishing were their main occupations, with particular emphasis on the latter.

The reindeer-breeding Lapps live in easily constructed wooden-framed tents; in earlier times these were covered with reindeer hides, but sailcloth is now commoner. In winter they use thick woollen coverings. From this type of tent there developed the more permanent four or six-sided hut covered with peat, which gives greater protection against the cold. The number of such dwellings has declined rapidly during the present century; tents are now used only by the herdsmen as they follow their animals. Timber houses have been built by them since the eighteenth century, and the majority of Lapps now live in these.

In matters of dress, the Lapps have retained their traditions. Their costume is more or less of one kind. Typical is the cloth or hide coat, with no opening in the front, and pulled on over the head. The men's coats are knee or thigh-length, the women's somewhat longer, and both are belted. In bad weather they used to put on over this an oval poncho of bearskin, covering shoulders, back and chest. Formerly it was only the men who wore trousers, but now most of the women wear them also. On their feet they wear short leather or hide boots with pointed and upturned toes; above these are leggings of reindeer hide which reach the knee. Boots and leggings are tied tightly at the calf with long, wide and usually decorated puttees. Their headgear varies from district to district. It is chiefly the Finnish and Norwegian Lapps who wear the well-known 'Four Winds' hat, with its four peaked flaps. In the Kola Peninsula they wear round caps, while in Sweden they have peaked caps of cloth. The women's hats show even more variety: there are numerous types of close-fitting cap with earflaps to be found in Norway, Sweden and Finland, while the Kola women wear high, crown-like headdresses. In Finland the Lapps wore 'horned' caps with ear flaps, so called because they ended in a horn shape, but they are no longer in use. The Lapps decorate all their clothing with coloured stripes, appliqué work and pearls. Their designs are chiefly geometrical, in their favourite colours of red, blue and yellow.

As for folk art, they are noted for their bone and horn carvings. Many domestic objects are made of these materials and are beautifully decorated.

Lapp folklore provides a rich treasure ground for the scholar. Oral tales, legends, proverbs and superstitions reveal traces of ancient customs and beliefs. The songs known as *juoigos* present the most remarkable feature of their folk poetry. These vary considerably in content; the longer ones tell of events in the lives of individuals, while shorter songs describe actual occurrences affecting the community, or sing the praises of nature. The particular interest of these songs is their spontaneity: a good singer will improvise both text and melody, and the better ones then spread and survive. There are many 'refrains' in the *juoigos*. They are often several lines long and offer a clue to the nature of the song. One type is used in an ironic song, another in a song of thanksgiving, for example. The reindeer breeders of Lake Inari introduce a boastful song with *läl-Läl-lä*, while *nŭ-nun-nŭ* or *jō-jō* indicates that the singer does not wish to relate anything bad about a character, though it would be possible to do so. The text of the *juoigos* often has nothing whatever to say. In some of them there are only one or two intelligible words or names; the rest of the song is made up of refrains, thus showing the subordinate rôle of the text to the melody. The archaic melodic line of these songs is constructed of very small musical intervals, but has many changes of rhythm. Here again changes of rhythm are often used to signify changes of subject and meaning. The melodies in use among the Lapps are quite different from anything else in Europe; similarities have been found among the Nenets. Both are probably relics of some very old Arctic or sub-Arctic musical culture.

During the present century the Lapps made immense cultural progress, with teachers, scholars and writers emerging from their ranks. The first works in the language date from the seventeenth century and consist of biblical translations, catechisms, prayer and hymn-books, calendars and alphabets. Today books and periodicals appear in two literary languages, the western and eastern variants of Norwegian Lapp; the former is used in Norway and Sweden, the latter in Finland. Apart from textbooks and newspapers, literary works have appeared, especially since Johan Turi's pioneer work *Muittalus samid birra* (Tale of the Lapps, 1910), which has been translated into English and other languages.

The Samoyeds

The ancestors of the Samoyeds broke away from the Uralic community in the fourth millennium BC. At this period they were probably living in the forest regions of Western Siberia.

Since research into this period has not yielded satisfactory results, it is impossible to give an accurate idea of their habitat or their early history. It is however certain that they still spoke a common language, Proto-Samoyed, and that they were chiefly engaged in hunting and fishing. They used arrows tipped with bone or stone, or simply with wood, but also used traps to catch wild animals. They also used primitive nets to catch fish. Their domestic animal was the dog, and this they harnessed to pull their sleds. They had not yet begun to breed reindeer; this began during the last few centuries BC. They knew the use of skis, sleds and boats made out of tree trunks, which played an important part in their communications. Their life thus reflected conditions similar to those of the Uralic period.

The first contact between Samoyeds and Turkic peoples took place during the Proto-Samoyed period, during the last centuries BC. This assumption is supported by historical data. According to Chinese chronicles certain Turkic tribes, driven westwards by the pressure of turbulent peoples, reached the borders of Europe in about 200 BC. The areas furthest to the west and north-west were occupied by a people called in these sources *Ting-ling*, and usually regarded as Uigurs. They settled in the Irtysh and Ob region, in the Altai mountains and to the north and north-west of these. The ancestors of the Samoyeds probably lived among the Ting-lings. There are Turkic loanwords in Samoyed; moreover the Wei-lio chronicle records that among the Ting-lings there lived a foreign fur-hunting people who on their 'hooves' travelled faster than a horse. This description probably refers to folk who travelled on skis; the idea of 'hooves' becomes comprehensible when it is realized that the Tavgi-Samoyeds or Nganasans still wear a type of boot whose foot does not project forward, but continues straight down in line with the leg, and whose sole is not unlike the hoof of a horse.

The Samoyeds migrated eastwards, as can be demonstrated by their connections with the so-called Yenisei peoples, the Kets, who still exist today (and whose other name 'Yenisei-Ostyaks' is misleading, since they have no connection with the Chanti), and the defunct Kotts, Arins and Assans, whose ancestors lived then in Southern Siberia, in the Altai and Sayan mountain areas. From the evidence of Yenisei loanwords in Samoyed, the Proto-Samoyeds reached the Altai mountain region immediately before the time of Christ.

The Samoyeds next began to disperse and groups of them became scattered through Siberia. The northern group, comprising the ancestors of the Nenets, Enets and Nganasans, became separated from the southern group and moved northwards, arriving in Northern Siberia around 500 AD. Some of them later settled in the tundra coastal region of North-East Europe. One of the southern Samoyed groups, the Sayan Samoyeds, settled in the Sayan mountains, while the ancestors of the modern Selkups moved north-eastwards to the middle Ob valley, settling to the south of the northern Samoyeds. This dispersal of the Samoyeds and their migrations, as well as their association with Arctic and Turkic peoples in Siberia, resulted in the formation of the Samoyed language-group, consisting of four living and numerous dead ones.

The most important representatives of the northern group and of the Samoyeds as a whole are the Nenets or Yurak-Samoyeds. They number 29,000 and live scattered along the coast of North-East Europe and Western Siberia from the mouth of the North Dvina to that of the Yenisei. This comprises the tundra region along the shores of the White Sea, the Kanin Peninsula, the Little Tundra between the mouths of the Mezen and Pechora, the Great Tundra between the Pechora and the Ural Mountains, and the Yamal Peninsula. They are also to be found on the offshore islands and along some of the river valleys of the Ob system. Of the total number of Nenets, 85·7 per cent speak the Nenets language. Administratively they belong to the Nenets National Region and the Yamal-Nenets National Region.

Linguistically the nearest to the Nenets are the Enets or Yenisei-Samoyeds, who live north and south of Dudinka on the Lower Yenisei. In 1926 they numbered only 378.

The third people forming the northern group are the Nganasans or Tavgi-Samoyeds. Their home is the Taimyr Peninsula, one of the most barren regions of Siberia, and they number about 1,000 of whom 93·4 per cent speak Nganasan. Together with the Enets, they live in the Taimyr National Region.

The only representatives of the southern group of Samoyeds still extant are the Selkups. There are 4,300 of them, but only one half speak this language. They live in two groups, the southern fragment in the Narym district, along the Narym, Tim, Ket, Vasyugan and Parabel rivers, which all flow into the Ob, and the northern Selkups along the Taz valley and beside the Turuhan, which flows into the Yenisei. The Selkups are administratively divided between the Yamal-Nenets National Region, the Chanti-Man'si National Region, and the district of Tomsk.

The Sayan-Samoyeds are now extinct. The best-known language in this group was Kamassian, which in 1914 was spoken by eight elderly folk in the village of Abalakova in the Sayan mountains. When they died in the twenties, the language died with them. From older sources it is known that there were several Samoyed-speaking peoples in the Sayan region, notably the Karagass, Koibals, Motors, Soyots and Taigis. There are traces of their Samoyed languages from the end of the eighteenth and the beginning of the nineteenth century, and from these it is clear that they were close to Kamassian. They gave up their own original languages in favour of Turkic, a process which was completed in the first half of the last century.

'Samoyed' is thus a collective name for the living and dead languages mentioned above. The modern form of the name is undoubtedly Russian, but it may be postulated that this cloaks some earlier non-Russian word which might be connected with the Lapp word *sabme*. At one time Samoyed was analysed as 'self-eater', but this is most probably an explanation devised to account for the earlier forms of the word (*Samoyad*', *Samogedi*, *Samogeti* etc.), coupled with the rumour that the Samoyeds were cannibals.

Nenets, Enets and *Nganasan* all mean 'human, man', and are derived from one and the same Northern Samoyed root. *Selkup* is a compound of *sö* 'earth'+*l*' formative+*qup, qum* 'human, man' (cf. Hungarian *hím* 'male').

These names are of recent use in literature concerning the Samoyeds. The Nenets are generally termed Yurak-Samoyeds, the first element of which is a Russified form of Ob-Ugrian *jaran, jorn* (their name for the Nenets), and in the first instance is probably a Forest Nenets tribal name, *jar*. The Nganasans are called Tavgi-Samoyeds, and here the first element is the Nenets *tāwyʔ* 'Nganasan'.

Ethnically the Samoyeds show many traces of racial mixtures.

No detailed analysis of their anthropological features has been attempted; the Selkups are best known. The Nenets are nearest to the Ostyaks, short in stature and with small heads. They have more mongoloid features than the Selkups, but are quite distinct from the Tunguz. The Nganasans also have small heads, dark hair and eyes, and clear skin. Their noses are not flat, like those of the mongoloid types, but they are broad. Their hair, however, is typically mongoloid, stiff and straight. They are taller than the Tunguz people, and possess many Europid characteristics. The Selkups are short and small-headed, but have soft hair, light skins, and generally lighter eyes than those of the Eastern Siberians. They are nearest to the Ob-Ugrians in their anthropological characteristics, while the Nenets have somewhat stronger mongoloid features.

The first historical reference to the Samoyeds appears in the Kievan chronicle, where Rogovich (1096) mentions them as the northern neighbours of the Jugra. These are presumably the Nenets. From this record, it appears that the Nenets had reached the borders of Europe and Siberia in the eleventh century, and had even penetrated the European side of the Ural mountains. After this there is a dearth of records until the gradual conquest of Siberia. Although after the conquest of the Ob valley in the fourteenth century there was doubtless occasional taxation of the Samoyeds, it was not until two centuries later that regular taxes were demanded. The Russians established numerous military trading settlements in the area, e.g. Tyumen (1586), Tobolsk (1587), Berjozov (1593), Surgut (1594), Obdorsk (1595), Narym and Ket (1596), Mangazeja (1601) and Turuhansk (1607). These fortified settlements, each with a voivode at its head, became not only administrative, but also economic and cultural centres. With the establishment of Turuhansk, the whole of the Yenisei area came under Russian control, and the way was open for further conquests. The Russians penetrated the Taimyr Peninsula and by 1614 the Tavgi-Samoyeds were paying taxes to them. With the foundation of Yeniseysk and Krasnoyarsk (1628), all the Samoyeds became subject to the Russian Empire.

The slow beginnings of civilization among the native peoples of Siberia can be traced to the Russians; they came to know new implements, new metal wares and means of making fire. They paid the price for this knowledge in taxes, which only from the eighteenth century onwards were paid in money (the Selkups were so taxed only from the end of the last century). Until then they were in the form of furs and hides. In some districts, as among the Nenets of the Pur and Yamal areas, no limits were set on taxation. The Samoyeds were thus forced to pay as much as they could, or even more, so that they remained in debt and had their reindeer herds seized in pawn. Gifts and tithes created an additional burden, and unrest grew; it found expression in attacks on the Russian settlements. The statute of Speransky (1822) promised the Nenets land and a degree of autonomy, but neither promise was fulfilled.

The native tribes had their own leaders, whose duty it was to collect the taxes and often to act as judges. The majority of the folk, however, sank into abject poverty, and were employed by the more affluent owners of herds to tend their animals. There was a series of insurrections in the nineteenth century, notably that of Vauli Piettomin (Vavljo Nenang) in the thirties, when the reindeer belonging to the large owners were seized and distributed among the poor; taxes were also refused. The leader was imprisoned in 1838, but escaped and three years later attacked the town of Obdorsk with a band of four hundred Ostyaks and Nenets; here, however, he was trapped into submission and sentenced to forced labour.

In the latter half of the last century, large traders from Archangel, Tobolsk and Krasnoyarsk penetrated far into Siberia, taking not only the lion's share of the fur trade, but also the best fisheries for themselves. This process was aided by the frequent diseases which decimated the reindeer herds and put their owners in debt to the traders. Thus most of the herds passed into Russian or Zyryan hands. In 1895 230,000 reindeer were in 'foreign' hands in the Pechora district, and only 50,000 were left to the Nenets.

The Nenets

The Nenets are divided into two groups, whose language and mode of life display many differences. The reindeer-breeders of the tundra are called Tundra Nenets, while the Yuraks of the taiga region north of the Middle Ob are known as Forest Nenets; these number only about 1,000.

The Tundra Nenets dialect is subdivided into numerous smaller ones (Kanin, Little Tundra, Great Tundra, Yamal, Ob, Nadym and Taz), but these are relatively close to each other and to the norm, despite the vast distance separating the eastern and western limits of the Nenets region. This relatively homogeneous linguistic state is explained by their nomadic existence. The Forest Nenets have more difficulty in understanding Tundra Nenets, and rarely come into contact with them; their dialect is subdivided into eastern and western types, which are fairly close to each other.

Nenets life and language have influenced their neighbours. There are many Nenets loanwords in Ob-Ugrian and Zyryan, and of these some have been further transmitted to Russian. The reverse is also true; Nenets contains words from all these languages. Forest Nenets has been strongly influenced by Ostyak, which is spoken by many of these folk, while some of their eastern groups have adopted Selkup.

Reindeer are the mainstay of life among the Tundra Nenets. Their herds graze on the tundra the whole year round, and are moved with the seasons to precisely defined areas. In winter they remain near to the forest region where the tundra is studded with bushes and shrubs; here the snow is less hard-packed and the reindeer can reach the lichen more easily. In spring the herds are driven north to arrive in summer on the shores of the Arctic, where the cool breezes protect them from their greatest enemies, mosquitoes and gnats. There is also good fishing here for the herdsmen. In autumn they return southwards. Dogs are used to round up the herds, and have proved indispensable; with the aid of huskies, two or three herdsmen can look after a herd of 2,000 animals. Reindeer attempting to escape are either brought back by the dogs or lassooed by the herdsmen. The owners of the herds or their men follow the deer throughout the year, accompanied by their families. Their tents and belongings are carried on sleds, and they themselves camp by the herd while it grazes; when the pasture no longer suffices their needs, the herd moves on, accompanied on sleds by the men and their families.

Reindeer provide food, clothing and tent-covering; antlers,

bones and sinews can all be used. The Nenets do not make use of reindeer milk, however, and this distinguishes them from other reindeer-breeding peoples of Siberia. Without these animals, existence would be impossible in the tundra region, hence the extensive breeding and use of them among the Samoyeds. The Zyryans followed the example of the Nenets and began to develop large scale reindeer breeding as a profitable occupation; for this they employed Nenets herdsmen and adopted their methods. Some of the Ob-Ugrians also began to breed reindeer under Nenets influence; these were mainly Ostyaks in the north, of whom whole tribes adopted this mode of life, some of them becoming completely assimilated to the Samoyeds in the process.

The modern form of reindeer breeding among the Tundra Nenets appears to be a secondary development. The methods used by the Forest Nenets, Selkups and Forest Enets probably represent an earlier form. In the forests large-scale breeding is impossible, and the inhabitants are not totally dependent upon reindeer, for other meat and fish are available. Single families keep small herds of twenty to thirty reindeer at the most. In summer, when there is an invasion of gnats, the Forest Nenets allow their herds to wander at will, while they go to the rivers to fish. Only in autumn do they round up their herds and then set out with them on their winter hunting-expeditions. They do not move further than 40–100 kilometres from their summer quarters and camp en route wherever opportunity offers. The reindeer are used primarily as draught animals, to pull sleds and carry goods. Hunting and fishing supply their needs in clothing and food. It was from this type of reindeer breeding that the Tundra Nenets developed their present methods, based as they are on the hard fact that their very existence depends on this one animal.

Many centuries ago the Yuraks of the tundras began to sink into poverty as they were unable to keep herds large enough to maintain their existence. The fifty to one hundred reindeer in their possession would be guarded by them during the winter, but driven with the larger herds to the north for the summer, while they themselves settled by the lakes to fish. Fishing is important for the Nenets of the Ob, Pur and Taz river valleys and essential to the life of the Forest Nenets. Sturgeon, salmon and other fish are trapped in various kinds of nets, weirs, pots and traps.

Hunting has been purused by Forest and Tundra Nenets alike. The most useful quarry was the wild reindeer, whose importance can be seen from its name *jil'ēpéP*, whose meaning is virtually identical with 'life'.[1] The result of their activities has been the extinction of the wild reindeer from the Nenets region. They also hunt the arctic fox, squirrel, ermine, wolverine, beaver, otter and more rarely the wolf and bears of the brown and polar varieties. Today they normally use the rifle, but not long ago they still hunted with bow, arrows and spear. Traps and snares are frequently found. Seals and walrus are also hunted on the sea coast. For hunting waterfowl, wild geese and wild duck they have devised ingenious nets with which a few men can catch as many as 2,000 birds in a few days.

Their diet is monotonous. Although they have known bread for a century, only within the last few decades has it begun to become popular. Their chief food consists of meat and fish; with the exception of totem animals, almost any kind of meat is eaten, normally raw in fresh blood. They also like dried or frozen and cooked meat and fish. In summer they slice these and dry them, sometimes smoking them a little and salting them to preserve them better. In winter large stores can be kept frozen without any special preparation. Palatable soup is made from meat, fish and rye flour. Fat is rendered down from fish and eaten with roe, pieces of fish and crushed berries. It is customary to eat the marrow and blood of a freshly killed deer, but sometimes the blood is frozen and preserved; it is later melted in boiling water and mixed with flour and berries to make a kind of cake. A special delicacy is young deer antler, which is still soft in spring. Their drink is tea made from compressed tea bricks.

As for dress, the most important articles of the men's clothing are the so-called *māl'ée*, a hooded, reversed reindeer-hide fur coat, and the *sawak*, which is worn over this, with the fur outside in very cold weather. Their trousers reach to the middle of the leg, and on their feet they wear high-heeled fur boots stuffed with hay. In summer they wear discarded winter clothing. The women wear a long fur coat (*pany*) which is a double reindeer skin decorated at the bottom with a separate fur border. On their heads

---

1 The word is derived from a cognate of Hu. *él-* 'live'. In colloquial Hungarian *élet* 'life' is used to mean 'corn' in many places.

they wear fur caps decorated with metal ornaments and glass beads. For special occasions they merely wear a more decorated version of their everyday dress.

The Nenets are compelled by their nomadic or semi-nomadic mode of life to live in portable tents, whose frames consist of thirty to forty poles; in winter these are covered with double reindeer hides, and in summer they use birch bark boiled soft for this purpose. The tents are very simply equipped. The fire is laid on an iron plate in the centre, the smoke escaping through the top of the tent. Over it hangs a pot suspended from a system of iron poles. Planks are placed to the left and right of the fire, and sleeping-places consisting of willow osiers covered with hay and reindeer hides are arranged on each side of the entrance. Opposite the entrance is the place for the domestic goods, vessels and other household equipment. The size of the tent indicates the wealth of the owner.

The Tundra Nenets carry their tents with them on their sleds, and it is the women's task to erect them. Owners of large herds have three or four tents for themselves, their herdsmen and their families, and their possessions sometimes need as many as eighty to one hundred sleds for their journeys. The Nenets do not live in villages; at most they might form a tented community in the summer when they fish by some lake. Since the Forest Nenets do not travel long distances and then mainly through forests, they do not need to carry their tent poles with them; they can be cut in the forests wherever necessary.

On all their journeys, both types of Nenets build wooden storehouses on stilts at their camp sites. In these they keep clothing, food and tools. Since their travels are usually by sled, they have developed numerous types for all purposes – for men, women, goods, tent poles, domestic gods and hides. These types are widely used among other Samoyed groups, and differ greatly from those of other Siberian reindeer breeders, such as the Tunguz and Koryak peoples. They are constructed of pine or birch without the use of nails; although they look fragile, they can carry great loads. The reindeer are harnessed to such sleds fanwise, with the trained leader on the extreme left. The driver also sits on the left, watching the leader, and he guides with a leading-rein and a long stick – a method of driving characteristic of the Samoyeds. Baggage-sleds are normally pulled by only two reindeer, and these are tied by the neck to the preceding sled. This method of transport is used also in summer in the slippery marshland areas. Dogs are very rarely used in harness.

The tribal system of the Nenets survived until the most recent times. Each tribe had its own strictly defined area for pasture, hunting and fishing, as well as its own migration route. These tribes were banded together in clans, and both were exogamous, to such an extent that certain Tundra Nenets could not take wives from the four Forest Nenets tribes, because all knew that there was a clan relationship between them. At the beginning of the present century there were over one hundred tribes. Each tribe had a common burial ground, a common sacrificial place and its own totem; mutual assistance and blood-revenge were also part of tribal life.

Characteristic of their system was common hunting and fishing. This existed until the present century. All the prey was shared, not only among those who had taken part in the expedition, but also among the sick, the old and the orphaned. Some of the larger necessities for such expeditions, such as the more valuable nets and larger boats, were the common property of the tribe. This does not imply an idyllic form of communism; centuries ago there were cases of Nenets who enriched themselves at the expense of their less fortunate neighbours, and at the end of the nineteenth century 75 per cent of the reindeer in the Great Tundra region were owned by 17 per cent of the population.

Family life was patriarchal. At times there would be ten to fifteen folk living in one tent and working together under the supervision of the head of the family. Women played a subordinate rôle, as with the Ob-Ugrians, and were subject to various taboos. They were regarded as unclean, and might enter a newly-pitched tent only when they had purified themselves and their utensils with the smoke of burning reindeer hide. They might not step over weapons, nets, snares, and other articles used by men. Bear meat, certain types of fish and the head of reindeer were forbidden food to them. The bride had no voice in arranging her marriage, and found it difficult to divorce her husband. In early times polygamy was practised but only among the richer folk who could afford the *kalim* or bridal-fee, consisting of a number of reindeer (varying from five to two hundred), furs and other useful articles. Women could not inherit. Their household duties were many, from setting up the tents to preparing fires and food, making clothes, looking after the children, and performing certain menial tasks connected with the deer and fishing; the more important tasks were forbidden to them.

The Nenets practise a shamanistic religion. Their chief god, *Num* (which also means 'sky') created the earth and rules both heaven and earth. The welfare of mankind depends on him. His son *Nga* is the god of death, from whom *Num* defends men only if they offer sacrifices to him. There are intermediaries between humankind and *Num*, spirits called *tädebcjo*, with whom only shamans can communicate to discover the will of *Num*. Spirits can also be found in all natural phenomena – lakes, rivers, hills and forests. Some are evil, such as the water-spirits, and these must be continually propitiated with sacrifices. The spirits of the dead are also worshipped. The Nenets believe that man consists of body, soul and shadow-soul; when he dies, his soul leaves him, but his shadow-soul or guardian spirit which has watched over him in life lives on in the next world. The spirits of famous shamans become *tädebcjos*, so images of shamans are made and respected.

Special honour is given to the ancestor of the tribe, who is generally represented as a totem animal. At one time members of the tribe were forbidden to kill or eat the flesh of such an animal. The bear and wolf are also taboo animals; they are rarely hunted or even named.

The spirits are represented by images of wood or odd-shaped stones, which are draped in cloth or wool and carried everywhere with the family. In the sacrificial places wooden images are kept. Many kinds of sacrifice are recorded, and these are of two main types, blood-offerings (reindeer, dogs) and bloodless sacrifices (food, drink and money). The ceremonies were conducted by the shaman (*tädibe*), who was believed to possess supernatural powers. His shadow-soul could leave his body and through the *šimši* pole (a separate tent pole round which the images were placed) could reach the world of spirits and obtain knowledge of their wishes, of the future, and of how to avert disasters. The shamans thus acted as intermediaries between men and spirits; they could fore-tell the future, heal the sick, talk with the spirits of the dead, reverse ill-fortune and find lost articles. The greatest shamans were able to slash and stab their own bodies without suffering.

At one time the shamans had their own distinctive dress, but in the nineteenth century only their headdress distinguished them from ordinary mortals. The most important item of their equip-ment was the drum of reindeer hide stretched on a round wooden frame; when struck with a wooden drumstick, it gave a hollow, mysterious sound. It accompanied songs and spells, and the shaman's wild dance which led to a trance; when he collapsed on the ground, his shadow-soul left his body to discover the will of the gods; and when he returned to life, he related his experi-ences and the desires of the gods in song.

At one time the shamans exercised considerable influence over the people; their advice was sought in all matters and they were well rewarded. Their power declined at the beginning of the present century, though the memory of former great shamans lived on. Among the Nenets, for example, the Enets shamans were considered more powerful than their own, and occasionally a shaman would receive payment only after a sick man had been fully cured.

Closely connected with their religious beliefs are the folk traditions of the Nenets. There are mythological tales, songs of spirits and animals, shamanistic songs, spells and prayers, and songs on many everyday themes. They have no musical accom-paniment, and often last throughout the night. To the European ear they seem somewhat monotonous, with a very limited melodic range and frequent repetition; variety is given by rhyth-mic changes. The content of the songs is generally improvised – or at least constructed in an easily-remembered form – and made to fit a fixed rhythmic pattern. This is achieved by repetition or the addition of line-filling syllables which have no grammatical or semantic rôle. A similar phenomenon has already been noted in Ob-Ugrian, but in their songs the additional matter is not so extensive. In the case of the Nenets songs the basic text is often so distorted by the additional syllables that it is extremely diffi-cult to decipher. As an example, many songs begin with the words *mańi P jil'ewɛwa P* 'we were living'; in one song they are modified thus to fit the rhythm:

mańńōw | jil'l'ow- | ɛwwōw | ŋāɛ-āɛ-āɛ-āj

and in another thus:

ma-a- | ńo-ōw | jil'l'o-wɛwow | ŋā̃-äj.

The Enets

The majority of the Enets roam the tundra near the mouth of the Yenisei and between this river and the River Pyasina in the summer; in winter they move further south. These are known as the Tundra Enets. The Forest Enets, a smaller group, inhabit the taiga region south of Dudinka. They are subdivided into four further groups: the Chantaysk Samoyeds or *maddu*, the Bayicha Samoyeds or *baj*, and the *muggad'd'i* and *juči* or Karasino Enets. The *maddu*, together with most of the *muggad'd'i* and *baj* groups live in the tundra region, while the *juči*, with some of the *muggad'd'i* and a few *baj* families constitute the Forest Enets.

Their language is known only from a brief grammatical sketch and a few word-lists, and appears to be fairly close to Nenets. Between the *baj* and *maddu* dialects, the only ones so far investigated, there are certain phonological variations of interest.

In the seventeenth century they were living west of their present habitat, near the rivers Taz and Turuhan. An influx of Nenets, Selkups and Kets forced them to move further east. At that time they numbered about 3,000, but in the intervening period many of them have become assimilated to their neighbours, the Selkups, Nenets, Dolgans and Nganasans.

Their life resembles that of the Nenets and Nganasans; those on the tundra breed reindeer, and the Forest Enets are chiefly engaged in fishing. Their tents are of the Nganasan type, and their clothing varies from the Nganasan style of the Tundra Enets to the Nenets *māl'ée* (though somewhat shorter) found in the forests.

The Enets are divided into tribal groups. The *maddu*, for example, once comprised ten exogamous tribes, while the other three groups were separate exogamous units. They too practised polygamy, and demanded bridal-fees; the levirate was also customary. While the Nenets considered their shamans better than their own, they themselves frequently consulted Ket or Selkup shamans in the belief that they were more powerful. At all events shamanism retained more of its original characteristics among the Enets than among the Nenets. The shamans were divided into three clearly defined categories according to their powers. The highest – who were able to communicate with the greatest spirits – were called *budtode* and could be recognized by their clothing, drum and stick. The second category possessed only a drum to distinguish it; known as *djano*, the shaman of this class defended humans against the evil spirits. The lowest category consisted of *sawodes*, who communicated with the spirits of the departed and took part in burial rites, but had neither drum nor special clothing to distinguish them.

From the travellers who have visited the Enets, it appears that they have a very rich folk tradition, but there are no original texts available and therefore no study has been made of it.

The Nganasans

The Nganasans are the northernmost people of the USSR, and live in the Taimyr National Region, a vast area of 860,000 square kilometres and (in 1959) only 34,000 inhabitants. These include Dolgans, Yakuts, Tunguzes and Nenets as well as Nganasans. The Taimyr Peninsula is one of the coldest regions of Siberia, with an average temperature in January of $-32°C$ and in July of $+2°C$. The bleak climate is intensified by more or less continuous gales and snowstorms.

The Nganasans consist of two tribes. In the west of the peninsula live the Avam-Samoyeds, who may be further subdivided into two groups, the Pyasina Avams, who are nomads in the river valley of this name, and the Taimyrs or Taimyr Avams who in the winter live between the tributaries of the Pyasina and Hatanga rivers and in summer migrate to the Taimyr valley. The other main group is the Vadeyev tribe, which lives a nomadic life on the tundra between Lake Taimyr and the Gulf of Hatanga. In addition to these two groups, there is a third, once independent, tribe called the Okos, probably of Dolgan origin, who became completely assimilated to the Nganasans at the beginning of the nineteenth century; they live amongst the other two groups. Scholars believe that the Nganasans are ethnically a mixture of Samoyeds, Palaeo-Asiatic (possibly Yukagir) and Tunguz peoples. At all events, their culture has been strongly influenced by their neighbours.

Until very recently reindeer breeding was of secondary importance to them. Their main occupation was hunting wild reindeer, and this they did almost all the year round. Their nomadic life was governed by the movements of the wild herds; after spending the winter on the edge of the forests, they moved northwards in March after the herds, and spent the summer hunting them. Some reached the coast, while others fished and caught waterfowl inland. In early autumn they once again moved south, reaching the forests by December; here they settled for the winter, setting up fox traps and collecting wood. Since the hinterland of the Taimyr Peninsula is barren, the Nganasans had to take their stocks of wood with them when they returned.

Various methods of hunting are pursued, and are varied according to the seasons. In summer they shoot the reindeer, either alone or travelling on foot in small groups. In order to conceal their approach, they often use a shelter made of planks and fitted on skis, the front of which is plastered with lumps of snow. In the centre is a small hole, through which they aim at the quarry. In spring and autumn they adopt an ancient form of hunting, called *ngatangiru*; they set up two lines of poles in a V formation, each decorated with scraps of hide or partridge feathers. One hunter on a sled drives the herd into the mouth of the V, where the deer are scared by the flapping of the decorations and by the shouts of the other hunters. As they approach the neck of the V, two or three men armed with bows and arrows shoot them down. A variation of this method is to drive the deer through the same formation of poles into a lake; as they swim towards the middle, a party of hidden hunters on the opposite bank enters a boat and kills them with spears. In winter they use a net of hide, sometimes fifty metres long, into which the deer are driven. When their antlers are caught in the net, they are easy prey. With the rapid decrease in the stock of wild deer, these methods of mass-slaughter have been forbidden; only the gun may now be used.

At one time another archaic method was used. A tame female or an unbroken bull was used as a decoy. With the former, the herd was not scared by her approach; the hunter held the end of a rope (which might be 300 metres long) and followed the decoy behind his shield until he found a suitable quarry. In the case of the bull, an animal with well-grown antlers was selected and a noose of deer sinews tied to these; as it approached the herd, it was met by the leader, who engaged it in battle, but was unable to escape from the noose. The hunter then arrived to dispatch it.

Nets are used to catch wildfowl, and arctic foxes are caught in traps, though fur-trapping has never played an important rôle in their economy. The Taimyr Avams are the only Nganasans to fish extensively; the rest merely supplement their diet in this way.

Reindeer breeding is second in importance to hunting. Unlike the Tundra Nenets, the Nganasans do not breed them for their flesh and hides, but to use them as beasts of burden. The reindeer sled is the only means of transport in the winter. During the present century the stock of reindeer has increased considerably, and even the poorer families own at least fifty of them (among their Dolgan neighbours such a number counts as wealth). Their methods are similar to those of the Nenets, down to the way in which they drive. The only difference is in the unique women's sled, used also for carrying goods.

Their diet is monotonous, consisting of wild reindeer meat in autumn and winter, wildfowl and fish at other seasons. During the brief summer and autumn they lay in large stores of meat and fish; the meat is sliced and dried, then chopped and preserved in fat, which is kept in reindeer bladders or skins. Fish is generally eaten raw, but the dried meat is cooked.

Both in type and furnishings, their tents are like those of the Nenets. From two to five families live in each. Their winter tents are strongly made and covered with several layers of sailcloth and reindeer hides in order to withstand the frequent storms in Taymyr.

Their clothing is made entirely of reindeer hide; red and black cloth is used merely to decorate it. Since they travel much more on foot than the Nenets, their clothes are shorter and lighter. The boots they wear are unique in Siberia; known as *fajimu*, and made of reindeer hide, they are high and cylindrical in shape, the length of the foot being the diameter of the cylinder. They are stuffed with hay, and have hoof-shaped soles. To protect themselves against snow-blindness, they wear metal 'spectacles' provided with horizontal slits. For special occasions, both men and women wear clothing decorated with red, white and black appliqué work, fur borders and metal ornaments. Only geometrical designs are used.

The Nganasans have retained their patriarchal tribal system. The Avams are divided into five exogamous groups, the Vadejevs into six. In the vast area where they live, there is no question of economic unity or tribal regions. The families who travel together do not necessarily belong to the same tribe; they are good neighbours of similar fortune, working together as a community. Despite the rigours of the climate, some of them manage to become relatively rich, and the poorer families depend upon them. In 1926 over half the reindeer were owned by 11 per cent of the Nganasans.

Their shamanistic beliefs spring from the same roots as those of the other Samoyeds and preserve similar features. Their folk poetry is believed to be rich, but no texts have been noted or published. They sing their heroic lays in a somewhat monotonous recitative-like style; these epics are of considerable length and may take several evenings to complete.

The Selkups

The only remaining members of the southern branch of the Samoyeds are linguistically quite distant from their northern relatives. A further sign of their separation is that their culture and traditions are closer to those of the neighbouring Eastern Ostyaks and Kets than to the Samoyed norm. This explains why geographers of the eighteenth and nineteenth centuries regarded Selkups, Kets and Ostyaks alike as 'Ostyaks'.

We have already seen that some of the Selkups live in the Taz and Turuhan valleys. This northern group settled here only in the seventeenth century; before this all the Selkups lived along the Middle Ob and its tributaries, from the River Chulym to the Vah. The southern Selkups who lived near Narym were bilingual in Russian and Selkup at the beginning of the present century, and most of them have now adopted the former language, leaving the majority of Selkup speakers in the Taz and Turuhan districts. Originally they had no collective name. *Söl'qup* is used by those in the Taz valley, and *šöl'qup* is found along the Turuhan. Of those in the Narym district, the Selkups in the Ket valley are called *süsse-qum*, and those in the Tim region *t'ūmel* or *čumel-qum* 'earth-man'. These three names, *šöl'qup*, *süsse-qum* and *čumel-qum*, give an indication of their grouping. The southern Selkups consist of two groups, the Tim Selkups, who live by the river of that name and also in the Vasyugan valley, and the Ket Selkups. The northern group live along the Taz and its tributaries, mingled with Ostyaks; their eastern branch in the Turuhan area is some-times called Baycha Selkup. In 1970 there were 4,300 Selkups.

There are three main dialects corresponding to their geographical locations, but these are subdivided into many smaller variants. Kai Donner, who in 1912 collected linguistic material among the southern Selkups, declared that virtually every jurt had its own separate dialect, and that this jeopardized the future of the language as a whole. The differences were such that Russian had to be used as a medium of communication. Today only about half the Selkups use the language of this name.

Their main occupations are hunting and fishing. To the southern Selkups squirrel hunting was of prime importance, a relic of the days before money was in general use and bundles of squirrel furs, bound together in tens, were used as units of barter. One mink, for example, was worth three bundles. The Selkup numerals preserve the memory of this type of trade; the Turuhan Selkups use *sitt-sar < sede-sārm* (20), *nassar < nak sārm* (30), *tiēssar < te sārm* (40) etc., where *sar < sārm* is the name for a bundle of ten furs.

The Taz Selkups hunt mainly the arctic fox, though wild deer and mink are valuable prey and various kinds of waterfowl are caught for their meat. Larger animals were hunted with bow and arrow, or with nets and traps. Tame decoys were also once used – such as a live bear cub, kept in captivity, then released to attack a wild bear; during the ensuing struggle it was comparatively easy to kill the wild bear.

Formerly the Selkups kept a variety of tame animals, partly as cult objects and partly for food. At the time of the spring floods, they would catch fox cubs, and feed and train them all the sum-mer. Before the hunting season in the autumn they would kill and eat them, presumably as sacrifices to ensure success. They also tamed wild geese, wild duck and other birds, some of which would return to their cages when released. These too were killed when the first snow fell in autumn. This treatment of animals and birds is ultimately derived from the respect in which the supposed animal-founder of the tribe was held; the domesticated animals or birds originally symbolized this respect, but with the decay of totemism more practical use was made of them.

Fishing is of more significance in the southern Selkup area than in the north, where reindeer are bred on a small scale. The herds are not guarded even in winter, when they are constantly needed either for food or as draught animals. At night they merely hobble them and leave them in the open. In summer, when the gnats begin to swarm, the deer are left to wander at will. They seek the woods, away from marshes and rivers, and their owners lose track of them completely. When the autumn fishing season is over, they follow their tracks into the forests and round up their animals. The deer are all marked, and strangers are returned to their rightful owners. This method of breeding was probably adopted from the Forest Nenets, a supposition which is borne out by a Selkup tale. One of their number strayed into a foreign land and there met a headless man (*olykytyl' qup*), who gave him a whole herd of reindeer for a bow. The 'headless man' is a translation into Selkup of the name of a Forest Enets tribe, the *ŋaɛwašata*.

The northern Selkups use dogs in harness as well as reindeer. In the south, dogs are used, but the horse is also found. The poorer Selkups by the Turuhan often pulled their own sleds, wearing broad, short skis; at most they might be assisted by a couple of dogs.

The southern Selkups have a somewhat more varied diet than their northern relations. Bread, flour, salt and tea have long been known among them, thanks to their Russian neighbours, but meat and fish still provide the staple food. In summer they lay in great stores of dried fish-meal and meat from various kinds of fowl. The women collect edible roots. To hold these stores, they make containers of wood and birch bark, as do the Ostyaks. Earthenware was once unknown among them. Now they use metal pots for cooking and obtain their domestic utensils from markets. Their settlements are more permanent in character than those of the nomadic reindeer breeders. They live on the high banks of rivers in 'villages' of eight to ten houses or jurts, but are not confined to one place; they change their habitat for the winter hunting season and the summer fishing, but do not travel far.

There are many styles of building. The northern Selkups live in winter quarters of ancient design. These are square timber huts, set about half a metre into the ground and packed with earth to seal the holes between the logs. Opposite the door is a small window 'glazed' with a piece of ice which is replaced when it melts. In the middle of the hut, or to the right of the door, is a clay stove built on a wooden framework. In addition to this kind of house, tents of the Nenets type are in use. In summer they live in tents covered with birch bark or, on their fishing trips, in covered boats.

The southern Selkups live in a variety of permanent houses, from the primitive huts just described to better built versions with wooden floors and Russian type stoves; those in the Ket valley live in Russian style wooden houses. The Narym Selkups live in huts of birch bark or round tents of pine bark in the summer; they, too, use covered boats during the fishing season, and cook in the open air.

Their dress is not uniform. In the north they are not distinguished from the other Samoyeds; in the south they have adopted Russian habits, but prefer to make up their own clothes from bought materials. This replaces their former practice of wearing waterproof garments of sturgeon and other fish skin.

The Selkups were organized in exogamous clans. Traces of a dual-fraternity system can still be found among the northern Selkups. Each clan consisted of a number of tribes, and these were still living in strictly defined areas in the seventeenth and eighteenth centuries. Later this organization disintegrated, giving rise to communities consisting of families from various tribes. The tradition of communal work, however, lived on, particularly in the Taz area, where wild reindeer and geese were hunted in common. Women do not occupy such a lowly place among the Selkups as among the other Siberian peoples; though they are subject to their husbands, they take an active part in hunting and fishing.

Since the eighteenth century they have nominally belonged to the Orthodox faith, but in many places they have retained their shamanistic practices, with their own images and sacrificial places. One ceremony is particularly worthy of note: the 'resurrection' of the shaman's drum. In their belief, the drum changes into a reindeer, on whose back the shaman travels to the world of the spirits. This newly constructed drum must immediately be 'brought to life' to make it suitable for this purpose. The ceremony lasts for some ten days and takes place when the birds migrate in the spring.

Their folk traditions are reflected mainly in legends, tales and riddles which have a concrete historical background. One of the central figures of their legends is the hero Itje, whose life depicts the struggles of the Selkups. It is interesting that in tales of their warfare the Ostyaks and Kets figure as their allies against the Nenets, Tunguzes and Tatars.

The Selkups are the only Samoyeds to use musical instruments. The Narym Selkups use a swan-shaped, two-stringed 'harp' which probably came to them by way of the Ostyaks; in more general use there is a Jews' harp made of reindeer bone.

The Samoyeds Today

After the Russian revolution, the area inhabited by the Samoyeds gradually obtained autonomy. Tribal councils were still in existence during the twenties, but in 1929–30 the Nenets, Yamal-Nenets and Taimyr national regions were created, embracing the majority of the Samoyed population. Collectivization was introduced in 1929 and completed in 1950, overcoming problems such as the tribal collective and the employment of women. Reindeer remain the chief source of income and there are numbers of nomadic collectives, particularly in the tundra regions. In order to increase the number of settled communities a regulation of 1951 offered long-term loans to those nomads who wished to settle, and introduced new activities, such as the growing of potatoes and cabbage. To exploit the rich mineral resources of the Taimyr region a new town, Norilsk and a new port, Igarka, have been built, and communications improved.

The first Samoyed (Selkup)-language school was opened in

1925. An alphabet was devised for it, and the foundations of two literary languages were laid during the following decade. The Nenets literary language is based on the Tundra dialect, and the Selkup equivalent on the Taz dialect. No separate textbooks were provided for the small numbers of Enets and Nganasans. Nenets is the more advanced of the two languages; Selkup, which like Nenets is written in Cyrillic characters, is confined almost entirely to elementary textbooks. Writers and scholars have begun to emerge from among the Nenets in recent years, though one of the most remarkable men of the present century was self-taught. He was Tyko Vylko (Ilya Konstantinovich Vilka), who for thirty years was president of the council of Novaya Zemlya; he made a map of the island, studied its natural resources, and had a great reputation as painter, singer and translator.

Select Bibliography

🙟🙟🙟🙟🙟🙟

THE following bibliography is intended to be a general guide to the literature available. Detailed bibliographies are to be found in the general works and in the periodicals given below. Entries have been restricted as far as possible to works in English, French, German and Russian.

A. PERIODICALS AND SERIES

Acta Linguistica Academiae Scientiarum Hungaricae, Budapest, 1951–.
Finnisch-ugrische Forschungen, Helsinki, 1901–.
Journal de la Société Finno-ougrienne, Helsinki, 1886–.
Mémoires de la Société Finno-ougrienne, Helsinki, 1890–.
Nyelvtudományi Közlemények, Budapest, 1862–.
Ungarische Jahrbücher, Berlin, 1920–43.
Ural-Altaische Jahrbücher, Wiesbaden, 1952–.
Uralic and Altaic Series, Indiana University Publications, Bloomington, 1960–.

B. GENERAL WORKS

Collinder, Björn, *A Handbook of the Uralic Languages:*
    Part 1 *Fenno-Ugric Vocabulary*, Stockholm, 1955
    Part 2 *Survey of the Uralic Languages*, Stockholm, 1957
    Part 3 *Comparative Grammar of the Uralic Languages*, Stockholm, 1960.
Collinder, Björn, *An Introduction to the Uralic Languages*, Berkeley & Los Angeles, 1965.
Décsy, Gyula, *Einführung in die finnische-ugrische Sprachwissenschaft*, Wiesbaden, 1965.
Steinitz, Wolfgang, *Geschichte des finnisch-ugrischen Vokalismus*, 1944.
Szinnyei, József, *Finnisch-ugrische Sprachwissenschaft*, Leipzig, 1910, 1922.[2]
Vuorela, Toivo, *The Finno-Ugric Peoples*, Bloomington, 1964.

Select Bibliography

INDIVIDUAL LANGUAGES

The entries are divided into Grammars, Dictionaries, Texts and General works. In the case of Hungarian, Finnish and Estonian, where texts and general works are readily available and generally known, the entries have been restricted to the first two categories only.

Hungarian

Grammars: Bánhídi, Z, Jókay, Z, and Szabó, D; *A Textbook of the Hungarian Language*, Budapest/London, 1964.

Lotz, Janos, *Das ungarische Sprachsystem*, Stockholm, 1939.

Tompa, József, *Ungarische Grammatik*, The Hague, 1968.

Dictionaries: Országh, László, ed., *Hungarian-English Dictionary*, Budapest, 1974[4]; *English-Hungarian Dictionary*, Budapest, 1970[3].

Benkő, Lóránd, ed., *A magyar nyelv történeti-etimológiai szótára*, Budapest, I (A-Gy) 1967; II (H-O) 1970. (Historical and etymological dictionary)

Lakó, György, ed., *A magyar szókészlet finnugor elemei*, Budapest, I (A-Gy) 1967, II (H-M) 1971.

Sauvageot, Aurélien, *Esquisse de la langue hongroise*, Paris, 1951.

Benkő, L. and Imre, S., ed., *The Hungarian Language*, The Hague, 1972.

Ob-Ugrian

Grammars: Balandin, A. N. and Vahrusheva, M.P., *Mansijskij jazyk*, Moscow-Leningrad, 1957.

Steinitz, Wolfgang, *Ostjakische Grammatik und Chrestomathie mit Wörterverzeichnis*, Leipzig, 1950.

Dictionaries: Balandin, A. N. and Vahrusheva, M. P., *Mansijsko-russkij slovar'*, Leningrad, 1958.

Rombandjejeva, J., *Russko-mansijskij slovar'*, Leningrad, 1954.

Karjalainen, K. F. and Toivonen, Y. H., *Ostjakisches Wörterbuch* I–II, Helsinki, 1948.

Texts:

Vogul

Kannisto, A. and Liimola, M.; *Wogulische Volksdichtung*, I–VI, Helsinki, 1951–63.

Munkácsi, Bernát, *Vogul népköltési gyűjtemény* I–IV, Budapest, 1892–1921.

Munkácsi, Bernát and Kálmán, B., *Vogul népköltési gyűjtemény*, Vol. III part 2, Budapest, 1952, Vol. IV part 2, Budapest, 1963.

Kálmán, B., *Vogul Chrestomathy*, Bloomington, 1965.

Ostyak

Pápay, J., *Osztják népköltési gyűjtemény*, Budapest-Leipzig, 1905.
Patkanov, S., *Die Irtyschostjaken und ihre Volkspoesie*, 2. *Ostjakische Texte mit deutscher und russische Übersetzung nebst Erläuterungen*, St. Petersburg, 1900.
Reguly, A. and Pápay, J., *Osztják hősénekek*, Budapest, I, 1944; II, 1951; III, 1, 1963; III, 2, 1965.
Steinitz, Wolfgang, *Ostjakische Volksdichtung und Erzählungen aus zwei Dialekten*, I–II, Tartu-Stockholm, 1939–41.
General: Austerlitz, R., *Ob-Ugric Metrics*, Helsinki, 1958.
Ahlqvist, A., *Unter Wogulen und Ostjaken*, Helsinki, 1883.
Kannisto, A., *Materialen zur Mythologie der Wogulen*, Helsinki, 1958.
Karjalainen, K. F., *Die Religion der Jugra-Völker*, Porvoo-Helsinki, 1921–27.
Patkanov, S., *Die Irtyschostjaken und ihre Volkspoesie, 1. Ethnographische-statistische Übersicht*, St. Petersburg, 1897.
Róheim, Géza, *Hungarian and Vogul Mythology*, New York, 1954.

Zyryan

Grammars: Lytkin, V. I., ed., *Sovremennyj komi jazyk* I, Syktyvkar, 1955.
Lytkin, V. I., *Istoricheskaja grammatika komi jazyka*, Syktyvkar, 1957.
Dictionaries: Fokos-Fuchs, D., *Syrjänisches Wörterbuch* I–II, Budapest, 1959.
Komi-russkij slovar', Syktyvkar, 1948.
Wichmann, Y., *Syrjänischer Wortschatz*, Helsinki, 1942.
Wiedemann, F. J., *Syrjänisch-Deutsches Wörterbuch*, Bloomington, 1964.
Texts: Fokos-Fuchs, D., *Volksdichtung der Komi (Syrjänne)*, Budapest, 1951.
Fokos-Fuchs, D., *Zürjén népköltészeti mutatványok*, Budapest, 1913 and *Zürjén szövegek*, Budapest, 1916.
Lach, Robert, *Wotjakische, syrjänische und permische Gesänge*, Wien-Leipzig, 1926.
Wichmann, Y., *Syrjänische Volksdichtung*, Helsinki, 1916.

Votyak

Grammars: Emeljanov, A. I., *Grammatika votjackogo jazyka*, Leningrad, 1927.
Pozdeeva, A. A., *Udmurtskaja grammatika*, Izhevsk, 1951.
Wiedemann, F. J., *Grammatik der wotjakischen Sprache*, Reval, 1851.

Select Bibliography

Dictionaries: Borisov, T. K., *Udmurtsko-russkij slovar'*, Moscow, 1948.
Perevoshchikov, P. N., *Russko-udmurtskij slovar'*, Moscow, 1956.
Munkácsi, B., *A votják nyelv szótára*, Budapest, 1896.
Texts: Munkácsi, B., *Volksbräuche und Volksdichtung der Wotjaken*, ed. Fuchs, D., Helsinki, 1952.
Munkácsi, B., *Votják népköltészeti hagyományok*, Budapest, 1887, and *Votják nyelvtanulmányok*, Budapest, 1884.
Wichmann, Y., *Wotjakische Chrestomathie mit Glossar*, Helsinki, 1954.[2]
General: Buch, M., *Die Wotjaken*, Helsinki, 1883.
Wasiljev, Johann, *Übersicht über die heidnischen Gebräuche, Aberglauben und Religion der Wotjaken*, Helsinki, 1902.

Cheremis

Grammars: Lewy, E., *Tscheremissische Grammatik*, Leipzig, 1922.
Sovremennyj marijskij jazyk, Joshkar-Ola, 1960.
Wichmann, Y., *Tscheremissische Texte mit Wörterverzeichnis und grammatikalischen Abriss*, Helsinki, 1953.[2]
Dictionaries: Paasonen, H., *Ost-tscheremissisches Wörterbuch*, Helsinki, 1948.
Sebeok, T. A., and Zeps, V. J., *Concordance and Thesaurus of Cheremis Poetic Language*, 's Gravenhage, 1961.
Serebrennikov, B. A., ed., *Marijsko-russkij slovar'*, Moscow, 1956.
Texts: Beke, O., *Mari szövegek*, Budapest, I, 1957, III–IV, 1961.
Beke, O., *Texte zur Religion der Osttscheremissen*, Wien, 1934.
Beke, O., *Tscheremissische Märchen, Sagen und Erzählungen*, Helsinki, 1938.
Beke, O., *Tscheremissische Texte zur Religion und Volkskunde*, Oslo, 1931.
Lewy, E., *Tscheremissische Texte* I–II, Hannover, 1925–26.
Paasonen, H., *Tscheremissische Texte*, Helsinki, 1939.
Seboek, T. A. and Ingemann, F. J., *An Eastern Cheremis Manual*: Phonology, Grammar, Texts and Glossary, Bloomington, 1961.
General: Holmberg (Harva), U., *Die Religion der Tscheremissen*, Porvoo, 1926.
Sebeok, T. A. and Brewster, P., *Studies in Cheremis*: Games, Bloomington, 1958.
Sebeok, T. A. and Ingemann, F. J., *Studies in Cheremis: The Supernatural*, New York, 1956.
Sebeok, T. A. and Raun, A., ed., *The First Cheremis Grammar* (1775), Chicago, 1956.

Mordvin

Grammars: Koljadenkov, M. N., *Grammatika mordovskih (erzjanskogo u mokshanskogo) jazykov*, Saransk, 1954.

Paasonen, H., *Mordvinische Chrestomathie mit Glossar und grammatikalischen Abriss*, Helsinki, 1953.[2]

Wiedemann, F. J., *Grammatik der Ersa-mordwinischen Sprache nebst einem kleinen mordwinisch-deutschen und deutsch-mordwinischen Wörterbuch*, St Petersburg, 1865.

Bubrich, D. V., *Istoricheskaja grammatika erzjanskogo jazyka*, Saransk, 1953.

Dictionaries: Koljadenkov, M. N. and Cyganov, N. F., *Erzjansko-russkij slovar'*, Moscow, 1949; and *Russko-erzjanskij slovar'*, Moscow, 1948.

Potapkin, S. G. and Imjarekov, A. K., *Mokshansko-russkij slovar'*, Moscow, 1949; and *Russko-mokshanski slovar'*, Moscow, 1951.

Texts: Lach, Robert, *Mordwinische Gesänge*, Wien-Leipzig, 1933.

Lewy, E., *Mordwinische Märchen in erzjanischen Dialekte*, Leipzig, 1931.

Paasonen, H., *Mordwinische Volksdichtung* I–IV, Helsinki, 1938–47.

General: Harva, U., *Die religiösen Vorstellungen der Mordvinen*, Helsinki, 1952.

Shachmatov, A. A., *Mordovskij etnograficheskij sbornik*, St Petersburg, 1910.

Väisänen, A. O., *Mordwinische Melodien*, Helsinki, 1948.

Finnish

Grammars: Atkinson, J., *A Finnish Grammar*, Helsinki, 1955.

Fromm, H. and Sadeniemi, M., *Finnisches Elementarbuch: Grammatik*, Heidelberg, 1956.

Dictionaries: Alanne, V. S., *Finnish-English General Dictionary*, Porvoo-Helsinki, 1968.

Katara, Pekka, *Finnisches-deutsches Wörterbuch*, Porvoo, 1957.[3]

Hurme, R. and Pesonen, M., *English-Finnish General Dictionary*, 1973.

General: Hakulinen, L., *The Structure and Development of the Finnish Language*, Bloomington, 1961.

Harms, R. T., *Finnish Structural Sketch*, Bloomington, 1964.

Sauvageot, A., *Esquisse de la langue finnoise*, Paris, 1949.[2]

Sauvageot, A., *Les anciens finnois*, Paris, 1961.

Estonian

Grammars: Harms, R. T., *Estonian Grammar*, Bloomington, 1962.

Saareste, A., *Die estnische Sprache*, Tartu, 1932.

Select Bibliography

Dictionaries: Saareste, A., *Eesti keele moisteline sonaraamat.*
Dictionnaire analogique de la langue estonienne, I–IV, Stockholm, 1958.
Silvet, J., *An English-Estonian Dictionary*, 1956.
Silvet, J., *Estonian-English Dictionary*, Tallinn, 1970.
General: Eisen, M. J., *Estnische Mythologie*, Leipzig, 1925.
Loorits, O., *Grundzüge des estnischen Volksglaubens* I–III, Lund, 1949–1959.
Manninen, I., *Die Sachkultur Estlands I–II*, Tartu, 1931–33.
Saareste, A., *Petit atlas des parlers estoniens*, Uppsala, 1955.

Carelian, Vepsian, Vodian, Livonian

Grammars: Bubrih, D. V., *Grammatika karel'skogo jazyka*, Petrozavodsk, 1937.
Hämäläinen, M. and Andrejev, F., *Vepskijan kelen grammatik*, Leningrad, 1934.
Ariste, P., *A Grammar of the Votic Language*, Bloomington, 1968.
Sjögren, A. J., *Livische Grammatik nebst Sprachproben*, St Petersburg, 1861.
Dictionaries: Kettunen, L., *Livisches Wörterbuch mit grammatischer Einleitung*, Helsinki, 1938.
Texts: Ariste, P., *Wotische Sprachproben*, Tartu, 1935.
Loorits, O., *Volkslieder der Liven*, Tartu, 1936.
Mägiste, J., *Woten erzählen*, Helsinki, 1959.

Lapp

Grammars: Itkonen, E., *Lappische Chrestomathie mit grammatikalischen Abriss und Wörterverzeichnis*, Helsinki, 1960.
Lagercrantz, E., *Sprachlehre des Nordlappischen*, Oslo, 1929; *Sprachlehre des Südlappischen*, Kristiania, 1923; *Sprachlehre des Westlappischen*, Helsinki, 1926.
Nielsen, K., *Laerebok i lappisk. I. Grammatik. II Tekster. III Glossar*, Oslo, 1926–29.
Dictionaries: Collinder, B., *Lappisches Wörterverzeichnis aus Härjedalen*, Uppsala-Leipzig, 1943.
Grundström, H., *Lulelapsk ordbok* I–IV, Lund-Uppsala, 1946–54.
Lagercrantz, E., *Lappischer Wortschatz* I–II, Helsinki, 1939.
Nielsen, K., *Lapp Dictionary* I–III, Oslo, 1932–38; IV, *Systematic Part*, Oslo, 1956.
Texts: Collinder, B., *Lappische Sprachproben aus Härjedalen*, Uppsala, 1942.
Grundström, H. and Väisänen, A. O., *Lappische Lieder*, Uppsala, 1958.

Lagercrantz, E., *Lappische Volksdichtung* I–VII, Helsinki, 1957–66.
Ravila, P., *Reste lappischen Volksglaubens*, Helsinki, 1934.
General: Collinder, B., *The Lapps*, Princeton, 1949.
Collinder, B., *The Affinities of Lapp*, Uppsala, 1945; and *Proto-Lappish and Samoyed*, Uppsala, 1954.
Lagercrantz, E., *Synopsis des Lappischen*, Oslo, 1941.
Manker, E., *The Holy Places of the Lapps* (*Lapparna heliga ställen*), Uppsala, 1957; and *The Nomadism of Swedish Mountain Lapps*, Stockholm, 1953.
Toivonen, Y. H., *Zum Problem des Protolappischen*, Helsinki, 1950.

Samoyed

Grammars: Castrén, M. A., *Grammatik der samojedischen Sprachen*, St Petersburg, 1854 (Reprint: Bloomington, 1966).
Kuprjanova, Z. N., Chomich, L. V. and Shcherbakova, A. M., *Neneckij jazyk*, Leningrad, 1961^2.
Prokofjev, G. N., 'Neneckij (jurako-samjedskij) jazyk', 'Nganasanskij (tavgiskij) jazyk', Enetskij (jenisejsko-samojedskij) jazyk' and 'Sel'kupskij (ostjako-samojedskij) jazyk' in *Jazyki i pis'mennost' narodov Severa* I, Moscow, Leningrad, 1937.
Dictionaries: Castrén, M. A., *Wörterverzeichnisse aus den samojedischen Sprachen*, St Petersburg, 1855.
Donner, K., *Kamassisches Wörterbuch nebst Sprachproben und Hauptzügen der Grammatik* (ed. A. J. Joki), Helsinki, 1944.
Lehtisalo, T. V., *Juraksamojedisches Wörterbuch*, Helsinki, 1956.
Pyrerka, A. P., and Tereschchenko, N. M., *Russko-nenetskiy slovar'*, Moscow-Leningrad, 1948.
Texts: Castrén, M. A., *Samojedische Volksdichtung* (ed. T. V. Lehtisalo), Helsinki, 1940.
Castrén, M. A. and Lehtisalo, T. V., *Samojedische Sprachmaterialen*, Helsinki, 1960.
Décsy, Gyula, *Yurak Chrestomathy*, Bloomington-The Hague, 1966.
Hajdú, Péter, *Chrestomathia Samoiedica*, Budapest, 1968.
Lehtisalo, T. V., *Juraksamojedische Volksdichtung*, Helsinki, 1947.
Szabó, L., *Selkup Texts with Phonetic Introduction and Vocabulary*, Bloomington-The Hague, 1967.
General: Castrén, M. A., *Reiseberichte und Briefe aus den Jahren 1845–1849*, St Petersburg, 1856.
Donner, K., *Bei den Samojeden in Sibirien*, Stuttgart, 1926.

Select Bibliography

Hajdú, Péter, *The Samoyed Peoples and Languages*, Bloomington The Hague, 1968².
Popov, A. A., *The Nganasan*, Bloomington-The Hague, 1966.

ADDENDA (Unclassified)

Congressus Internationalis Fenno-Ugristarum Budapestini habitus 1960 (ed. Gy. Ortutay), Budapest, 1963.
Congressus Secundus Internationalis Fenno-Ugristarum Helsingiae habitus 1965, Helsinki, 1968.
Gulya, J., *Eastern Ostyak Chrestomathy*, Bloomington-The Hague, 1966.
Pimenov, V. V., *Vepsy*, Moscow-Leningrad, 1965.
Rédei, K., *Northern Ostyak Chrestomathy*, Bloomington-The Hague, 1966.
Tauli, V., *Structural Tendencies in Uralic Languages*, Bloomington-The Hague, 1966.
The First Votyak Grammar (Introduction: Gy. Décsy), Bloomington-The Hague, 1967.
Ostjakische Heldenlieder aus József Pápay's Nachlass, Budapest, 1972.

Index of Persons

🙖🙖🙖🙖🙖🙖

Index of Persons

247

Subject Index

𑀍𑀍𑀍𑀍𑀍𑀍

248